BALKAN
BLUE

BALKAN BLUE

FAMILY AND MILITARY MEMORIES

by

ROY REDGRAVE

LEO COOPER

First published in Great Britain in 2000 by
LEO COOPER
an imprint of Pen & Sword Books
47 Church Street, Barnsley, S Yorks, S70 2AS

Copyright © 2000 Roy Redgrave

ISBN 0 85052 755 4

A CIP catalogue record for this book
is available from the British Library

Typeset in 10½ on 12½pt Plantin
by Phoenix Typesetting, Ilkley, W Yorks
Printed by
Redwood Books Ltd, Trowbridge, Wilts.

CONTENTS

ACKNOWLEDGEMENTS

It was not until I began writing this account that I realized how foolish I had been not to have asked more questions from my elders or listened more carefully to what they had to say. The lack of notes on the back of photographs has been to some extent mitigated by my sister Ioana Hart's recollections.

I am much indebted to the late Alan Hill, Dorian Dennis, and Ilinca Bossy for their comments and suggestions. I am most grateful to Selina Walker for encouraging me to persist with the venture and to Tom Hartman for his keen interest and meticulous research which has brought this endeavour to a successful conclusion.

Finally I recognize the great help I have always received from my wife, Valerie, who has corrected my grammar and checked the proofs.

Chapter One

ROMANIAN CHILDHOOD

On the far side of the crowded room I could see someone pointing me out. They had already tried to compromise me and I felt uneasy. The Athene Palace Hotel in Bucharest had seen better days, especially between the two world wars. In the spring of 1945, whilst a Russian military band played outside in the square, a "liberation committee" debated inside how on earth to get the British and Americans to re-establish themselves in Romania quickly. Little did they realize that at the Yalta Conference these two countries had already agreed to allow the Soviet Union to exercise complete control over Eastern Europe.

It was now 1973 and I was attending a reception given by the Communists in honour of a visit by the National Defence College of Canada. A distinguished-looking Romanian general approached me and was introduced as Chief of the General Staff. It seemed that his intelligence officers had not done their home work, because he asked me,

"I understand that you were born in our country. Would you be so kind as to tell me where?"

"Of course, Sir," I replied, raising my glass up towards the chandeliers, "in this very hotel, on the second floor in the corner room."

He smiled weakly and wandered off shaking his head and muttering, "*Vai de mini*" (goodness gracious).

To my Romanian mother, Bucharest was the centre of her world, a city whose charm and vitality was only equalled by its capacity for intrigue and violence. Known as 'the Paris of the Balkans', it had attracted people from all over the world until the cataclysmic events of the Second World War scattered my entire family like the burst of a star shell, full of bright hopes, which dimmed rapidly as we began to feel that we would never be together again.

My mother took great pride in the fact that she had given birth to me in a famous hotel and in the knowledge that I was then washed in the first

1

French bidet ever to have been installed in the capital. My grandfather, Mihail Capsa, was born in 1845, before the Crimean War. He was a captain with a yellow plume in his cap when he fought the Ottomans at the Battle of Plevna in 1877. On his return he married and had two daughters, Gabrielle and Marie, and four sons, Jean, George, Nicu and Cotan. Then a tragedy occurred; his young wife died of cancer, leaving him with six children.

Grandfather was a pink-faced, gentle and conscientious man, intensely proud of his country, who rose to the rank of General. He met my grandmother, Alexandrina Rallet, in 1895 when he was a Colonel at Headquarters 2nd Army Corps. He was fifty-one years old and she was twenty-seven when they married, but she was the last unmarried daughter and there was no dowry.

They were married in the Orthodox church of Saint Spirodon in Bucharest by the Metropolitan Primate and two years later, 23 March 1897, my mother, Micheline Jeanne, was born. Twelve days earlier, two thousand kilometres away, my father Robin Roy Redgrave, had been born in Brighton, England, the son of a struggling young actor and actress. The chances of these two children from such totally different backgrounds ever meeting must surely have been remote.

In 1902 my Romanian grandmother was at last given a dowry which included a Bechstein grand piano. This was to have a great influence on my mother, who, in 1906, was left by her aunt, Anna Rallet, a country house at Doftana near Cimpina which was our home until the Germans occupied Romania in 1941. In the First World War it had become a hospital for contagious diseases and it became a German general's head-quarters in 1941.

When she was eleven years old my mother's musical ability was recognized by George Enesco, pianist and composer, who wrote to a friend in Paris, on Royal Palace stationery, asking if there might be a place in his music school for Micheline Capsa, "*pour une petite étrangère qui serait grande artiste un jour*". There was, but it seems that there was not enough money to support her. By the beginning of 1914, now a vivacious golden-haired sixteen-year-old, she had proved that she had a real talent for music. She never went to school but was entrusted to an English governess whom my grandmother disliked on principle.

My grandfather, General Capsa, had one last duty to perform before leaving his Command in Constantza, which was to arrange the State Visit by Tsar Nicholas of Russia on 13 June 1914. It was hoped that Crown Prince Carol might show interest in the Tsar's daughter Grand Duchess

Olga. The visit went like clockwork, but by the time the Russian Imperial ship cast off it was clear neither of the young were in the least impressed with each other. Had it been otherwise she might have been spared her awful fate in the cellar at Ekaterinburg in 1917.

After retirement Grandfather became Governor of the District of Prahova which included being responsible for the construction of a new circular prison at Doftana which is now visited by tourists. He had a fall and died six months later. At his funeral in 1916 an ornate hearse draped in black was drawn by a team of black oxen with black plumes; there were no horses left because of the war, They were led by soldiers wearing blackcocks' feathers in their caps. He lay in an open coffin, his face uncovered and his military cap on his chest. The soldiers were followed by bearded Orthodox priests wearing tall hats, clad in splendid black robes, and then by the mourners. Somewhere in the procession two boys carried plates of bread and salt to help him on his way and, bringing up the rear, a solitary gypsy fiddler played a sad doina.

When Romania entered the war in 1916 she was unprepared and the ancient planes in the Romanian Air Force were no match for the modern battle-tested three-winged German Taubes. It was while flying the very last fighter to defend Bucharest that my uncle Nicu was killed. Uncle Jean survived the war and later became an Air Marshal. As the German, Austrian, Turkish and Bulgarian armies advanced, thousands of people besieged the railway station and the roads were blocked with refugees. It was bitterly cold as thousands of elderly people, women and children began to trudge towards the distant mountains. Somewhere among those frightened people was my mother, aged nineteen, fortunate in the knowledge that Doftana was only a hundred kilometres away.

By Christmas Day she had reached the comparative safety of Doftana, visited occasionally by German patrols, which soon left, with my grandmother hissing "*Sales Boches*" at their backs. Fortunately the grand piano was there and she practised daily. Next spring she obtained a permit from the "Kaiserliches Kommandant" in Cimpina to visit her father's grave in Bucharest, but when she got there she became a Red Cross nurse in the American Hospital.

Eighteen months later, after one last orgy of looting, German carts clattered over the cobbles and out of Bucharest. The citizens could hardly believe that the nightmare was over. After being cut off for two years in Moldavia the Royal Family and the Army returned to wildly cheering crowds.

Queen Marie reopened her country palace at Cotroceni and invited my mother to give a recital in a room which, she recalled, was full of stupendous flower arrangements and that the Queen presented her with a signed photograph in a silver frame.

In June 1920 Mother went to Sofia where she was to play at the Russian Embassy. She wrote to her mother, "I have been practising Beethoven Sonatas until two or three every morning with Colonel Mealin, who has been showing me how to interpret the movements." One can just imagine the gallant colonel turning the pages and warming to his task with her golden hair brushing against his side-whiskers.

If my mother's love life may have been just beginning, that of Crown Prince Carol had become more and more complicated. Mother told me that she had spent two hours in 1919 on a Danube steamer alone with the lovelorn Prince, who "poured out his heart to me". He was miserable, it seemed, at having been forcibly separated by the King from his great love Zizi Lambrino. Carol, however, had the knack of making the best of a difficult situation and found another mistress, a gentle and pretty shopgirl who soon became pregnant. Queen Marie became alarmed, arranged for her to have her baby and be paid off and then reluctantly allowed Zizi to come back into Prince Carol's life. There was more consternation when she learned that Zizi was also pregnant and that the Crown Prince wished to resign from all his responsibilities and leave Romania with her. "And all that," my mother added, "was before he married Princess Helen or met his mistress Magda Lupescu!"

In 1921 Western capital, engineers and geologists began to pour into Romania. These were a tough bunch of men employed by large international companies. Into this exciting situation stepped my handsome easy-going father, aged 22, who did not possess a single technical qualification or any experience in oil exploration. He would never have survived this challenge but for the financial help he received from his stepfather, F.J. Nettlefold (FJN), in England.

As far as I have been able to discover, the Redgrave family were cordwainers, shoemakers and farm workers who settled around Crick in Northamptonshire about four hundred years ago. The key figure in the change from these mundane occupations to the theatre was Cornelius, born in 1824. One of thirteen children, he died in 1922. He was a publican, a bagatelle maker and finally ran a theatre ticket agency at 16 Brydges Street in Covent Garden.

His son Augustus married Zoe Elsworthy Pym, whose children included my grandfather George Edward Redgrave. When Augustus died, Cornelius secretly married Zoe, his daughter-in-law, and moved to Canada. This was a hideous experience for them all, especially for George, who was much relieved when they returned to England in 1879 and Zoe married a young actor, Adderly Howard.

George, now aged 17, must have been influenced by his actor step-father, because he too wanted to act. In order to improve his image he exchanged 'Edward' for his mother's name 'Elsworthy' and adopted a stage name, 'Roy', instead of George. His sister, Harriet, flourished as a vaudeville actress known as 'Dolly Elsworthy' and his brother, Christopher, became a stage manager.

Roy Redgrave was a charming happy-go-lucky person and a versatile actor. In 1894 he married Ellen Maud Pratt, an actress, who bore him three children, Nellie, Jack and Robin (my father). In 1900 he volunteered to go to South Africa to fight the Boers. My father remembers him returning suntanned and wearing a wide-brimmed bush hat. After his military adventures, he decided that a life of domestic bliss was going to be quite impossible and, although he adored his children and especially my father, he deserted them all in 1904 and went off to seek work in Australia.

He returned to England a year later but never settled down. In 1906 he had a son, Victor, by Miss Esther Cooke (Ettie Carlisle), daughter of a well-known circus proprietor. Their identity was only revealed in 1982 when Victor wrote from an old people's home in Vancouver. Once again Roy fled and in 1907 went through a form of marriage with yet another actress, Margaret Scudamore, known as Daisy, whom he also deserted after three years. Their only child became the distinguished actor Sir Michael Redgrave who married Rachel Kempson. In due course their children, Vanessa, Corin and Lynn, and numerous grandchildren all chose to make the stage their career.

There seemed to be no trace of what had happened to Roy after he left Daisy, until 1979, when Lynn Redgrave lunched with me in Hong Kong where I was Commander British Forces. Lynn and her husband John Clark had settled in California and were on their way with their children to visit Australia. We sat on the terrace of Headquarter House on The Peak overlooking Hong Kong harbour and determined to discover what happened to Roy after 1909.

I too had to visit Australia and my arrival coincided with a report in the *Canberra Times* about a tin box discovered buried in the permafrost near Dawson City in the Yukon which contained a number of old films. A still from an Australian silent film, *Robbery Under Arms*, showed Roy

Redgrave with a pistol in his hand holding up a stage coach. This prompted me to visit the excellent Australian National Film Library, where I discovered that his first film was *The Christian* in 1911, then *The Crisis* in 1912, followed by many others, including *Robbery Under Arms* in 1920. Meanwhile Lynn unearthed a mass of press clippings. He had, it seems, written a play about the historic arrest of the murderer, Dr Crippen, on board a liner bound for New York, called *By Wireless Telegraphy*. He had also acted in four plays in Melbourne between 1914 and 1915.

Lynn was able to find his unmarked grave in Sydney, a plot which had been purchased by a 'Minnie Redgrave', and she promptly ordered a gravestone. 'Minnie' was probably a popular actress called Minnie Titell Brune with whom he first acted in Australia. Roy Redgrave's excessive drinking had left him with few friends and he died in 1922, just a few days after his first wife, my grandmother Ellen Maud, died in London, and the same year that his grandfather Cornelius died in London aged 98.

The *Sydney Morning Herald* of 25 May 1922 described Redgrave as "an actor of brilliant power who for some years past had got out of touch with his admirers owing to the necessity of filling minor roles through ill health and advancing years". *The Bulletin* said he was "a recognised good actor rather than an accepted favourite" and that "he was terribly hoarse-voiced and, when he became unemployed, his voice became even hoarser". The last time he had done well was at the Theatre Royal, Sydney, on 22 Jan 1921 in *The Maid of the Mountains*.

"Shortly before his death (from cancer of the throat and scalp) in a Sydney hospital on May 25th (1922), Roy Redgrave, the popular actor, wrote the following:

> One of the best! Held his own 'in a crowd',
> Lived like the rest (when finances allowed),
> Slapped on the back as a jolly fine sport
> Drank any tack from bad whiskey to port.
> Fool to himself – that's the worst you can say;
> Cruel to himself, for the health has to pay
> Months back he died, and we've only just heard,
> No friends by his side just to say the kind word.
> No relatives near and no assets at all,
> Quite lonely, I fear, when he answered the call.
> One of the best. Held his own while he could,
> Died like the rest, just when life seemed so good."

My grandmother, Ellen Maud, had been left by Roy to raise her three children. After a few years she married Frederick J. Nettlefold, a kind and wealthy but somewhat austere man who had ambitious plans for her. He rented a theatre in the Strand where he financed his own productions which were seldom successful. My father adored his mother, who, thanks to her marriage, was now able to give him a good education. He joined the Royal Field Artillery in 1916 and was rapidly commissioned. His battery sailed from Liverpool to Palestine where they came under command of General Allenby, who, unlike his fellow generals in Flanders, conducted a brilliant mobile campaign against the Ottoman Turks.

Lieutenant Robin Redgrave was a Forward Observation Officer at the Battle of Beersheba, where he directed gunfire in support of an epic cavalry charge. His ability to speak French soon led to an attachment to the French Army who awarded him the Croix de Guerre with a silver star after a battle in which a bullet passed through his cap, leaving a scar in his scalp. In 1919 he was demobilized and, like so many other young men at that time, was at a total loss what to do next. FJN suggested he should spend a year in Kenya learning the business at his farm at Juja, where the main crop was sisal. However, he was far more interested in the big game and wild life which was abundant on the estate than planting sisal and fruit trees. He walked into a pride of lions and while his companions shinned up trees he killed five with six shots. FJN then suggested he should join his new petroleum company, 'Dacia Romana', at Ploesti in Romania. But working in an oil refinery was probably going to be just as depressing as the sisal grass-shredding machines in the tin sheds at Juja, so my father soon decided that he would prefer to work in the oil fields.

He found lodgings in a small wooden house in Telega, a village through which Texan oil drillers sometimes walked with a pistol in each hand, just as if they were back home in 'Dead Man's Gulch'. They could keep a square jerrycan rolling ahead of them by firing well-aimed shots at the top corners, which then hit the dusty road only to ricochet over the heads of screaming peasant women, crying children and barking dogs.

Sitting alone at the end of a day's work on the wooden veranda of his house in Telega my father must have missed his friends until he discovered that there was a 'swimming pool' just two kilometres away along the road to Doftana. This was the remains of a flooded salt mine dating back from the years when salt was Romania's second greatest export, beaten only by oil. The warm green water was so saline and buoyant that it was quite impossible to sink. Michelene Capsa used to walk from

Doftana to join her friends beside the pool and it was there, her hair tied back with a blue ribbon and wearing a long bathing dress with blue and white hoops, that she met Robin Redgrave. Their common language was French and within weeks they became engaged.

They were married in the Mayor's office in Telega in 1923, a civil ceremony witnessed by Jean Ghika, mother's uncle, and Lawrence Rutherford, manager of FJN's refinery. The Mayor had made a big effort to sweep around his house with a long-handled straw broom and placed a large vase of red and white dahlias on his desk. The villagers felt a little cheated because the church wedding was to be in Bucharest, but mother promised a celebration at Doftana later. This turned out to be such a success that it became an annual event in aid of the Red Cross. After a lengthy Romanian Orthodox service in Bucharest the British contingent, which included FJN, were glad to step out into the sunshine. They all stood at the top of the church steps; father, with mother on his arm, wore his old Royal Artillery uniform, his old wartime boots and well-fitting breeches. It had been a very long day and nobody noticed that on the vestry table lay the wedding certificate on which father had declared his age as 25 and his bride as 24, which was fair enough seeing that he was all of twelve days older.

My father now formed his own company which carried out contract oil drilling for larger companies. The capital was provided by FJN. The general euphoria of being his own master with apparently large sums of money to spend prompted him to rebuild Doftana, which they did not wish to occupy because of the risk of contagious diseases left behind from its use as a hospital. The privy was among the apricot trees, a delightful place to sit in the sunshine with the door ajar, especially when the blossom was out. The first priority was to provide running water and install a bathroom and sewage system. A pump was installed and a wooden storage water tank built on the hill behind the house. I once found a dead red squirrel in the tank which I fished out with a wooden rake. Lots of men with long-handled spades moved vast quantities of earth and rocks to lay out the garden, plant lawns, rose beds, rock gardens, create a lily pond and lay a concrete tennis court which was ideal for the village fête and dancing the *Hora*.

In December 1924 my mother returned from her first visit to England on the Orient Express. She told me years later that I was conceived on that famous train as it thundered across Europe. A few hours before I was due to be born, on 16 September 1925, mother took another look at the local hospital and insisted that only the Athene Palace Hotel in the centre of Bucharest was suitable for the delivery of her first child. Mother and I checked in at the hotel almost simultaneously. There was barely time to reach the bedroom before a scratch team consisting of the head porter, hotel laundry lady and an elderly seamstress delivered me, whilst father ordered the champagne. For years afterwards whenever I returned the staff would ask, "Is he ours?" I was allowed to ride up and down in the lift, like Barbar the elephant, then visit the kitchens to taste the most wonderful '*caracs*', small chocolate cakes on a firm sponge base, covered in hard green icing.

I am not quite sure into which faith I was actually baptised, but the ceremony took place on the lawn at Doftana and was attended by bearded Romanian Orthodox priests wearing high black hats and the Anglican chaplain from the British Embassy, Chalmers Bell, who wore a white dog collar. By all accounts it was a good party and I survived the indignity of being dipped into a silver bowl of Cotnari wine punch. Very soon after I was born, red-headed, hot-headed Nurse Greaves, 'Nini', arrived from Jamaica where she had lived on a large sugar cane plantation. To begin with she treated all Romanians as she had done the 'natives' and ruled the household at Doftana with a rod of iron, but she mellowed quickly and soon earned their affection and respect. She was always immaculate in a starched white and red uniform. My grandmother, Madame la General Capsa, whom we called 'Gui', resented her arrival because she considered, having once held my naked body at arm's length, that only she knew what was good for small boys. They spoke no common language and disliked each other intensely, at any rate until after my sisters were born, Mary Maud in 1927 and Ioana in 1931. Nini ran the house with a jingling bunch of keys tied to her uniform belt and a pungent, fluent vocabulary of Romanian, picked up from the kitchen staff.

I did not see much of my father and so was absolutely thrilled on those rare occasions when he took me with him to the oil fields. He would leave the car after a rough and dusty journey in some small village and we would soon be surrounded by curious children. Two miserable-looking horses would be led out and I was lifted onto the smallest. These mountain horses were small, thin and ugly, but their redeeming feature was that they were incredibly sure-footed and good-natured. There was an uncomfortable wooden saddle with a high pommel covered by a bit of red carpet, which I was told to grip only as a last resort. I soon established an understanding with my horse which was happy to amble along up to a kilometre behind my father. We followed the swift-flowing streams up into the foothills of the Carpathians; it was another world. There were otters and water rats and the little kingfishers which sat on branches overhanging deep pools. As we got closer to the oil wells I was aware of a peculiar but not unpleasant smell. This was the greenish black crude oil which invariably seeped out around any drilling site, whilst in the distance I could hear the steady thump of a diesel engine. Soon the immense wooden oil derrick came into sight, towering above the silver birch trees. Steel pipes were being lifted up and attached to a drill which then slowly disappeared into the ground.

I was introduced, with some pride I sensed, to my father's cheerful workmen and then left to explore the site. The men let me taste their cold *mamaliga* (a maize flour dish) and I listened fascinated to stories of wartime adventures and how packs of wolves were seen in their village last winter. The real treat came when my father's business was over and we rode back briskly to the car and stopped on the way home at Giculescu's, a grocer in Ploesti, in whose cool cellar father drank *tuica* with his friends and washed it down with cold bottled beer from Azuga, whilst I was allowed to nibble freshly made potato crisps and drink lemonade from a bottle with a marble in its neck. On the pavement outside Giculescu's there were wooden barrels bound with brass bands which contained many different sorts of caviare: small glistening black beads, dull grey translucent pearls and huge globules of orange caviare. Most of the caviare came from fishing villages on the North side of the Danube Delta where the Lipovans, who were of Russian origin, lived. Carefully lifting the lids, I dipped a potato crisp into each barrel in turn and then slipped behind the nearest parked car where I sat on the running board with my back against the spare wheel to nibble unseen. These were moments of sheer bliss.

Doftana was renowned for its hospitality; the gates were never closed and guests arrived at all hours. As a child I remember the animated conversation and laughter, the sound drifting upstairs into the children's nursery. But, tucked away at Doftana with my sisters, I grew up with very few friends and, except for occasional contacts with the children of diplomats and oil men, who lived miles away, we were left very much to our own devices. The garden was a paradise, combining a formal layout with a dense wilderness which clung to a steep slope and was crossed by a path which I was certain nobody except we children knew. We picked apples and peaches, together with handfuls of pea pods and crawled deep under the soft feathery foliage of the asparagus beds to eat in secret.

When the apricots and cherry trees were in blossom the orchard was thick with bees. They lived in a long line of hives whose entrances faced away from the sandy footpath, so that no one should disturb their flight path. We watched fascinated as the drones were dragged out by the soldier bees to die, wondering what had gone wrong with their happy lives.

There was a little summer house on a steep wooded slope which overlooked the Doftana River. We called this delightful place the Eagle's Nest where grown-ups could disappear for a nap, or so we were told. Behind the house amongst the beech trees there was a deep pit dug into the hillside with access through two heavy trap doors. Every winter blocks of ice were cut out of the Doftana River and dragged up to the ice house on a sledge to be stored between layers of straw. Some of the ice was used in the wooden ice cream bucket, packed round a cylinder which contained equal portions of fresh fruit and cream, then slowly rotated by a handle. It took a long time to make the ice cream but the result was sensational.

In spite of momentous events taking place in Bucharest during the early 1930s, we continued to be brought up in a sort of cocoon at Doftana. My sisters and I rode our Opel and Peugeot bicycles along dirt roads through little villages ringing our bells and scattering flocks of turkeys and chickens, whilst mongrels, with kinks in their tails, yapped at our heels. In summer we bathed naked in dark pools beneath gentle waterfalls in the Doftana River and in winter we rode toboggans down the steepest slopes we could find into the valley.

Mother loved walking and picnics. I am not sure that I always did. The car would drop us in a mountain valley near Sinia where chestnut trees, maples and hornbeam flourished. We walked past huge oak trees, their roots covered in deep moss and giant mushrooms, and then climbed through beech woods into splendid forests of pine and larch. Eventually we reached the bright green pastures right on top of the mountain, overlooked only by spectacular grey peaks. The picnic was spread out on a rough wooden table outside a shepherd's log hut. He seemed really happy to have some company.

These mountain huts must have been miserable places in which to live, even during the summer. The walls were logs through which the wind blew and the roofs were rough wooden slats. A large iron cooking pot of boiling maize was suspended over an open log fire, which filled the hut with smoke and steam. The sparse furnishings included equipment for making cheese and a beautifully carved flute which was balanced on two nails in the wall. Draped over a nail in the door hung the shepherd's

11

embroidered sheepskin cloak and a leather water bottle. I loved to hear the melancholy tunes he played and the stories of how, "only last night", he had driven six wolves away from his sheep. There was no fencing, so, to prevent his cows and sheep from straying too far, he tied a slab of rock salt to the saw-horse, knowing that they would always return to lick it; indeed he claimed to have seen a wolf lick the salt before cocking his leg.

I was frightened of wolves, quite unjustly it now seems. I shivered with fear when I heard them howl on a winter's night. Once on the Ploesti to Cimpina road I had been left alone in a broken-down car with my sister Mary Maud, while the driver went for help. In the light of a half-moon we could see the eyes of shadowy creatures around the car and we pulled the car rug over our heads when they began to howl. Years later, in an Inuit village in North-West Greenland, I was reminded of the sound when packs of huskies took up the same eerie cry.

One afternoon at Doftana I was in the hay loft when I heard an awful howl, but it was different, a human cry. I peeped through a crack in the boards at the drama taking place below. Dimitri, the gypsy chauffeur, lay squirming on his back on the cobbled forecourt, sobbing and moaning. Two Gendarmes held his feet up, and a corporal beat the bare soles of his feet with a cane. This punishment, called 'bastinado', was administered on the spot by local police without any sort of trial. In this case Dimitri had been caught once again with stolen property in his room and justice was swift. As soon as the Gendarmes had ridden off on their bicycles and Dimitri had hobbled off to wash the blood off his feet, I scrambled down the ladder and ran back into the house, just bursting with the news. As was usual I suppose with grown-ups, nobody seemed the slightest bit interested and all reckoned that, in view of his many other misdemeanours, Dimitri had got off very lightly.

I have always been fascinated by Romanian gypsy music. I only have to hear a *Tzigane* play his violin to feel emotional and shed a tear. The gloomiest gypsy tune ever written was a tango called "Gloomy Sunday" which was composed by a Hungarian, Rezsoe Seres. It had a sad haunting melody and was blamed for many suicides during the 1930s. I discovered a few years ago that the composer, when he was 68 years old, jumped eight floors to his death in Budapest, on a Sunday of course.

Whenever a gypsy caravan passed through the Doftana valley it was as if a swarm of locusts had landed. They plundered the orchards, cut the sunflowers, plucked the corn cobs and discovered under which bushes the villagers' hens laid their eggs. They usually parked their carts and horses in a circle on the water meadow beside the Doftana River.

One morning Mary Maud and I were cycling along a path which followed the line of the single railway track from Doftana to Cimpina. We noticed that there was a commotion in the gypsy camp so we stopped on the embankment overlooking the meadow to watch two men fighting. They were surrounded by a silent ring of gypsies. Suddenly one was knocked down and, as he lay on the grass quite still, the other man stood defiantly over him and very slowly drew a knife from a fold in his clothing. There was a high-pitched wail from someone in the crowd and a young woman holding a baby in her arms dashed into the ring and stood panting in front of the man holding the knife. She screamed and spat at him, then, gripping the baby by its legs, swung it around her head like a club and hit him, causing him to lose his balance. Pandemonium broke out as the crowd of gypsies surged forward and we cycled off as fast as we could. Dimitri assured us later that the battered baby still had a father and that nobody had been killed.

Once a year gypsies came up the drive to Doftana leading two brown Carpathian bears on a chain. They played a jig on a flute and beat a tambourine which prompted the poor bears to dance on two legs, picking up their feet. On one memorable occasion we saw a bear dance on a man with a sack over his back. The back 'cure' was accompanied by a jig on the flute, pitiful moans from the man and bear grunts, while the tambourine player and spectators all shouted encouragement. I can still see the man's fingers digging deep into the dirt. The look of sheer relief on the unfortunate fellow's face when the bear stepped off his back may have induced others to believe that every coin they put into the gypsy's black purse was worth the anguish and pain of such a bruising cure.

I learnt later that bears endured a brutal training during which they are made to associate music with hot coals under their feet. I also learnt how brutal life was when I saw two headless chickens fly out of the wood cellar. A gypsy tinker, who sold the birds to the cook, had been asked to despatch them, which he did, somewhat messily, with the large axe used to split logs.

Once a month my sisters and I were driven to Ploesti where Padre Bell from the British Embassy ran a Sunday School with such a light touch that we believed he was really a magician and that his black beard was

13

false. We sang a few happy hymns, listened agog to his stories and left clutching a handful of sticky labels to put into our Sunday School attendance books. The Romanian Orthodox priest, who also had a beard, came to Doftana to flick holy water around with a small brush made from twigs of various herbs. When his task was over he was given a glass of cold water and a spoonful of sticky sweet sherbet "*dulceata*"; the twigs were treasured by unmarried girls who placed them under their pillows, hoping a romance might follow.

Behind the house there was a grassy slope which stretched right down to a line of willow trees which traced the course of the river. It was the greenest grass I have ever seen and it was known as Bondi's Garden. Bondi had once been a handsome bay in the Royal Palace stables and drew a smart black carriage with brass oil lamps which mother used when father had taken the car to the oil fields. He hauled slabs of ice cut from the river, logs for fires, rocks for garden walls and barrels of plums to the secret distillery behind the garage, where father made his own '*tuica*' in the dead of night, some of which had to go in bribes to keep the Gendarmes happy. I believe that Bondi was happiest when all the terrible ruts and potholes in the roads around Doftana were packed hard with snow and the sledge slid effortlessly. My sisters and I put on skis, clung to a rope behind the sledge and, shrieking with delight, sped through the village with bells jingling and Dimitri cracking his whip.

Sadly the day came when Bondi was deemed too old for all the work he was expected to do and it was decided to send him to the vet in Cimpina to be put down. Dimitri, of course, was our ally, in that he reckoned that there was still some life in the old horse, but as things turned out his motives were different. We awoke one grey morning to discover that Dimitri had moved off at dawn with Bondi and were horrified to find two fat sows in Bondi's stable. Our parents deemed it prudent to disappear for the day whilst arrangements had been made to distract us by inviting lots of American children who lived beside the refinery at Ploesti to spend the day at Doftana. By the time the sows had given birth to fourteen piglets we had forgotten all about Bondi. A month later Mitzi, the Hungarian maid, came running into the drawing room to say she had seen a ghost on the lawn. Sure enough there was a ghost of a horse, a mere skeleton grazing with a broken rope still hanging round his neck.

My irate father telephoned the vet in Cimpina, who replied equally vexed, "Of course I put your horse down last month. I am not in the habit of presenting fictitious accounts." He paused and added, "Furthermore, I am amazed that you ever allowed an animal to get into such an awful state." This, needless to say, hurt my father to the quick because Bondi may well have been old but he was certainly well cared for and loved. "Thank you, I think I now understand. It's time I had another word with Dimitri."

Dimitri was summoned, but he claimed he had done exactly as he had been ordered. My father threatened to fetch the Gendarmes who would beat him if it appeared that he was once again telling a lie. Seeing that there was no escape, Dimitri confessed that as he descended into the valley at dawn he had seen smoke curling up from fires in the gypsy camp and stopped to take a cup of tea from a gypsy lady. It appears that she had beguiled him into exchanging Bondi for an even more decrepit animal and offered one hundred lei. The gypsies had travelled over 180 kilometres before Bondi broke loose and wandered back. And so he spent another year or two in Bondi's garden, whilst Dimitri's star grew a little dimmer in my father's eyes.

Sadly Dimitri's star was extinguished six months later when he was asked to mend a telephone bell. Unable to resist the temptation to forage around, he found a loaded .45 service revolver under my father's bedside table and accidentally killed himself. I have no idea how my father explained the matter to the Gendarmes, but I was shocked to realize that my happy-go-lucky father felt himself threatened even at peaceful Doftana.

There was tension even in the kitchen where Mitzi the Hungarian cook thought little of Elena, a Romanian maid. One Easter there was no coffee served after lunch because the two had had a terrible row in the kitchen. The coffee was thrown at the cook who seized a saucepan full of green dye in which the hard-boiled Easter eggs had been left to cool and splashed it at the maid. A little white cockerel who always sat in the open window had green feathers ever afterwards.

The laundry at Doftana was done by Vetta, a washerwoman who lived nearby. Everything was put into a huge cauldron and boiled, then rinsed and laid on the grass to dry until my father erected a line between the poplar trees. Vetta was a war widow, living with her horrible drunken son who used to beat her. My father found her in tears one day and was so appalled at her injuries that he whipped the boy. Nevertheless after we had left Doftana in 1940 we heard that poor Vetta had died as the result of yet another assault.

Life in Romania was changing rapidly, not just because King Carol's policies were ruthless but also because of the emergence of a Fascist Youth Party, who wore green shirts and whose venom and violence were directed against Jews and at all foreign interests, other than those which were pro-German. The authorities therefore allowed my father to keep his revolver beside his bed just a little longer.

Chapter Two

STORM CLOUDS

When I was eight years old my father realized that I must be educated. I could speak three languages, but I was illiterate. Despite King Carol's decree that all children in Romania must go to school, my education had been forgotten. I had never been inside a classroom. So Miss Rushton came from Stroud and set me to work. She was magnificent; she aroused my curiosity and enthusiasm with the exciting books she had brought with her. I soon learnt to read and looked forward to the *Children's Newspaper* which came each month from England. I began to appreciate that there was lots to do in the world beyond Doftana and I looked forward keenly to the prospect of going to a boarding school.

My uncle, Colonel Georges Capsa, considered it was his duty to educate me in two matters which he knew instinctively were not in Miss Rushton's lesson plan, the seduction of women and the joys of soldiering. "The women in this country are all beautiful and quite irresistible," he once confided to me, "and when you grow a little older you too will discover just what I mean."

He took me on 10 May 1934 to the Independence Day Parade in Bucharest to watch a noisy and colourful display. King Carol feared that there might be an attempt on his life and so, for the first time since his return to Romania, invited his Mother, Queen Marie, to ride with him in the procession and hopefully diminish the threat to himself. She rode side-saddle, wearing a red Hussar tunic, a wide blue skirt and fur busby with a red plume, the uniform of Uncle George's regiment, the Rosiori. The much-loved Queen Mother received a tremendous ovation from the crowd, to the obvious chagrin of her jealous son. Indeed a few days after the parade he banished her close friend Prince Stirby from Romania for life and cancelled all arrangements to celebrate her 60th birthday just in case it detracted from his own fading popularity.

Uncle George had served in both the Rosiori, a regular cavalry regiment, and in the Calarashi, a unique regiment of volunteer horsemen, whose peculiar traditions he took great pains to explain to me. A volunteer for the Calarashi had to bring his own horse, and both then appeared before a regimental selection board. The slightest flaw in either resulted in disqualification for both. Once selected, both had to give five years' part-time service to their country. If either were sick, both were returned to their village until fit again. If the horse had to be destroyed then the trooper was discharged and was never allowed to re-enlist in the regiment, even if he turned up with another fine horse.

Thus a soldier in the Calarashi became a sort of Centaur; man and horse were quite inseparable. Once a volunteer completed five years' military service he could resign, but without his horse. This was blackmail because few men could bear to part from their horse and so they re-enlisted. Eventually when the horse was too old for active service, both were discharged.

"A Calarashi only really lives once," explained Uncle George. "The age of his horse matches the best years of his youth. He can truthfully say, 'Once I was a Calarashi, but now I am just a man'." I nodded my head and tried to understand.

It was with Uncle George that I witnessed one of the most beautiful spectacles imaginable; a whole regiment of those peasant horsemen riding through a whirlpool of white snow flakes, heads erect and each man wearing a long goatskin cape which fell from his shoulders in a long oblique line to cover his horse's quarters. Thirty years later when I was commanding the Household Cavalry Regiment at Hyde Park Barracks, I watched The Queen's Life Guard ride back from Horse Guards along the South Carriage Way one wintery morning. Each trooper's dark blue cape stretching back covering his horse's quarters was covered in white powdery snowflakes which fell from a leaden sky. I was hypnotized and remembered the proud Calarashi in 1935 riding through flurries of snow, while Uncle George held my hand and returned their salute.

When my education reached the minimum standard needed to enter an English preparatory school, I was put onto a train in the care of Uncle George who was making his first visit to England. He was in charge of King Carol's racing stable and under orders to buy British bloodstock so as to ensure that eighty percent of the races at Baneasa continued to be won by the King.

We stayed at the Regent Palace Hotel and I was amazed to see the way he attacked his first English breakfast, eating everything on the menu, kippers, eggs, sausages, bacon and mushrooms, and as an afterthought waffles and maple syrup. We then rushed around London sight-seeing in a most haphazard manner, into red double-decker buses, down into the underground, into taxis and on one memorable occasion down into the ladies' lavatory at Leicester Square. We had lunch at Simpson's and tea at Gunter's and then hurried to Waterloo station just in time to catch the school train to Bracknell. I waved Uncle George goodbye and watched him stride off eagerly into the crowds and bright city lights and into Soho to discover if London girls were as friendly as those in Bucharest. As he slept after his endeavours his wallet was stolen by "a lady from the shadows, a most impatient Celtic lady, with no finesse".

Lambrook School in Winkfield Row was surrounded by magnificent beech and chestnut trees and huge clumps of rhododendron bushes. It was a happy place, thanks to the interest that the masters' wives took in the small boys, in particular Flora Forbes. My letters home always reflected acute embarrassment at my dismal position at the bottom of every class which seldom numbered more than eleven boys.

"Now don't think my marks are too bad, because actually my place was higher than it usually is, which is 10th."

"Last term I was top because nobody knew more than I did, but this term I am in a higher form and the people who were here last term are more experienced. So that's why this week I am 9th."

"It is almost impossible for me to be in the first three, because try as I can (which I do), the other boys, who are better than me, have been in the form longer, and are also trying."

If I flourished in any subject it was Current Affairs, taught by Mr Squarey, and French, taught by Mr Bentley. Letter-writing on Sundays was a messy ordeal, dipping a steel nib on the end of a small stick into a china inkwell, recording incomprehensible cricket scores and a few morsels of news.

"I am still a Wolf cub but a very seinor one, I have passed all the tests I can passe." "Well here is a mirical, I am in the top game for criket. I wrote to Gui two pages in French, I think every word was correct with the aid of a dickshonry."

Letters to Romania cost two and a half pence and only took five days. We were encouraged to take part in stage productions, which I much enjoyed, and to write a story. I began a tale called "Black Michael Defeated". The manuscript cover was illustrated with a confused naval battle in which blood and water were depicted in equal proportions. It began dramatically: "The man was running in thier derecton with a peace of papper in his hand, he handed it to Jackson and he red it 'Black Michael twenty miles away, engage at once.' Jackson looked at Milnep and Milnep looked at Jackson, for Black Michael was the most dreded pirate ever to haunt British shores." Needless to say the pirate, his mouth full of battered yellow teeth, perished when the flames of his burning ship reached the magazine "and blue them all to smithereens".

During my five years at Lambrook I was only taken out twice; this was by an old friend of my mother, Hubert Jakins, who was British Consul in Djibouti and often spent his leave at Doftana. He drove me to Oxford, filled me with crumpets and cakes and held my hand in Windsor Park, returning me to school on time but slightly puzzled.

I spent nearly three weeks a year on the Orient Express and thus had less holiday than other boys. Since 1906 the Orient Express stopped at Cimpina, ten kilometres from Doftana, for two minutes before making its final run to Bucharest through fields of maize and sunflowers and past clusters of tall oil derricks. There was great excitement at Cimpina station before the train made its twice-weekly stop. The platform was swept with straw brushes, the geraniums and petunias were watered and the station master brushed down his best tunic and glanced at his chronometer. Smart horse-drawn carriages lined the approach roads while spectators crowded onto every vantage point to catch sight of the first whisp of smoke.

The train's arrival was followed by frantic activity. The first problem was to find the blue Wagon-Lits coaches among the motley selection of other rolling stock. The sleeping cars were high off the ground and porters preferred to load through open windows rather than to drag a school trunk up the steep steps while hanging onto a brass rail. Mother always managed to delay our departure, to the stationmaster's despair and to my embarrassment, by inspecting my berth and checking whether there was paper in the WC. Then a shrill whistle blast, a loud hiss of steam, much spinning of engine wheels before they began to grip and we pulled away with handkerchiefs fluttering from every window until we disappeared into the Carpathian foothills.

After my trip with Uncle George I was allowed to travel alone. My father took the brown-uniformed attendant aside, gave him a tip and asked him to keep an eye on his nine-year-old son, but it soon became evident that he had other things to do. There were tickets to check, passports to collect, baggage to move, bells to answer and business to be arranged for the ladies who travelled further down the train. After all, three days alone in a first-class compartment could be very dull indeed, without those ladies who chatted, played cards and provided far more than today's in-flight entertainment.

My first trip alone started well; at each stop I lowered the window to watch the milling crowds, the fresh walnut and yoghurt vendors and the engineer tapping the wheels with a long hammer. The dining-car attendant announced first and second service and was followed by a column of my fellow passengers. But this was something for which I was totally unprepared. I could not enter that awesome dining-car alone, sit opposite a stranger and select from a menu. For the next day or so I eked out a packet of biscuits and two bars of chocolate which Grandmother had slipped into my bag. By lunchtime on the third day I was feeling very hungry and sorry for myself as the by now familiar line of passengers passed along the corridor. Suddenly the door slid open and a lady said, "Do excuse me, but would you like to accompany me? I do so hate eating alone." I leapt to my feet and followed. She was something to do with Missions to Seamen and had guessed my predicament. The waiter saw my unused meal coupons and gave me generous helpings. That lady became my idol, a dream in pale blue and she completely restored my self-confidence.

One of the hazards of travelling alone was that I never knew with whom I might have to share the compartment. In 1936 an enormous Turk got on at Berlin. All my life I had been brought up to fear the Turks; they had skinned an ancestor alive in 1714. My grandfather had fought them in Bulgaria in 1877 and my father had been wounded by them in Palestine in 1917. They had massacred Greeks and Armenians just before I was born and I was now terrified. Poor man, he tried so hard to be friendly, showing me a huge box of cigars which he hoped to take through customs, a wooden box with six cut-throat razors and a book of photographs of the Olympic Games in Berlin. Perhaps he was a weight-lifter or judo wrestler. Anyway I lay in the bottom bunk too scared to disturb him, let alone to use the remarkable china sauceboat which was stored beneath the wash basin. Long after dawn I was still motionless, longing to lift the blind and see where we were. Eventually the attendant looked in and told me that the Turk had been taken off the train during the night by Customs officers. I heaved a sigh of relief and dived for the receptacle under the washstand.

My good friend the late Philippe Daniel Dreyfus once described how, as a young man, he had had to share a Wagon Lits compartment with an uncouth stranger. Lying half-asleep on the top bunk, Philippe was surprised to see that the man had taken a red toothbrush out of

Philippe's sponge bag and was happily cleaning his teeth with it.

Next morning Philippe was the first to wash and shave. Then, making sure the fellow was awake, he picked up his red toothbrush and vigorously set about cleaning every crevice in his backside and in between his toes, just centimetres from the, by now horrified, stranger's nose!

Among my Romanian uncles there was one whose photograph did not stand among the great and favoured on the grand piano at Doftana; this was Cotan, a fat, delightful extrovert who had been discharged from the Army for various escapades. The last straw seems to have been when he tied up his charger to the latch of an open french window of a young lady's bedroom in a grand country house. Unfortunately, while they embraced they were disturbed and, with little time to gird up his loins, let alone get "collected" in the saddle, he applied his spurs too hard and departed from the french windows like a space rocket. He cleared the terrace, but his horse fell on him when it landed in the soft earth among the geraniums. Poor Cotan, badly injured, managed somehow to clamber back into the saddle and the horse made his own way back to its stable in barracks but Cotan was pronounced too injured ever to ride again.

It is possible that Cotan was just as relieved as was the Army at his premature discharge, but he was now obliged to live entirely on his wits, which he did by organizing parties for Bucharest society, special entertainments and marvellous picnic lunches for which he hired carriages or boats and of course gypsy musicians. He had tremendous charm and a wonderful sense of humour. He was much in demand. My mother slightly disapproved of him, but I loved him almost as much as I loved his mongrel dog, Pouffi. Half-Pekinese, half-Dachshund, Pouffi was a highly intelligent and unusual dog. If Cotan was short of money, Pouffi, who was just as much a gourmet as Cotan, was soon aware of the problem. When it came to the serious business of making money they would act as a team. Cotan would bet that wherever a banknote was hidden, Pouffi would find it and naturally, if successful, be allowed to keep it. As soon as someone opened their wallet Cotan would select as large a denomination note as they were prepared to wager, preferably a well-used one. He would then show it to Pouffi who looked at it with watery eyes and sniffed. He then whispered in Pouffi's ear, who was sent out of the room whilst the note was hidden. This could be anywhere provided it was within reach of a small dog. On being summoned back into the room he would begin to sweep the room systematically, like a sapper clearing a minefield, lifting carpets, moving cushions and searching pockets.

Eventually he would find the banknote and only part with it to Cotan after being rewarded with a substantial titbit.

Occasionally Cotan went for high stakes, taking care to choose victims who were preferably female and of a nervous disposition. He casually suggested that if they were ever to be left alone with the adorable little harmless Pouffi they would never be able to escape unharmed, unless they stuffed Pouffi's mouth with a wad of banknotes. This possibility was invariably treated with scorn and laughter, and so Cotan, showing visible signs of having second thoughts about placing such a large bet on a hopeless cause, would nevertheless increase the bundle of notes being wagered, show them to Pouffi and then leave the two alone. Now Pouffi had been trained, so to speak, in reverse. He did not mind who came into a room, but no one was ever to be allowed out. After a few minutes of patiently looking at each other, the victim might start to edge towards the door. Instantly Pouffi became incredibly ferocious, snarling and snapping at her heels. She would be forced to sit down again and reflect. From then on every time she dared move, the dog's lips curled back to display a set of evil yellow fangs and he uttered extraordinary blood-curdling growls. Few people lasted more than twenty minutes, and only when the dog's mouth was stuffed with a wad of money so that he could no longer bite did they rush for the door. I was determined that one day I too would have such a dog and make a fortune.

Europe was becoming a suspicious and dangerous place. Whereas only Turkey had required a passport in 1876, now every country imposed its Immigration and Customs controls. There was always tension as officials in an array of different uniforms tramped through the Orient Express at every frontier crossing. The journey was no longer fun; my letters began to contain descriptions of searches for Jews, of people being dragged off the train and of lots of black uniforms, jackboots and skull and cross bones cap badges.

Not a word of the disturbing events taking place in Romania and elsewhere was ever discussed by my parents in my presence, even though I asked about the memorial stone to the Prime Minister Duca which I had seen at Sinia station. He had been assassinated by Corneliu Codreanu's Iron Guard, a fanatical pro-Nazi group whose policy was violently anti-Jewish and anti-democratic. They wanted Romania to break off all contact with the League of Nations, France and Russia, and to establish close links with Germany. The Government gradually became destabilized until in 1937 an unusual event occurred in

Romanian politics: the government in power failed to rig the election. In desperation King Carol appointed an eccentric poet called Goga to be Prime Minister, who caused such havoc that after a short while the King suspended the government and set up a Fascist military dictatorship. He had Codreanu arrested and then rashly allowed him to be shot "trying to escape". On 18 July 1938 Queen Marie died. She had had an internal haemorrhage and her son was suspected of delaying calling in foreign doctors who diagnosed liver damage. Her body was taken from Bucharest to Curtea de Arges to be buried next to her husband, King Ferdinand. Thousands of people lined the railway track holding candles and it took the train six hours to make a two-hour journey. In a final attempt to ignore the important part she had played in sustaining national morale during the First World War, King Carol ordered that there should be no inscription on her tomb.

Visitors to Doftana either ignored events taking place in Romania or more likely had begun to be very discreet now that the Secret Police were very much a power in the land. The British, along with the French and American community, were worried at what seemed to be a total failure by their governments to heed the direction in which King Carol was, albeit pragmatically, taking his country. The British Ambassador, Sir Reginald Hoare, suggested to London that King Carol should be invited to make a State visit as soon as possible. This was postponed no less than three times, because King George V was dying, because of the abdication of Edward VIII and because of Hitler's invasion of Austria.

However, in November 1938 the King and his 17-year-old son, Prince Michael, left Bucharest in the Royal Blue train drawn by three locomotives. At Lambrook School I began to bask in the reflected glory of the occasion. There were 127 pieces of hand luggage, forty trunks containing uniforms and tons of royal silver and plate. The destroyer *Sikh* and escorting warships and Royal Air Force escort planes were delayed by thick fog. The driver of a gleaming steam engine, called Leatherhead, complained that fog prevented him going more than 60 mph. The Life Guards escort, whose horses had been waiting at least an hour and a half, were unaccustomed to the dimly lit streets and troopers had a difficult ride. But it was the first time a State Visit had ever been televised in Britain and the principal actors rose to the occasion. King Carol wore a splendid white cloak over one shoulder with the black and gold cross of St Michael the Brave, contrasting with the cocked hat and dark blue uniform of an Admiral in the Romanian Navy. Prince Michael wore the grey uniform of Romanian Mountain Troops which already carried fifteen medal ribbons on his tunic! He had endeared himself to the dining car steward on the train by asking for a second helping of orange soufflé, speaking fluent English, as did his father. The visit received a lot of Press coverage and I was delighted to see that Mother's cousin, Matila Ghika, was a special attaché to the King. The visit was deemed successful by the British press, but no defence agreements or arms sales were reported. King Carol then went on to meet President Lebrun of France and Chancellor Adolf Hitler in Berchtesgaden. The meeting with Hitler was not cordial. In spite of Carol's Hohenzollern background, it seemed he was no longer to be trusted. His triumphant return to Bucharest was a National holiday and the start of "British Week". My parents left Doftana to attend the many social events arranged.

In 1938 I returned to Doftana for the summer holidays to find that my bedroom in the eaves of the house now had fitted cupboards, book shelves, bright coloured curtains and specially made furniture. Opposite my bedroom was the attic, known in Romanian as the *"pod"*. This was full of an astonishing variety of objects including Russian samovars, Turkish helmets, swords, Hussar tunics and my father's army tin trunk with a 1918 photo of Marlene Dietrich and a map showing Turkish positions at the Battle of Gaza. I never grew tired of exploring the *'pod'* and knew every cranny which eventually, when the Iron Guard were watching my father, proved useful.

From the window of my room I could see the wooden veranda of Gui's cottage, and beneath it the wood store and the room where Florica, the maid, lived. She was a dark handsome girl and there was something volcanic about her which seemed to suggest smouldering fires. She sang sad songs which our Hungarian cook hated. Next to the sloping roof stood an old walnut tree beneath which Fetitica, a mongrel, had dug a deep cavern between the roots where, in its dark inaccessible depths, she chose to have puppies. One morning, when I was aiming my air gun out of the window, Florica came up behind me and put her hands on my shoulders,

"I bet you would never climb out onto the roof in the dark and then climb down the old walnut tree. There is something very secret I could show you, but that's only if you dare," she purred.

"Of course I dare," I protested, "but what is it?"

"Just wait and see. You are a big boy now. It's a special surprise."

That night when everybody was asleep and the half-moon was hidden by a cloud, I climbed out of the window, crossed the roof and climbed down the great walnut tree. It was easy to slip down its smooth bark and I began to tiptoe along the sandy path towards Florica's room. She had left her door ajar and a pale shaft of light beckoned me. I paused a moment outside her door to listen; there was not a sound to be heard. Gently I pushed the door open and there in the warm yellow light lay Florica, like a sleek contented seal, basking beneath an array of wall carpets, icons and crosses. She was submerged in a heap of white bed clothes, eiderdowns and huge feather pillows.

I could scarcely believe that this was the same prim housemaid in a starched red and white uniform whom I saw every day, who folded my pyjamas so carefully and breathed deeply when she helped me to button my shirt. Alas I had no more time for idle comparisons, because with a husky cry of "*Ai venit!*" (so you have come), she rose from her bed, drew me into the room and then closed the bolts of the door behind me with a sickening thud. Trapped between her bed and the washstand, with a pink chamber pot underneath, I never stood a chance. With a flick of her shoulders and two wriggles of her hips she was undressed in a flash and bore down on me with her arms outstretched, murmuring "*Draga*" (darling).

A little later, lying with my head firmly clasped to her bosom, I just managed to avoid suffocation and had time to reflect on my extraordinary predicament. Maybe this was what Uncle George meant when he said Romanian women were irresistible, certainly there was a pleasant warm tumescent feeling and I began to look at Florica in a completely different light. For the rest of those holidays she left her knickers in the '*pod*' before coming to make my bed. I was proud that, although I might still be only 10th in my class at school, in this particular subject, at just under twelve years old I was now way ahead of my peers.

Before I left Lambrook School in the spring of 1939, I was summoned by Mr Cameron, the headmaster, to receive his advice on how to face the moral hazards that lay ahead of me. I was warned not let people 'take advantage of me' and to note the dangers inherent in the use of public lavatories. My future relation with women should be akin to a bee climbing into a snapdragon, but somehow I just could not reconcile this to my adventures with Florica. Finally he gave me a bible, which I still possess, and suggested I took note of Corinthians XVI 13, an exhortation to "Stand fast in the faith, quit you like men, be strong," which would cover all dilemmas that lay ahead in life.

In March 1939 my mother made her second visit to England in order to select my wardrobe from a long list provided by Sherborne School in Dorset. She spent a great deal of time and money at Gieves in Bond Street where I was fitted with two oversize dark grey suits, a straw hat, blazer and several stiff white collars with collar studs front and back. I grew to hate those dreadful stiff collars. I was put into a house called The Green, an old coaching inn at the top of Cheap Street. Our housemaster, Sam Hey, was a cheerful rotund unmarried Yorkshireman who taught geography and chain-smoked, spilling ash over his blue suits. I do not believe that he ever understood our unhappiness. Our welfare and creature comforts depended greatly on the goodwill of Matron, whom we seldom saw and was also unmarried.

After a while my confidence returned and I gradually began to discover how to make the best of what the school had to offer, and of course there was plenty. Nevertheless I became resentful of authority and distinctly rebellious. I hated the injustice, petty rules and lack of encouragement from anyone in authority.

For the summer holidays of 1939, instead of travelling on the Orient Express, I was driven to Romania by American friends from Ploesti, Ray and Gertrude Walters. We sailed on the German liner *Deutschland* from Southampton to Cuxhaven and I watched a propaganda film of singing German soldiers marching into the Saarland, then into Austria and recently into Czechoslovakia, through streets of cheering crowds waving swastika flags. I felt uneasy, remembering the effect that the entry of Nazi troops into Vienna the previous year had then had on my travelling companions.

We climbed into the car on the quayside and took the road towards Stade. Donald Walters, from a Quaker school in England, and I looked out for German Army trucks and sang the National Anthem at the top of our voices every time we passed a marching column. Little did I realize that six years later I would again be looking out for German troops on that very same road, advancing cautiously towards Cuxhaven in command of an armoured car reconnaissance troop from the 1st Household Cavalry Regiment.

My father met me in Bucharest and took me straight to the airport whence we flew in Savoia-Marchetti aircraft to Constantza. This, although we did not realize it, was to be our last family holiday together. Mother had rented a villa from the Stirby family, complete with a minaret beside the golden sands of Mamaia beach. My father made sure we never had a dull moment. The tension building up in Europe was forgotten and I do not believe he or any of our many friends who visited us listened to the radio or read a newspaper during those last three idyllic weeks of August 1939.

Shortly after we returned to Doftana Adolf Hitler ordered his troops to invade Poland and three days later, on 3 September, Neville Chamberlain declared that Great Britain was now at war with Germany. We listened to his broadcast on the BBC World Service, standing in silence around the tall mahogany radio in the drawing room. This will make a whole difference to our lives, I thought; who knows, I may not have to go back to school.

A week later my sisters and I leant on our bicycles beside the main road outside Cimpina to watch a seemingly endless column of silent misery streaming south. They were Polish refugees, exhausted old men, women and children, pushing prams, handcarts and bicycles, leading a cow or a goat, riding on farm carts piled high with bundles of bedding and household effects. There were motorcars with battered sides, broken headlights and mattresses tied to the roofs, all crammed with grey faces. There were smart carriages with huddled figures in fur coats drawn by tired horses whose heads hung low and a few Polish soldiers who trudged past in mudstained uniforms, conspicious in their distinctive diamond-shaped caps. These people were not just fleeing from the Germans advancing from the west but also from the Russians, who, having made a secret treaty with Hitler, had chosen the same moment to invade Poland from the east. It was a shattering experience seeing those refugees and I do not believe any of us children spoke. War suddenly seemed so very close, a war which at our age we could not understand. When we got home my father told us that he had seen the sides of Bucharest airfield lined with battered Polish warplanes.

Father was now worried because the Iron Guard, whose pro-Nazi beliefs were no longer hidden, had begun to harass those few Englishmen remaining in Romania, whom they suspected of planning to sabotage the oil fields. This may well have been true but would have been an impossible task. It is possible that he was being protected by Rica Antonescu, a childhood friend of my mother who had married a young officer just after the liberation of Transylvania in 1920. He was now an ambitious general with very pro-German views and plotting secretly to overthrow King Carol. General Antonescu later became a ruler acceptable to the Germans until he met a singularly unpleasant death at the hands of the Communists in 1946.

Not wishing to jeopardize the delicate relationship which my mother still had with Rica, my father took me to his study and unlocked a cupboard which contained a shotgun and two sporting rifles which he had used in Kenya many years before.

"Hide these guns, son, anywhere you want, but don't ever tell me or anybody else where you have put them. One day when this wretched war is over they will be yours, so grease them up well." With that he walked out of the house and drove off to the oil fields. It was the first time he had asked my help. I felt now I was an adult, entrusted with a secret task. I was elated.

I ran down the drive through the pine trees to the garage where I found a can of grease and then back to the hothouses, where, dodging the enormous toads who chose to live there, I picked up some sacking. Making sure no one saw me, I took the weapons up into the *pod* and locked the door. I smothered each gun in grease, wrapped them carefully in sacking and then wound a piece of oilskin around each weapon. After stacking up tin trunks and boxes I was able to climb to the top of a tall wardrobe from where I could peer down into the narrow gap between the roof tiles and the wooden planks which formed the overhanging eaves of the house. Gently I let each sticky package slide down ten feet into the darkness before returning the grease tin to the garage and cleaning myself with a petrol-soaked rag. Curiously, my father never mentioned those guns to me again.

Mussolini's Italy had not yet decided to enter the war on the side of Germany and so, very much to my disappointment, it was decided to send me back to England on the Simplon Express via Yugoslavia and Italy. After a tearful farewell to my sisters, to Gui and of course Florica, I was driven to Cimpina station. Mother slipped a small icon into my pocket and after father had given me a hug and whispered, "Stick it son", advice which was going to prove more useful than Corinthians XVI 13, I climbed into a crowded carriage and waved goodbye. Seven days later, which included an air raid alert in Paris, I reported to Miss Elsie Tomlinson, my step-grandfather's secretary in Cannon Street, London. She was to take a keen and kindly interest in me from then on. She gave me half a crown, a cup of tea, one of FJN's digestive biscuits and sent me off to catch a train to Sherborne from Waterloo Station.

The train was packed with Reservists who were rejoining their units, so I stood in the corridor. The station at Sherborne was deserted. I heaved my suitcase out of the guards' van onto the platform and began the long slow walk up Cheap Street to The Green where I knew I would have to face all the inconveniences suffered by small boys returning to school several days after term has begun.

"So Redgrave has at last bothered to come back. Well, don't hang around boy, hurry up and get unpacked."

Later, in the dormitory, I lay beneath my tartan blanket and watched the dark storm clouds scudding past the open window. I felt cold and very miserable. Little did I know that I was not going to see any of my family again for six years. I felt under my pillow for the little icon mother had given me, clasped it tightly and wept.

Chapter Three

SCATTERED TO THE WINDS

One glorious summer day soon after the withdrawal of British troops from Dunkirk in France I was taking part in a Field Day with the Sherborne School Cadet Corps in the grounds of Sherborne Castle. I had been given a most important message to deliver to a beleaguered platoon. The journey through enemy territory was fraught with danger and excitement. Suddenly the sun flashed on the brass belt buckles of a mounted gentleman who was scanning the valley below through his binoculars. I could scarcely stop myself trembling as I quietly eased my rifle through the undergrowth to rest on top of a bank. I was so close that I felt sure he could hear my heart thumping.

Placing my cheek on the butt of my old Lee Enfield rifle, I lined up the sights and squeezed the trigger gently, first pressure, then harder; a single shot, he stiffened and was then practically catapulted out of sight as two inches of lead pencil propelled by a .303 blank cartridge hit the flank of his grey mare. Brigadier Moberly, retired Indian Army, galloped away out of control into the far distance and for the time being gave up his duties as an umpire. Taking advantage of his absence, I cut across 'neutral territory', arrived at my destination minus one puttee and minus the vital message, which had been lost while evading capture on the way. Nevertheless the information I had gained proved to be of such great value that from then onwards I was always assigned to scouting duties and, without realizing it at the time, my military career had begun.

There can be few small towns which have a school with such beautiful buildings as Sherborne. There has been a school there for eleven hundred years, ever since the reign of Alfred the Great, but the present school was given its charter by King Edward VI, son of Henry VIII and Jane Seymour. The colour of the stone, the exquisite cloisters and the soaring columns of the Abbey were a joy to behold. I had never seen anything like it. It was impossible to be educated in such lovely and peaceful

31

surroundings without acquiring a sense of continuity and stability.

The North Dorset countryside is full of small combes and gentle hills. I explored these and many little villages on my bicycle. Next to my icon, my bicycle had become my most treasured possession. I had paid one pound for the frame and then with difficulty constructed the rest of the machine from bits found on a scrapheap. The result was a sturdy old-fashioned bike with no gears, an awful saddle and brakes which needed delicate adjustment, but I no longer had to walk to the playing fields and on Sundays I could escape from the school and search for fossils in small escarpments and quarries. That old bicycle became my salvation, especially during the school holidays when I had no money for bus fares. Initially I spent my holidays with my Uncle Jack at Cockwood, a tiny village on the estuary of the River Exe. He was a big man with only one arm, having lost the other in a boyhood accident in a school gymnasium. With ginger hair and bright blue eyes, it was easy to imagine that if he had worn a helmet with a pair of cow horns he could well have been mistaken for a Viking warrior, a direct descendant of those who had once pillaged the Norfolk coast. It soon became obvious that his wife Paula did not cherish the idea of looking after me for the duration of the war and so holidays at their bungalow in Devon became less frequent.

I was staying at Cockwood when Exeter was bombed for the first time. The distinctive drone of what seemed like hundreds of German bombers had brought us out on to the lawn and three minutes later we heard the explosions. There were no anti-aircraft guns around the city, which took a terrible pounding; the sky was red with fires which burnt all night. The next morning my cousin Douglas and I went to see the damage. I was appalled by what we saw and began to understand what those Polish refugees I had seen in Romania must have been through. Our favourite cinema, the Rougemont, unique in that it provided double seats and curtains for those sitting in the back row, had been flattened. We returned to the village thankful that we did not live in the city.

German fighter aircraft then began to carry out daylight hit and run attacks on targets either side of the River Exe. One morning, standing on the lawn which overlooked the river, I watched rooted to the spot as a single fighter streaked in low from the sea straight towards Cockwood. I did not dive for cover until I saw machine-gun fire cut through the earth in the vegetable patch. On a second occasion Douglas and I were sailing in an 18-foot 'Sharpie' across to Exmouth, a hazardous journey in itself because the estuary was full of steel scaffolding triangles placed there to deter seaplanes from landing and disgorging a vast invasion force, when two Messerschmitt 109s came in low over Dawlish Warren. We both jumped into the water as they opened fire, probably at a totally different target, before flying on towards the Royal Marine Depot at Topsham. Douglas saved the day by just preventing our drifting boat from hitting one of the dreaded triangles.

As the war crept closer to Sherborne the boys took turns at Fire Watching on the roof of The Green whenever the air-raid sirens sounded. Night after night we were disturbed as German bombers flew over to attack cities like Bristol and those boys not on duty picked up their helmets and gas masks and trooped down into the shelter where we slept as best we could. At weekends we made long cycle rides to look at the debris of crashed aircraft and to hunt for souvenirs.

At around five o'clock one fine autumn day we were still in class when the sirens sounded and almost immediately we heard a deep rumbling sound. There was no time to get to the air raid shelter and our master shouted for us to get under our desks. The noise of exploding bombs grew louder and ever closer. I don't believe I was frightened but I was certainly angry and indignant: "Why pick on us, why on Sherborne?" as bombs fell literally all around us, bringing down the ceiling and shattering the windows of our classroom. Three bombs had fallen within the school quadrangle beside the sandbagged cloisters in which boys were sheltering, others in the road beside the chemistry laboratories, outside the swimming pool, in the school gardens and several exploded on the school playing fields before cutting a swathe right through the town. Mercifully not a single boy out of five hundred was injured; indeed only seventeen people were killed and thirty-two injured in the whole town. We were particularly shocked that four small children had been blown to bits near the school playing fields and the corporation dustman, together with his horse and cart, had also perished. Apparently a force of fifty Heinkel bombers escorted by fighters had crossed the Dorset coast near Weymouth with the intention, it was thought, of attacking the Westlands factory in Yeovil. They were intercepted by Spitfires based at Warmwell and hurriedly dropped three hundred bombs in three minutes on Sherborne, damaging 807 houses, many quite close to the Abbey church of Saint Mary, which had been built twelve hundred years earlier. A tablet in the Abbey today reads, "Praising God that when the blast of hostile bombs fell on Sherborne 30th September 1940 this Abbey church was spared. A thousand years in thy sight are but as yesterday."

The main railway to London was cut, there was extensive damage to sewers and electricity, gas and water supplies were disrupted. The Government, for reasons unknown, put a news blackout on naming Sherborne until years later. The next morning delayed action bombs exploded and then we were put into teams to clean up the town and to help people salvage their belongings. By the end of the war, in 1945, air raid warning sirens had sounded in rural Sherborne 386 times.

I felt homesick as a second Christmas away from my family approached. I longed for the magic of Doftana deep under a mantle of snow and a Christmas Day ritual which never changed; the agonizing wait until the doors to the drawing room were flung open to reveal a fabulous decorated Christmas tree rising out of a tantalizing heap of parcels. The staff and their families came in and were given presents, then we sang songs and finally father handed out bottles of home-distilled tuica and boxes of Capsa chocolates to speed their departure. Only after they had left were we allowed to open our presents, and at that last Christmas before the war I had been given a blue Peugeot bicycle with gears, which alas I never saw again.

Junior boys at Sherborne school seldom had an opportunity to read a newspaper and so I never minded cleaning a prefect's study if I could listen to the six o'clock news on the radio. I began to take a keen interest in every report about events in Romania and started to keep a scrap book. The very first picture was from the *Illustrated London News* and showed the Romanian Prime Minister, Armand Calinescu, wearing a black eye patch, who had been assassinated outside his home by the Iron Guard just before Christmas 1939. They had put seventeen bullets into his body and also killed his detective before rushing to the Broadcasting Station to interrupt transmission shouting "Calinescu is dead. We have avenged the Iron Guard".

Retribution had been swift because there were also some grisly pictures of the twisted bodies of his nine killers who had been taken back to the scene of the murder at Elfefterie Bridge and executed in public. Their corpses were left in the road for 24 hours and then taken to Ploesti to hang from lamp posts where the public were forced into a queue and told to walk past the awful spectacle.

Most of the British community chose to leave Romania soon afterwards, although the Foreign Office had still been unable to issue any clear directive, in spite of the fact that the Americans, who were not even at war with anyone, had already decided to leave Romania.

I was often teased by other boys about Romania whose interests I now defended fiercely. In helpless frustration I wrote to my father:

"There are lots of chaps who say a lot of silly things about Romania and I feel like knocking their blocks off, only they are all bigger than me. At least I manage to out-argue them."

However, it was not only the boys who infuriated me because a term later I wrote in despair:

"It is really a bit much when even the Headmaster who takes us for current affairs says, 'Now if Mr Redgrave really wants to set his oil wells on fire he had better hurry up because the Germans have already set up a bockwurst and beer stall in Ploesti,'" and so on. I finished the letter, "Once again I wish I were with you and I do so hope Romania is not invaded, so that I can come out for Easter." Letters still cost only 2½d, but now took twelve days.

It must have been clear to Adolf Hitler, long before King Carol's visit to London, that Great Britain was never going to help Romania. Germany increased its trade until it provided nearly 40 per cent of Romania's imports. When the remainder of Czechoslovakia was annexed by Germany in March 1939 this figure increased to 50 per cent. It is to Romania's credit that, when Czechoslovakia was threatened, King Carol was the first to offer support, but was dismayed at the total lack of courage or interest shown by the United Kingdom and France. Sadly this signalled the end of the Little Entente which had been one of the firmest alliances in Europe.

German propaganda in Romania, especially in Bucharest, then began to increase, but was never even remotely matched by the British. German newspapers, for instance, cost only 6 Lei, whereas a British newspaper cost 20 Lei, one fifth of a worker's wage. There were 3500 Romanian students enrolled at the Anglo-American Institute in Bucharest but they could not afford the exorbitant cost of British text books, whereas the Nazi literature was given away free.

Romania's isolation from her friends in the west increased after the Soviet Union joined Germany in the attack on Poland. King Carol realized that helping Poland would mean disaster, so he turned to his Balkan neighbours, but none wanted war and indeed two were waiting for a chance to settle old scores. In May 1940 the meticulously planned German invasion of Western Europe began and France, Luxembourg, Belgium, Holland, Norway and Denmark all fell. The collapse of the French Maginot Line was a mortal blow to all Allied supporters in Romania. How much reliance could now be placed on the much-vaunted Romanian defensive wall of 'liquid fire' on the River Sereth, which was the frontier with Russia?

35

On the 10th of June 1940 Italy declared war against Britain and France, thus severing the only remaining land link with Romania. I did not have to look at my school atlas to realize that now I was completely cut off from my family and that I was never going to spend holidays at Doftana again. Mother, who had abundant common sense, anticipated trouble and sent sums of money out of Romania with friends to pay my school fees which were £200 a year. Two months earlier she had wisely removed my sister Mary Maud from a convent school in Italy, the Poggio Imperiale in Florence.

Suddenly the Greater Romania created at the end of 1918 began to crumble with terrifying swiftness. The Russians took immediate advantage of King Carol's predicament to increase their empire. They massed an army on the northern border on 28 June 1940 and demanded that Romania should cede Bessarabia and Northern Bukovina to them. The King appealed to Adolf Hitler who, needless to say, had his own good reasons to advise Romania not to resist and to give up these provinces.

A few days later, in July, the Romanian cabinet was obliged to resign and was replaced by pro-German right-wingers which included Horia Sima. When he realized all was not going his own way he resigned and returned to lead his greenshirted Iron Guardists. He was popular with his men because at least he was a Romanian, whereas Corneliu Codreanu, who had founded the movement, was discovered after his death to have been called Zelinski, born of Polish and German parents.

Now the jackals began to move in. The Bulgarians, following the Russian example and no doubt acting on German advice, marched into Southern Dobrudja in August 1940 to reclaim their lost province. In September the Hungarians, again on German advice, rapidly occupied large areas of Transylvania. In a belated desperate attempt to save his country from any further loss, on 5 September King Carol denounced any guarantee that might still have existed with Great Britain and declared Romania to be pro-German but not yet a co-belligerent. However, it was no good. He was forced to abdicate and once again handed over the crown to his son, Crown Prince Michael. King Carol left Romania not only with Mme Lupescu and Ernest Urdarianu, his Lord Chamberlain, but also with nine railway coaches piled high with national treasures. This was noticed too late and pursuing cars missed halting the train at the frontier by just a few minutes. Power now lay in the hands of General Antonescu, an ambitious and competent soldier who gave himself the title of "Conducator" or dictator. He had been Commander of the Third Army Corps, but was dismissed by King Carol and imprisoned at the Monastery of Bistrita in Moldavia because he had protested against the mass executions which followed the assassination of Prime Minister Calinescu, but he is also said to have protested at the assassination of seventy statesmen and Civil Service officials by the Iron Guard in November. It was thought he had developed close links with the German Minister in Bucharest, Dr Wilhelm Fabricius, and with the Iron Guard. He had little political instinct, but felt humiliated because the Army had not been allowed to defend the national borders and he was determined to save what was left of his country from the long-term threat presented by the Soviet Union and Communism. In his eyes the only course remaining open was co-operation with the Nazi Germans.

In October 1940 German troops in great numbers began to arrive in Romania to 'protect the oil fields' and to train the Romanian army. They were accompanied by a small army of Gestapo officials whose activities, designed to establish complete control of the country, were thorough and intense. Thousands of intellectuals and local leaders were sent to prison or to concentration camps and the few remaining British were placed under close surveillance. Pressure on the few Western oilmen still left in Romania had increased after the Germans overran France in June 1940. They had been able to intercept a train leaving Bordeaux for Spain which contained French 2ème Bureau (Intelligence) documents which confirmed that plans existed for technicians to sabotage the oil refineries in Romania. This information had been passed to the Iron Guard, possibly by Baron Manfred von Buch Killinger, who became German Ambassador in Bucharest.

All British subjects had been ordered to leave Romania on 3 July, but a few, including my parents and an old friend Percy Clark, succeeded in getting their right to be domiciled in the country recognized, Percy because he ran the only company to make wire ropes for oil rigs. In August Father was in trouble because his heavy Bulgarian 12mm revolver had again been 'discovered' and he had to buy off the Gendarmes. Practically all their friends had left Romania, the French going to Syria and the Lebanon, the Americans back to the States, the Dutch to the East Indies only to be captured by the Japanese, whilst the British went to Greece or Turkey whence they hoped to reach Egypt or South Africa. Their position became hazardous after Italy chose to invade Greece from Albania, but fortunately Turkey remained neutral. Letters sent from Istanbul were full of depressing tales:

"If you ever have to make the same trip as we have had to do, for heavens sake keep clear of this town, unless you have an awful lot of money."

37

Not surprisingly Turkish banks were refusing to accept Romanian lei or French francs, which were now worthless. There is no doubt that conditions for British refugees in Turkish Thrace in the autumn of 1940 were difficult, but London already had too many problems of its own to be able to alleviate their hardships. Another old friend wrote:

"We all have our troubles and keep on discussing ways and means of getting out of here. We just pray that you too will still be able to get out of Romania."

After the arrival of German troops in Bucharest in October the Iron Guard felt encouraged to take the law into their own hands. Three men with revolvers broke into Percy Clark's room at the Athene Palace Hotel and kidnapped him. He was accused of being in the British Intelligence Service and was starved, punched and beaten, his arms and wrists cruelly twisted and rendered practically useless. They tried the old trick of leaving him with just one 'friendly' guard who offered to let him escape in return for a sum of money. He took the bait but luckily spotted the ambush waiting for him in the shadows across the street. He turned round and walked back into the house with bullets thudding into the door behind him. Eventually he was located by Norman Mayers, the British Consul in Bucharest, who got the police to rescue him and transfer him to hospital. Then at the end of October he was taken across the Danube by Padre Bell from the British Embassy who travelled with him to the American Hospital in Istanbul where he was nursed back to health.

My father had been advised by the British Embassy to move his family from Doftana to the comparative safety of a flat in Bucharest. Five days later there was a very strong earthquake which damaged both the house at Doftana and their flat. As if this was not an evil omen, there were also strong rumours that Romania might soon join the Axis Pact, with Germany and Italy, and declare war on Britain, yet my parents still did not seem to have made any move to leave Romania. Perhaps they drew comfort from my cheerful letters describing how in England we had been issued with gas masks after breakfast and how much I longed to possess a black steel helmet, marked with large white letters ARP (Air-Raid Precautions) for fire watching. Perhaps they were confident that Madame Rica Antonescu, the Conducator's wife, whom my mother had known for thirty-five years, would continue to protect them.

Great Britain may have been willing to help Romania, but, whatever transpired, it was certainly too little and too late. The British Government made two unsuccessful attempts to influence events. In the first instance, in the spring of 1940, a number of our most modern twin-engine Blenheim bombers were flown to Romania with great difficulty via staging points in Africa and the Middle East. As thing turned out, according to my uncle Jean, then a Colonel in the Air Force, Romanian pilots hardly had time to begin flying training before General Antonescu allowed the German Luftwaffe to fly them straight to their own airfields in Germany.

The second British intervention was an ambitious idea, but its execution was hopeless and inept. The plan was to block the River Danube at the Iron Gates where the river narrows and cuts through the Carpathians. If navigation could be interrupted on that great river then no more oil-laden barges would pass through to sustain the German war machine. British agents assembled four barges at Sulena at the mouth of the Danube and in great secrecy were able to fill them with explosives and concrete. Tug-boat crews manned by British sailors dressed in singularly un-Romanian plain clothes and a few Romanian-speaking agents were also gathered at Sulena. Unfortunately their loose talk before sailing and the noisy and strange behaviour of these crews whilst refuelling in the port of Georgiu soon drew attention to the expedition. Officials friendly to Britain in the Romanian Government, who had previously turned a blind eye to the adventure, were now placed in a most embarrassing position. The expedition had to be cancelled and all the British sailors were expelled, much to the delight of German agents already operating in Romania.

The inevitable result was that British nationals came under increased suspicion and that my father needed more and more permits just to be able to move about and carry on his business in the oil fields. Even my sisters, aged 8 and 10, had to report to the police station for identity checks. All this was no novelty to Mother and Gui who still retained German passes issued by "Der Kaisert Kommandantur" in 1917 in Cimpina. In December 1940 my father must at last have realized that time was running out and he rushed around trying to realize some of his assets. He scribbled hasty progress reports to his wife:

"Darling Mine, I'm having a hell of a time trying to sell my oil. Prahova only offered me the price of light oil, namely 11,000 lei, *imagine it*! So I'm on the run elsewhere. Have got an account of 5000 lei for you which I enclose."

While he was away my mother set about obtaining an imposing certificate stating that she had worked with devotion and skill in the Red Cross Hospital in Bucharest during 1917–1918 and that she was also President of the Telega Branch of the Red Cross. Armed with this document, she

39

had high hopes that she now possessed a talisman which would overcome all difficulties. The reality of the situation was that, but for protection from Madame Rica Antonescu, my father would have already been arrested or kidnapped by the Greenshirts in the Iron Guard.

General Antonescu has been portrayed as an honest soldier who tried belatedly to save his country from total collapse but failed because he had no political power base. Horia Sima, leader of the Iron Guard, soon decided that the General was not acting as a proper Fascist and that he was certainly not right wing enough to change Romanian society as they wanted. Sima therefore ordered his Greenshirts to rebel against the General on 20 January 1941. This action split the country, resulting in civil war which is well described by Clare Hollingworth in her book *There's a German Just Behind Me.*

The revolt began with no less than three attempts on the same day to murder General Antonescu. The Iron Guard took over parts of Bucharest and proceeded to commit the most appalling atrocities on the Jewish community. About five hundred Jews were taken from their homes in open cattle trucks to the town slaughter house, where fifty middle-aged women were impaled on hooks and hoisted up on the beams to bleed slowly to death. The crowd got tired of waiting for them to die and so put the rest to death in the street. The Jewish district of Bucharest, which had grown up during the previous twenty-five years, was then ransacked and burned. Entire Jewish families were taken into the countryside and shot, then the Greenshirts set fire to the synagogue and those Jews who tried to escape were strangled outside on the steps. Fighting between the Army and the Iron Guard rebels continued in the streets with bullets shattering windows in the block of flats where my mother and sisters were sheltering. After three days General Antonescu made some sort of a deal with the German forces who had already moved into Romania. They quickly put down the revolt and restored a semblance of order in all the troubled cities.

It must have surprised foreigners that the Romanians could be quite so anti-Semitic and so brutal, but they should have remembered that when Octavian Goga, the poet laureate and an ardent Fascist, was made Prime Minister by King Carol for ninety disastrous days in 1938 he did all he could to make life quite intolerable for the Jews. He explained to the English writer Hector Bolitho at the time that one million out of twenty million Romanians were Jews and that they had nearly all arrived since 1916. He complained that the bulk of the trade in the country was managed by Jews and that it was their greed which had caused the

Peasant Revolt of 1907; three-quarters of the bank clerks were Jews, half the lawyers and so on. He went on to say, "The Jews describe themselves as the salt of the earth, but our salt is not as refined as yours is in England, and at the present moment the dish is too salty for Romanian tastes."

The Germans now put intense pressure on the Romanian Government, and on General Antonescu in particular, to put an end to all British activities in Romania and to arrest all those who did not have diplomatic status. They skilfully set about uniting what was left of the country by spreading rumours that the Russians were about to invade when in fact they were planning to invade Russia themselves. Anti-British feeling increased, encouraged by a German propaganda story that we were about to bomb Ploesti, which was virtually impossible, being out of flying range of our bombers from any of the airfields in use at the time.

There was to be no Christmas at Doftana in 1940 and it must have been a lean and worrying time for my parents, who nevertheless did their best to make the little flat in Bucharest look festive. The tension increased during the next few weeks until at about 11 pm on 9 February 1941 the telephone rang in the flat and a voice speaking in French said, "Micheline, tell Robin he *must* leave the country *now*. He is in very great danger. No, *not* tomorrow, within the hour. Drive to the frontier; he might still escape." It had been Rica and the conversation ended abruptly. A quick call to the Embassy confirmed that there was every indication that not only were more attacks on Jews and British imminent but that Romania would be forced to declare war on Great Britain. My father put down the telephone and hastily packed two suitcases, collected his important papers, kissed his wife and sleeping daughters goodbye and slipped out of the back door from the block of flats into the empty street. There were a few agonizing moments when his motor-car would not start, but he was soon pushing the Buick as fast as it could go south towards Georgiu which he reached just as dawn was breaking. He abandoned the car, giving the keys to an astonished official who stood between him and the first ferry which was just about to cast off. As he crossed the Danube the first rays of sunshine touched the water, giving that brown river just for a moment a warm yellow glow. He heaved a sigh of relief and then realized that the first knock on the door of the flat in Bucharest was expected at any moment and he prayed that the British Consul had sent an officer round to collect my mother and sisters.

Romania severed all diplomatic relations with Britain on 10 February and the British Consulate became a hive of activity, with diplomats burning files and instructing their citizens to report to the Gara de Nord before 9pm on the 13th where a special train would take them to Constanta on the Black Sea. The outlook was bleak and uncertain, and time was short for my mother, who was worrying about her children. There were only two options. In the event she made a decision which she was to regret bitterly. The two girls were to remain behind with their grandmother, Gui, and uncles and aunts. Perhaps she thought they would be safer with their relatives than facing the unknown dangers which lay ahead. So with a hug and a kiss, and "It won't be for long, darlings," my mother put two suitcases into a taxi and was driven through empty streets to the station.

A night curfew had been imposed on Bucharest, so it was impossible for any Romanian to go to the railway station, which was guarded by German and Romanian soldiers, to see their British friends off. In any case, nobody could then afford to be seen to be pro-British. However, one solitary elegant figure in black, Princess Marthe Bibesco, had taken the risk and had come to wish her friends 'bon voyage'. Miss Clare Hollingworth combined her press reporting for the *Daily Express* with helping the Consulate staff to organize the evacuation. Mother was put into the third of the blue Wagon Lits Coaches which had been taken out of a siding where they had been stored ever since the Orient Express stopped running. She must have felt a qualm or two when she saw that two berths had also been reserved for my sisters.

There was much relief when the train steamed out at precisely 10 pm. Early next morning they arrived at a railway siding close to the docks in Constanta which was ringed by steel-helmeted German soldiers, backed up by six light tanks and several military trucks. There was an uncanny silence, no one was allowed off the train, no one spoke, all eyes were on the old Turkish ship *Izmir* which lay just fifty yards away, waiting to take them aboard. Unbeknown to them, there had been some delay in the departure of the Romanian Embassy staff in London, and so they waited with growing unease. Eventually they were ordered to step down and carry their bags towards the ship through lines of curious German soldiers and sinister men in leather coats, losing only one of their number to ever-vigilant Gestapo officers.

It was 14 February 1941, Saint Valentine's Day, when the *Izmir* cast off and moved cautiously through the minefield which protected the port and out into the Black Sea towards Istanbul. All the tension of the past four days disappeared and as Clare aptly put it, "It was one of the happiest journeys I can recollect." I doubt, however, that it was so for my mother who was sailing into a precarious unknown future, leaving her daughters and childhood home behind.

After many adventures my parents reached Cairo by mid-March. Barely a week later my father was a Captain in the Royal Artillery and sailing up the Nile to the Sudan where he was posted as Liaison Officer to the Free French Forces coming from French bases in Equatorial Africa to fight the Italians and who were under command of General Legentilhomme and General Catroux. Mother was left almost destitute and obliged to look for a job for the first time in her life. The ever helpful Norman Mayers managed to find employment for her in the accounts department of the British Repatriation Office at the Embassy in Cairo.

At last letters began to arrive from Romania. Ioana wrote,

"Darling Mummy I am nearly happy, but not quite . . . I miss you badly, I love you, I wont forget you."

Her elder sister had settled down quickly and was determined to enjoy life,

"We are going to Floresti because King Michael will be there. It's the second time I will have seen him. Ioana continues to sleep with your photo and letter under her pillow. She is still sore about you leaving . . . Florica has married, her husband is ugly, at least I think so." Gui wrote reassuringly in French, ending:

"Every night the girls beg God to bring you back. Rica sent us an enormous box of chocolates from Capsa's . . . I wish she had not done so."

Any hopes of Bucharest remaining a safe haven disappeared when the first air raid alarm sounded soon after the Germans, and their Romanian allies, attacked Russia on 22 June 1941. The Germans had had little difficulty in persuading the Romanians to advance and recapture their recently lost provinces of Bessarabia and Bukovina, but beyond that the soldiers had no wish to go, least of all to march to Odessa and on into the Caucasus. The German High Command therefore decided to split up Romanian units amongst their own formations and thus prevent a successful mutiny. They were thereafter to exploit Romanian troops shamefully, whose casualties during their Russian campaign were appalling. It is interesting to note that of the three-quarters of a million 'Saxons' of German descent who lived in Transylvania, only sixty-seven men volunteered to fight in Russia, Hitler being quite happy not to conscript them, but preferred to see a firm German presence established in the region.

The summer of 1941 was probably the darkest period of our family fortunes and appeared to offer least hope of us ever getting together again. We had by now all been touched by war. My sisters were trapped in Romania, my mother was penniless in Egypt, my father fighting Italians in Eritrea and I was fire-watching in England. We had indeed been scattered to the winds and suddenly each found ourselves in alien surroundings and very much alone.

Chapter Four

CALLED TO ARMS

I was dismayed when Sam Hey, my housemaster, suggested the time had come to decide what subjects to study in order to prepare for a career. My dream was to travel when I left school, to lead an outdoor life and never read Classics again. I went to Smith's bookshop and bought *Hugo's Teach Yourself German in Three Months*, because my elderly teacher was hopeless. My aptitude for languages and a vague desire to be a diplomat prompted Sam to place me in the Modern Languages Sixth form. Little did I know that the Foreign Office considered a degree in Classics to be mandatory.

FJN had other plans for my future and wrote to my Mother, "Unfortunately he is too like his father in one respect and that is he does not take life very seriously and is always happy-go-lucky. This is not a very good foundation to work upon when you have no money and will have to work for it."

He therefore decided that I was to join a firm of tea brokers in the City as a clerk. With immediate effect I was to take extra tuition in Pitman's Shorthand and in Book-Keeping. I hated both these subjects, bitterly resenting the erosion of my spare time and especially the idea of working in a city office.

I wrote to my Father in despair:

"Everybody is trying to make me decide about a *career*, but I feel lost like Alice in Wonderland. If only you were here. I am in an unholy muddle and only know that I do not want to work in an office." Elsie Tomlinson, FJN's secretary and my great ally, wrote to Mother, "Roy does not like the idea of an indoor life, as I think he prefers something more adventurous . . . maybe with his knowledge of languages he could be a foreign traveller . . . or join the Forces." She concluded with a perceptive forecast, "You know after this war there will be a lot of levelling up and your boy's future will depend much more on himself and his own efforts and personality than on money or birth. I enclose a letter from him which gives you an idea that he meets troubles quite lightly."

During the holidays I heard that I had passed the Oxford and Cambridge School Certificate Exam with credits and a distinction and immediately informed Uncle Jack and FJN who each sent me a pound. This unexpected wealth meant I was rich enough to invite a girl to the cinema before the holidays ended. Unbelievably at Sherborne School all contact with girls was strictly forbidden and was as grave an offence as being late for chapel. This did not prevent me waving to a cheerful band of young ladies who walked up Green Hill past my study window every morning on their way to work in the Sherborne Steam Laundry. Our conversation was limited to short sentences as they hurried to work and I could see no way of ever getting any closer to them.

In an inspired moment I thought of making 'a field study' and was able to persuade my English master to let me write an essay about 'Steam Laundries in our Society' and he provided me with a certificate to that effect. My study companion, Robin Butterell, and I were beside ourselves with excitement as we drew up a questionnaire to be answered by the Steam Laundry manageress, who the girls had warned us was "a proper old dragon". In the event the whole venture was a terrible anti-climax. The manageress examined our credentials and then went out of her way to show us every aspect of her empire, from the accounts section to the laundry marking system. Sadly when we got close to the girls, they were not as attractive as we had wishfully imagined and their hair and clothing smelt strongly of starch and steam. Worst of all, when we returned there was still the essay to write!

Playing rugby football brought out the best and the worst in me. I am horrified to read my letters now:

"We played against the team who broke my collar bone last term. We were short of six players because of flu, they were only short of one. Everyone expected us to lose but we soon found out their side was held together by one man. Well in the first few minutes he went through our forwards like butter, so I yelled to our threes to tackle low and went after him like a bullet myself. I was going flat out and judged I could just get him before the corner flag. Out of the corner of my eye I could see the captain of our side level with me, we did a flying tackle, it was a real corner flag smash up. He was carried off with a wonky knee. We won."

My dreadful arrogance and brutality evidently got worse as I wrote describing another tribal encounter:

"We played a really crack team, the one which won the competition. I had to play on the defensive most of the time. They beat us 20–3, my try, but their full back has a black eye, a forward has had to go to the dentist, the left wing limps, the scrum half wears a bandage round his neck and two others had nose bleeds. I also had a nose bleed, am bruised all over and covered in cuts, but I feel great."

After that first ferocious year I settled down to learn more about the finer points of the game. I got into the school first XV which gave me much-needed self-confidence and, at a time when sport seemed to matter more than academic success, status. Once, when we played Clifton College, I met my father's half-brother, Michael Redgrave. He had just left the Royal Navy and was then acting in *A Month in the Country* at the St James's theatre. We were photographed beside the rugby pitch by *The Tatler* and I promptly wrote to Miss Tomlinson begging her to buy me a copy. It was many years before I met him again. A week later I wrote to her explaining how expensive it was to take a girl out, what with cinema tickets, doughnuts and a sixpenny entrance fee to village dances, and that this was going to place an intolerable strain on my resources:

"I have had to put seven shillings and sixpence aside for my rail ticket back to school. I paid ninepence to the hospital for six stitches in my ear after the brakes failed on my bike, so I only have one shilling and ninepence left out of the ten shillings you sent me which is not really enough to take out this girl I met at Dawlish Warren next Saturday."

Ever sympathetic, she sent me a five shilling postal order and Mary, the innkeeper's daughter, and I had a wonderful time. We went twice to Exeter where we saw extracts from *Lilac Time* sung mainly by Polish airmen and a review full of jokes about rationing, air raid wardens, Hitler and the blackout. This last skit was so corny, about a pretty girl who is picked up in a dark street by a Chinese gentleman and ends up with a howling baby in her arms, the final line being:

"And all through a chink in the blackout."

As each term drew to a close there was always a nagging question of where to go next holidays. Sam Hey solved this by establishing farming camps for boys who could not go home. We set up base in an old barn in the hamlet of Fifield Bavant, near Salisbury, where we slept on palliasses and cooked on a field kitchen. Just behind the farm on a small rise stands a tiny stone chapel outside which the Bishop of Sherborne once held a Sunday service using a farm cart as an altar. Mother was to spot a photograph of this occasion in a magazine in a dentist's waiting room in South Africa. Each day we bicycled to the fields, which were often quite a long way away. We worked until an hour before dusk piling sheaves of corn or barley into stooks, turning wet hay, pulling weeds out of immense muddy fields of kale or pitching hay onto the elevator machine while ricks were built. Sweating away on top of the haystack with a pitch fork, I used to pray for the machine to break down and give us a break.

When I was seventeen I was allowed to join the 4th Battalion of the Dorset Home Guard. I was very conscious of the important part I now had to play in the defence of South-West England. Discarding the 1914 service dress tunic, brass buttons and putties of the school OTC, I was issued with modern battle dress, a black leather belt and gaiters, a gas mask strapped to my chest and a narrow forage cap. Armed with Canadian Ross rifles made in 1917 and long bayonets, we practised various contingency plans against Regular Army units who were then training in Dorset.

My role, as I had hoped, was that of a scout, with instructions to man an outpost covering the western approaches to the town and report all I saw on a field telephone. I chose my position with some care beneath a hedgerow in the south-west corner of Sherborne Girls' School playing fields. We were told to dig weapon pits and to camouflage them as best we could. No doubt my activities were viewed by the school authorities with some alarm but they were soon impressed by my determination to defend the school grounds to the last of my fifteen rounds of ammunition and not to harm the girls. These delightful creatures continued to play hockey and other games a few yards away in a distracted and desultory fashion.

About half-way through the summer term there was an invasion alarm on a Sunday afternoon. I went to my battle position neatly hidden under a hawthorn hedge and was joined in my lonely vigil by Helen, a handsome young amazon with a great sense of fun, unbridled curiosity and blue knickers. Our protracted discussions at the bottom of my slit trench, beneath a roof of twigs, became a source of constant delight on similar occasions during that long hot summer. Unfortunately an ill-concealed look or some gesture on my part as her 'crocodile' passed me on Green Hill alerted her mistress who complained to my Housemaster that I had been so indiscreet as to blow a kiss and make advances to one of her girls. As this was such an understatement I was quite prepared to accept the accusation and to his eternal credit Sam Hey stood up for me and said it took two even to blow a kiss. However, Helen moved on and so did I.

News of my encounter with Michael Redgrave at Clifton had got back to my English teacher at Sherborne who presumed that I too must have some acting ability which only needed liberating. This possibility had never occurred to me, but I reluctantly agreed to recite a lengthy Victorian melodrama about a runaway locomotive and then to sing "My Little Grey Home in the West" at a school concert. On the basis of these doubtful performances I was told to play Ferdinand in *The Tempest* which the school was going to perform at the end of term with help from Sherborne Girls' School. The girl chosen to play Miranda opposite me, was large, spotty, sad and terribly shy. I was expected to go down on one knee before her, draw my hand to my heart and plead, "Admired Miranda . . . indeed the top of admiration. . . . O you so perfect and so peerless . . .". I had an awful sinking feeling that my horrid friends would tease me terribly when it was over and as the day approached I became more and more worried. The play was to take place outdoors in a walled garden at the top of Green Hill. However, it rained for the last three days of term and the performance had to be cancelled. I now felt rather sorry for Miranda, and as we were both staying on for the first days of the holidays in our respective houses I asked her to be my partner in a local tennis competition. She was a far better tennis player than I and together we reached the finals. When I asked whether we could play in another tournament, her house mistress complained to Sam Hey that either I was a very forward young man or a very lonely one. In truth I suppose I was both.

The problem of where to spend the long summer holidays was solved behind the scenes and on the last day of term I was given a railway ticket to Dartmouth and the address of a Mrs Widger who would look after me on her farm. I wheeled my bicycle out of the guard's van at Dartmouth station and with difficulty tied my battered brown suitcase on to the carrier over the rear wheel. Asking the ticket collector for directions I was disappointed to learn I had only reached Kingswear and still had to cross the River Dart on a ferry and then bicycle ten miles or so towards Slapton. Two hours later, hot and tired, I rode into a muddy farmyard and was greeted kindly by Mrs Widger. The tiny farmhouse stood alone in a beautiful valley. There were only two cold water taps, one for the house and one for the cattle, and there was no electricity. I was to share a room with George, the cowman. Not only did I have to share the cupboard, the candle and the chamber pot, but also the bed whose lumpy mattress had a dip in the middle. He was a simple morose fellow who seldom spoke to me and would leap from bed when he could have crept out at five o'clock each morning to milk the cows.

On the first morning I was given a thick cheese and cucumber sandwich and a bottle of cold tea. I was then taken outside by the farmer and shown how to hone a scythe with a whetstone. "You see that there meadow on yonder hill?" he asked.

"You mean right up on the sky line beyond the wood?" I asked somewhat surprised because it looked so far away.

"Yes that be un. Cut all them thistles and nettles starting from round the gate. T"is easy if you keeps the heel of the scythe down and make sure you be back before dark."

Those were lonely days and, although I never really learnt how to handle the cumbersome scythe, I grew to love the Devon countryside and learnt much about the flight of duck to their feeding grounds. One memorable day I was allowed to carry into the fields a very old twelve bore, hammer shotgun with rust holes in both barrels and a pocketful of cartridges. I believe that Mrs Widger was pleased with the rabbits and pigeons which I brought back to the farm each evening. I was eternally grateful to have been given my first taste of rough shooting in such beautiful surroundings.

Quite early in the war I had volunteered for special duty during the holidays with the Devon Home Guard. In much the same way that a Romanian peasant presented himself and his horse to the famous Calarashi Regiment, I turned up with my trusty bicycle at headquarters of the Cockwood Platoon alongside the Anchor Inn and offered my services as a scout. However, as I was too young for combat duties, I was only allowed to be a despatch rider. I sat in the boot of the platoon Austin saloon whose lid opened downwards, with my bicycle inverted between my body and the rear window, ready to be dropped off and pedal away with the commander's orders (there being no radio communications). Later, after my 17th birthday when I had joined the Dorset Home Guard, I was allotted duties of more consequence.

The Cockwood Platoon was commanded by my one-armed Uncle Jack. He had had a rifle specially cut down in order to reduce its weight and fitted with a pistol grip so that he could hold it steady with three fingers and squeeze the trigger between thumb and forefinger. He presented a fearsome sight in all his war paint, face streaked with black and dark tan boot polish, rifle, binoculars, compass, pistol, satchel, map case and gas mask which were all attached to his person in some way or other. There was also an entrenching tool and a whistle on a lanyard which he seldom blew because he could never remember how many blasts to blow for each order.

Once I was part of the gun crew of a monstrous weapon called a Spigot Mortar which looked like a squashed tarantula, four cast iron pipes as legs and a fat green barrel. We were determined to see if it worked and assembled it one Sunday morning in a meadow outside the village. We inserted the projectile, pointed side up and then stood well back. There was a dull thud as the bomb rose unsteadily above our heads, wobbled, then soared off course towards the Dawlish road where it hit two telegraph poles before exploding in a field of anemones. The spigot mortar was hastily dismantled and stowed away in a barn.

All over Britain contractors had haphazardly sited 'dragon's teeth' antitank barriers and concrete pill boxes, but the position at Mount Pleasant Inn was specially chosen by my uncle because it had a magnificent field of fire over Dawlish Warren beaches and was next to the pub. Inside the pillbox an ancient six-pounder gun had been installed, together with forty-six shells. Benjamin, who had fired a similar weapon on a merchant ship in the First World War, was placed in charge of this vital weapon. Nobody was quite sure whether the gun could fire, let alone how to aim it. We had all studied the handbook carefully but it clearly referred to a different and much more modern piece of ordnance. The prospect of having to wait until the Germans invaded before we knew if the gun worked was too much, and so a target was selected among the deserted sand dunes below, just beyond the minefield. Three shells were fired; two fell well short into the minefield with spectacular results and the third, its trajectory having been adjusted by raising the barrel, just disappeared across the River Exe.

"Where be to, Ben?" asked the sergeant peering through the slit beside the gun.

"Cor lummey!" exclaimed Ben, as a puff of dust rose lazily, "Oi seen im, just in front of them black sheds beside Exmouth harbour." The explosion was attributed by Exmouth as another hit and run attack by German aircraft. So we left it at that, locked up the pillbox and reverted to a more mobile form of defence among the hedgerows.

One night we were called out to search for the crew of a German Junkers 88 bomber shot down after a raid on Exeter. It was nearly midnight when the platoon assembled outside The Anchor beside Cockwood harbour. It was cold and very misty, the tide was in and so while we waited for the section from Cofton to join us I checked the moorings of my uncle's boat. After some discussion as to where we should start the search, we fanned out and moved parallel to the railway towards Starcross. Then voices, foreign voices, were reported coming

51

from a railway wagon in a siding, there were whispered orders and we deployed with all the native cunning of local poachers. The PIAT anti-tank weapon was called forward and Sidney, who worked in a garage and who had never fired it, was shaking with excitement. As we closed in we saw a railway engine with a goods wagon either side, and quite definitely there were foreign voices. Once the ambush had been set and Sid had unpacked the PIAT missile from its wrappers, Uncle Jack leapt onto the railway track brandishing his pistol and shouting, "Come out, you are surrounded, surrender! *Sie sind Kaput!*"

There was a stunned, deathly silence on both sides, amazed perhaps at his unexpected grasp of the German language; then the cocking of many rifle bolts. Slowly one of the wagon doors slid back to reveal British tin hats and battledress uniforms. It was a Polish platoon waiting for dawn to break before starting an armoured train patrol to Newton Abbot along the line which follows the coast. Later we did find a German airman; the others had died. Walking back home I saw three badgers outside their set behind Cofton church. I loved those quiet woods and spent many hours alone there, overcome with homesickness for the silver birch and chestnut trees of Doftana.

Easter was never much of an occasion in England and when it came round once again I missed my parents and the breakfast table at Doftana covered in Easter cakes and bowls of coloured hard-boiled eggs. There were cries of '*Christos a inviat*' (Christ has risen again) as we knocked eggs against each other, rather like conkers, to discover whose egg was the hardest, except cheats who used red wooden eggs. A midnight service was held in the tiny church at Telega at which we lit candles from a twisted consecrated candle held by a chanting bearded priest. After the service the congregation snaked its way round the village until it was time for us to extinguish the flickering lights, climb back into the carriage and trot back to Doftana under the stars.

In May 1941 the American Ambassador in Istanbul, Franklin Gunter, was asked by the British Embassy in Cairo whether he could arrange for my sisters to leave Romania, but he said he was unable to organize trans-port. Mary Maud and Ioana were now confined to a flat in Bucharest because towns like Ploesti and Cimpina, where there were oil refineries, might soon be bombed. The previous month, when German troops were pouring through Yugoslavia to invade Greece, Britain, who had made great sacrifices to help the Greeks, tried to use Greek airfields from which the RAF might bomb Ploesti. Quite incredibly, the Greeks, although under Luftwaffe bombardment themselves, refused, saying that they were not at war with Romania. Thus the British lost their last chance to destroy the oil refineries. The Russians also tried three times in June 1941 to bomb Ploesti but only succeeding in causing damage in their third attempt which was made at twilight. Soon afterwards the German Luftwaffe caught the Russian bombers on the ground and destroyed them all.

An erratic international postal service enabled Gui to write to Mother asking what she should do with various family possessions, but Mary Maud's letters contained much more information:

"Everybody is OK in Romania. Nicu died of a bad heart. Vasilly is a filthy swine, Uncle Cotan is nearly finished, he is so badly off with his heart, the doctor says not much hope. Uncle George is fine always at Nestor's eating cakes . . . I hear you (Dad) are down in the blues, well change your mind, if I get to Beirut I'll soon put you OK . . . so long Daddy darling."

My father had every reason to be miserable because no sooner had he returned from Eritrea to Cairo, where he hoped to be reunited with Mother, than he was sent to Haifa Fortress in Palestine and thence, after the defeat of the Vichy French, into Syria and Lebanon. He numbered every letter he wrote throughout the war and chided her when she did not write as often as he did or if the mail was delayed.

In January 1942 the British Embassy in Cairo sent a coded signal to the Foreign Office in London saying that Mrs Redgrave had been "a very valuable connection with General Antonescu" and would they make arrangements to get her daughters out of Bucharest? She had evidently been writing letters on behalf of the British 'authorities' which were taken by a neutral courier through Istanbul to Rica Antonescu in Bucharest who presumably passed them on to her husband. These negotiations were successful and on 28 February 1942 my sisters left Bucharest in the care of the Swiss Delegation and an Egyptian, Madame Amin Fuad. It took them five days to complete the six-hour railway journey to Istanbul. Mary Maud, aged 14, wrote:

"In Sofia the Bulgars did not want to give us a visa because we were British and said we must go to the German Legation . . . but we got them somehow. At Svilengrad (Southern Bulgaria) they did not want to let us pass, so the Swiss Minister said if they did not let us pass he would not go either. We then travelled in a bus on roads worse than Romania for five hours. We spent a night in Andriopol in an awful hotel, the beds were FULL OF FLEAS, we sat up all night. Met a charming Turk in the Cavalry who bought me cigarettes and a newspaper." They were well looked after in Istanbul by Mrs Ellerington, the Romanian wife of a British diplomat, while plans were made for the rest of their journey to Cairo.

On 7 March the girls were once more on their way, stopping one day in Tripoli where they had a wonderful reunion with my father who had driven from Damascus to greet them. He then put them on a train to Egypt, but due to a delayed telegram the plan went wrong and Mary Maud wrote afterwards to her father:

"Mummy never even came to Kantara to fetch us! I had to go through all that stuff alone. I had to borrow money from the Wagon Lits Inspector to buy our tickets to Cairo. Well on the train some very nice RAF officer took us home and invited us to the cinema next day."

In fact there were several officers in their railway carriage who were astonished that two little girls should be arriving alone in an unknown city so late at night. So they drew lots among themselves as to who should take the girls to Mother's address.

My sisters settled down very quickly, but my mother, with two more mouths to feed, found herself desperately short of money. A month later my father, instead of being posted back to Cairo, was bitterly disappointed to be sent to Persia to look after War Correspondents in Tehran. Suddenly, after several British defeats, the situation in the Western Desert became serious and on 2 July 1942 my father wrote, "Rommel only 70 miles from Alexandria. What will my poor Jeanie do?"

On 14 July, "Letter today from my dear one announcing her departure for South Africa. When, oh when, shall I ever see them again? How miserable I feel."

The evacuation of British families from Egypt to South Africa was carried out in great secrecy. They left on 18 July on the *Queen Elizabeth* which had no escort, zig-zagging down the Indian Ocean and relying on her speed to evade enemy submarines. During the trip Mary Maud disappeared and was found standing on a table at a troops' concert singing "Smoke gets in your eyes", to cries of "Come on blondie, give us another one." Early in August they were offloaded at Durban and were found accommodation at Fields Hotel in Kloof, where the girls went to school and Mother got a job in the YMCA canteen at a military airfield.

A year later they were still in South Africa, my sisters at a boarding school and Mother once more working hard to pay the fees. She heard from her husband that he was expecting to leave Tehran for another posting and wrote:

"Sweetheart mine are you going to be transferred? I am all upset again, where are you going to be sent? I hope it is still in the Middle East and *not* the Western Desert. Who knows, we may come together again sooner than we expect. How marvellous it would be!"

But of course it was not to be.

Meanwhile Gui in Bucharest continued to write to Durban. Although food, she wrote, was still available, the situation in Romania was beginning to deteriorate. When Hitler invaded Russia on 22 June 1941 the Third Romanian Army had been placed under German command who used them to spearhead their advance on Odessa. They had not been fully trained or properly equipped and were unwillingly launched into an attack well beyond their national borders. By the time the Black Sea port was captured the Third Army had suffered 90,000 casualties, including 50,000 killed; thousands more Romanians perished in battles further north; it is no wonder 86,000 men were tried by court martial for refusing to enlist between June 1941 and June 1944. Every family in the land was touched by these losses which, it was said, included one-third of the able-bodied peasant farmers in Romania. Uncle George's cavalry regiment, the Rosiori, was decimated in the breakout from Stalingrad before the Russians finally closed the ring around General von Paulus's doomed 110,000 German soldiers.

In 1942 the British and the Americans were at a loss as to how to help the Russians, being in no position to invade the mainland of Europe. They were certain that the German drive towards Odessa was only a stepping stone in their main objective of seizing the unlimited resources of Russian oil at Baku. If only the oil refineries at Ploesti could be destroyed then the German armies might lose half the fuel they required to reach the South-East Caucasus.

By chance a group of American Liberator bombers had arrived in the Middle East. They had in fact been dispatched from the United States in a daring attempt to bomb Japan from China and were half-way through an incredible flight which had taken them via Brazil, across the South Atlantic, West Africa, Sudan and Egypt. It was a remarkable achievement to have travelled so far with no navigational aids or proper support and at times through appalling weather. Then news was received that the Japanese had captured Chengtu, the Chinese base whence they were to launch their raid and so the Allies changed their target to Ploesti.

The Russians were asked whether the American planes could land in the Soviet Union to refuel after the attack because the round trip back to Egypt, 2600 miles, was beyond the range of a Liberator bomber. The Russians did not reply. Nevertheless on 11 June the first American air attack on Europe was launched. No sooner had the aircraft become airborne than the Russians' agreement to refuelling was received, but as the planes were on 'radio silence' the message could not be passed. They flew over the Black Sea as far as Constanta and then along the Danube, but this happened to be in flood, so the little island which was to mark their turn to Ploesti was invisible. Other landmarks were shrouded by dense cloud and unbeknown to them a dummy set of refineries had been constructed ten miles east of Ploesti. Consequently bombs were dropped at random over Ploesti and Constanta with very little damage done. Some of the bombers landed in Turkey with empty fuel tanks, including at least one pursuing German Messerschmitt. The Americans were interned in a camp with a number of Russian aviators who taught them chess, until in due course they escaped into Allied-controlled Syria.

The German military commander in Romania was a distinguished aviator, General Alfred Gerstenberg, who took note of the abortive attack and determined to make Ploesti and Cimpina impregnable with a ring of anti-aircraft guns, many of which were placed on the estates of landowners who were secretly pro-British. Thousands of air defence troops arrived from Germany into a countryside where there was still an abundance of fruit, ham, chickens and wine, all of which were strictly rationed in their homeland. 70,000 slave workers were transported from other occupied territories in Europe to help construct concrete bunkers. German troops were happy to discover that there were thousands of lonely women in Romania, but General Gerstenberg, worried about security and the softening of his troops, demanded and received from Germany hundreds of German Luftwaffe girls and female typists and technicians, thus putting an end to fraternization with people who were technically allies. Anti-German feeling was growing among Romanians and, in spite of censorship, Gui's letters contained references to 'Les sales B' (Boches). General Gerstenberg, an intelligent and tolerant man who was never a Nazi, no doubt interpreted the way the war was going and therefore began to make plans to deal with a Romanian uprising which he regarded as inevitable.

In May 1943 my father was flown to Maison Blanche (Casablanca) to undertake liaison duties with the French. After the successful Allied landing in North Africa, the British and Americans held a conference to decide the course of the war. The British suggested that the next Allied invasion should be in the Balkans where it would take pressure off the Russians and where it was known that many Greeks, Yugoslavs and Romanians had pro-Allied feelings. This was strongly opposed by the

United States who wished the first landings in Europe to be made in Sicily and possibly cherished a desire to keep Western influence out of the Balkans. However, one thing they all agreed was that the destruction of Ploesti would placate Joseph Stalin, the Russian leader, and this was now within the range of US B24 bombers at Benghazi.

Unknown to the Allies, General Gerstenberg had, by the summer of 1943, managed to turn Ploesti into probably the greatest aerial defence complex in the world. It was now ringed by forty batteries each of six 88mm anti-aircraft guns which were interspersed with literally thousands of 37mm and 20mm quick-firing guns placed on bridges, roof tops, church towers, inside haystacks or dug into the ground. Amazingly, the Allies knew absolutely nothing about these defences because there was no active resistance movement in Romania until 1944 and because no photographic reconnaissance missions had been attempted. The Germans had also constructed a pipe line which encircled Ploesti with branches into eleven refineries, so that in the event of any one being damaged, crude oil could be switched to another. None of my mother's friends across whose land the pipe was laid realized the significance until much later.

Apart from this lack of intelligence, the Americans ignored information from a captured Romanian pilot that Ploesti was protected by many squadrons of German fighters. The RAF offered to provide four Pathfinder aircraft to guide the US bombers to their targets, but the Americans turned down the offer because they resented the implication they might get lost, which in the event many did. The American plan was to surprise the defence by attacking at low level, despite the RAF pointing out the dangers of heavy bombers attacking well-defended targets at ground level, citing as an example the British raid on the Mohne See Dam when only seven out of nineteen Lancaster bombers returned.

Nevertheless, preparations for the raid continued, but security around the US bases was poor, there was loose talk by air crew in Cairo bars and worst of all the Germans had already broken the 9th US Air Force secret codes. Consequently when four waves of B24 Liberators took off from Benghazi at dawn on 1 August 1943 the German radar stations on top of Greek mountains were immediately alerted. The air raid is described in great detail in *Ploesti* by James Dugan and Caroll Stewart. Of the 179 bombers that took part, fifty-three were lost and of those that returned ninety-two were unable to fly again the next day. The loss of over 500 aircrew, killed, wounded and captured, had been a high price to pay.

From the Romanian point of view here at last was visible proof that the Americans and British had not forgotten Romania. From the circular balcony at our home in Doftana the attack on the Steaua Romana refinery at Cimpina, outside the Ploesti defensive ring, was a spectacular sight. The low-level bombing was precise and the refinery was put out of action until after the war with very few civilians killed. However, in Bucharest and Ploesti, where no air-raid shelters had been constructed and the bombing was not accurate, many died in this and subsequent raids. The saddest death toll was when the women's prison in Ploesti received a direct hit, the warder with the cell door keys was blown to bits and one hundred women were trapped in their cells and burned to death.

In spite of such incidents the civilian population welcomed and gave help to the wounded US aviators except where they were mistaken for Russians. Some airmen spent their 'escape pack' money on drink for their benefactors before being taken in farm carts or marched to hospitals and prison. The Romanians were quick to claim sovereignty over the prisoners and refused to allow the Germans to keep them. A crew whose aircraft crashed onto Cantacuzene lands (where oil was first found in 1837) were rescued by Princess Caterina Caradja and taken to her home. Gui describes a line of bombers flying low over Bucharest. These had missed a navigational landmark and so followed the railway to Ploesti straight over a battery of 88mm guns hidden in a goods train.

Most Romanians took these events as proof that Germany was never going to win the war and the problem was how to disengage themselves from war in the Soviet Union and encourage the Western Allies to rescue Romania before the Russian army arrived. That summer Mr Maniu of the Peasant Party and M Brataniu of the Liberals sent a brave joint letter to General Antonescu saying that, now that the Provinces of Bukovina and Bessarabia had been reunited with Romania, there was no longer any reason to continue the war, let alone work towards the defeat of America and Britain. General Antonescu probably agreed, but by now he was totally subservient to the wishes of Adolf Hitler.

By the summer of 1943 the tide of war had turned in favour of the Allies and I was still at Sherborne, terrified it would all end before I had had a chance to join up. One morning the school assembled to listen to yet another talk about the Services. The speaker was Kenneth Shennan, a reserve officer in the Royal Horse Guards. He was not an inspiring lecturer but what he had to say about Reconnaissance and Armoured Cars had me enthralled. He concluded by asking whether anyone was interested in joining the Household Cavalry. I was the only boy in the school to step forward. I had no idea what the Household Cavalry was, but somebody must have put me wise because I wrote to Mother in South Africa telling her of my decision:

"On the whole it is not so bad. I can live on my pay, in wartime at any rate. In peacetime I believe the custom is to go grouse shooting, give big dinner parties and play polo at a cost of another £600 per annum. However, I doubt if you will see me in the Army once this war is over." (Little did I realize I would serve for 37 years!)

The large brass and leather bum-rack around the fireplace in the officers' mess at Combermere Barracks in Windsor was the first I had seen. My blue Sunday suit seemed tighter and more shiny than ever, as I sat uneasily on the edge beneath a portrait of the bald-headed Marquess of Granby, bravely sipping the first glass of port I had ever tasted. I was being vetted for a commission by senior officers of the Household Cavalry Depot and Training Regiment and was trying hard to find convincing answers to their searching questions. They did their best not to show disappointment that here was yet another wartime potential officer who did not ride, who had never hunted with any pack of hounds, who did not have a single relative or friend in the regiment, who did not have a country home anywhere in the United Kingdom and who received no private income or allowance. Nevertheless Colonel Andrew Ferguson of The Life Guards and Major Harry Legge-Bourke of the Royal Horse Guards (The Blues) must have been impressed by my enthusiasm and allowed me to see Humber and Daimler armoured cars which so attracted me to the Household Cavalry.

The papers and railway warrant telling me where to report were given to me by Sam Hey just before the end of term. I had become quite fond of Sam and believe that he did a lot more for me than I realized at the time or ever thanked him for. I was sad that I had never had a chance to show my parents around the school which had offered me so much. I wrote to my father in Egypt:

"I am so thankful that you sent me here, because even though it is clear I have not become a scholar, I have learnt so many things which will be worth their weight in gold later on in life."

A week later I wrote: "Things have hurried up somewhat. I must join up this afternoon: dont worry, remember I can look after myself, make friends and usually get along quite OK. I have to be at the barracks in Windsor by 1600 hours. Everything is just fine, at the moment."

But by 1615 hours things had changed for the worse. "Jump to

59

attention, young man. What's your name again?" "306300 Trooper Redgrave SIR."

My brief moment of self-confidence had vanished, and so too into a cardboard box had my civilian clothes. I was once again right at the bottom of the heap, alone in an alien world without any personal possessions except for one shilling and my precious silver-covered Romanian icon.

Chapter Five

THE BLUNT WHETSTONE

Having once had a glimpse inside the officers' mess when I was interviewed before leaving school, I now decided that the accommodation provided for recruits in the cavalry barracks at Windsor fell far short of my expectations. Twenty-four wooden double bunks stood on the black cobbled floor of a stable which contained no other furniture whatsoever. Our clothes at night were hung from saddle trees, attached to two rows of red metal pillars which ran the length of the stable. Every garment felt damp from the clammy mist which swept in over the open top half of the stable doors. At dawn, as soon as the trumpeter had blown reveille, we hastily picked up our boots and brown gym shoes off the floor, before an over-zealous corporal threw two buckets of water over the cobbles just 'to settle the dust', and we dressed quickly before he had time to refill the buckets from a tap in the stable yard.

I shared my bunk with a Great Western Railway worker from Slough, an experienced man of the world who took his girlfriends into the Spital cemetery just down the road. He claimed it was the quietest place in Windsor, "with none of them officious air raid wardens snooping around". I suppose I was the only person in that stable who owned a pair of pyjamas and suffered acute embarrassment every time I put them on. All other recruits wore khaki shirts, only boy soldiers were issued with pyjamas, which when they became a 'man' were replaced with a third shirt, but I was still under eighteen.

Uncle Jack wrote a few days after I had joined up to say that my 'call up' papers for the coal mines had arrived and what was he to do with them? Conscripts had stopped being taken by the Army because the priority now was sending 'Bevin Boys' to work in the coal mines. The only way to get round this was to volunteer to be a Regular soldier rather than wait to be drafted. I had therefore 'signed on' for twelve years, five with the Colours and seven with the Reserve, in the Royal Horse Guards

(The Blues). It was a contract I would have to fulfill if I failed to get a commission. "Hairy trousers for the duration if you don't make it," had warned the Adjutant.

I very nearly never got started because I did not have a Birth Certificate. The rest of my squad went off for basic training at the Guards Depot whilst I was left behind at Windsor in despair because bureaucracy had come to a grinding halt over this unexpected complication. Eventually a resourceful Corporal Major in the Orderly Room took me aside and asked me what evidence did I have that I was Me at all. I showed him a small medallion which had been struck on my christening day, giving my date of birth, my names and those of my godparents, all in Romanian. This precious bit of bronze, no bigger than a halfpenny, was sent off to the War Office, where no doubt it still resides in my file. The arrival of this weighty piece of evidence on a minister's desk must have done the trick, because I was told I could now leave Combermere Barracks where I had been confined since my arrival. The first time I strode out past the Guardroom wearing a neatly tailored battle dress I was very conscious that I was carrying the name of a famous regiment on my shoulder. An elderly postman stopped me outside a pub called 'The Trooper'. "Have you just joined up, son?" he asked. "Yes sir," I replied. "Well you look just grand, but do tuck your shirt tails in. Good luck," and he walked off with his sack on his shoulder.

Finally the great day came when all had been approved by the War Office and I was allowed to rejoin my squad. I took a train to Purley in Surrey, where, hot and tired, I carried a kit bag and sundry items of equipment up the hill to the Guards Depot, Caterham. The helpful corporal at the gate misdirected me, like countless others before me, to the next set of gates up the hill, to what was in those days called a lunatic asylum.

Passing through the training machine at the Guards Depot required resilience and unquestioning obedience. I learnt how to clean boots, brass, webbing and a rifle, but cleaning myself was very difficult. The 'ablutions' were few and in a dreadful state, two tiny basins to twenty-two men. There were no plugs, no soap, a cracked mirror and a damp roll of War Department toilet paper. In those first few weeks I learnt how to perform 'Double Sentry Drill' outside Buckingham Palace, how to 'Rest on my Arms Reversed' at a State Funeral and how to salute if I happened to be 'Improperly Dressed'. Every movement of an arm or a leg was accompanied by shouts of ONE, two three, ONE, but I was not taught anything remotely practical, such as how to fire my musket, until months later. Needless to say this archaic training programme which included many hours of monotonous foot drill was subsequently modified. Yet there were great benefits to be gained from such an austere grounding, as John Lyle wrote in 1579:

"The finest edge is made with the blunt whetstone."

The Guards Depot did not normally train the Household Cavalry and I was among the first groups of "Donkey Wallopers" to pass through Caterham. The Brigade of Guards consists of five distinguished regiments all with similar proud traditions and it was not surprising that the different traditions of the Household Cavalry were not always appreciated. Twice I was sent doubling to the Guardroom to hear the cell door slam behind me. The crime? Daring to salute an officer when I was not wearing a hat, a tradition unique to the Blues and now to their successors The Blues and Royals.

The origin of this custom is attributed to the Marquess of Granby, of The Blues, who in 1741 led a dawn attack against the French camped on a hill outside Warburg in Germany. He was determined to put the record right after his humiliation the previous year when, as commander of The Blues at the Battle of Minden, he had had to watch British infantry being hard-pressed by the French, whilst his urgent requests to charge and relieve them were turned down by his ever hesitant Commander in Chief, Lord Sackville. Subsequently Sackville was court-martialled, but he reappeared as Secretary of State for the Colonies, only to lose us the American War of Independence.

As soon as Granby heard that the French were again on the march he moved fast to catch them unawares. His approach was hidden by a low morning mist and he caught them with their shaving brushes out and frying pans cooking breakfast. During one of three great cavalry charges up the hill at the head of his squadrons, his hat and wig fell off, leaving a distinctive bald cranium reflecting the morning sunrise which may have given rise to the expression "to go at the enemy bald-headed". By the time the Prince of Hanover had brought up the rest of the Allied Army the battle had been won and Granby rode up to his commander and saluted, hatless. Thus are traditions made, but it was an explanation which only produced another discourteous display of anger from the Grenadier Guards sergeant in charge of the regimental police.

No one mattered more to me during that monotonous period at the Guards Depot than Guardsman Evans, Welsh Guards, for, although we were located in the Scots Guards Lines, we were looked after by staff from the whole Brigade of Guards. Evans was our 'Trained Soldier' who ruled our barrack room with firmness and a certain mystique. I never saw him without his cap on; even at night he would sit up in bed with his cheese-cutter peak resting on his nose and a cigarette between his lips whose glow could be seen long after a lone piper had blown 'Lights Out'. Exhausted and punch drunk from cleaning our equipment with blanco and polishing brasses for parade next morning, we slept soundly on narrow, cast iron beds, which had to be pulled out before use, taking care not to tangle the two sets of springs. Three horsehair 'biscuits' provided a thin bumpy mattress, which during the day had to be stacked, together with three folded grey blankets, on top of which a neat array of boots, hats, belt, mess tins or whatever the platoon sergeant dictated, laid out in a set pattern. There were no sheets, chairs or curtains and the lino-covered floors had to be waxed, then 'bumped' with a strange iron object attached to a pole around which a piece of army blanket was tied. At one end of the room stood a solitary black stove on whose side were the letters VR. Alongside it was a large square cast-iron tub containing a week's coal ration and some kindling wood, all of which had to be kept tidy and spotless.

We were so preoccupied with cleaning sundry objects and just getting through the drill and physical training which was our daily diet that any desire for female company seldom stirred our loins. This miserable state of affairs was blamed darkly by Trained Soldier Evans on the lavish quantities of bromide which he had seen the Master Cook pour into the tea urn. A trooper's pay was three shillings a day out of which iniquitous deductions were made for sports we did not play and 'barrack damages', just in case we broke a window or lost a mop.

It was a great day when we finished our basic training and rushed to the railway station clutching our leave warrants. The trains were packed so I sat on my kit bag in the corridor of a Great Western coach as far as Exeter where I offered my precarious seat to a vivacious blonde who had just boarded the train. All traces of the dreaded bromide vanished and I worked fast but not fast enough because she left the train before I could discover her name. I then had to ask my fat friend, the railway porter at Starcross Station, to telephone his mate at the previous station to find out who was the stunning blonde who travelled on the five fifteen each day. Thus a torrid romance started which ended just as suddenly as it had begun with the arrival of American troops in the West Country. I wonder if she ever married Walt and got to Cincinnati.

The Guards Armoured Training Wing was situated among the

heather and pines at Pirbright; it was much more relaxed and we soon got down to the serious business of learning about tank radios, guns and engines. After a few weeks we moved two miles up the road to Blackdown Camp, a pre-officer cadet training unit run by the Royal Armoured Corps who perhaps did not trust the training which the Guards had given us and went through it all again. This delay in getting to the Officer Training Unit at Sandhurst was nearly my downfall. I had been detailed for a weekend guard duty and had gone to the NAAFI canteen to buy an assortment of cakes for the guard. However, one of my companions opened a parcel which contained a large fruit cake, so we offered the NAAFI 'wads' to the guard sergeant and duty trumpeter who said they would gladly dispose of them. Four days later we were all 'on a charge' and marched into an office to stand before our squadron leader, Major Strang Steel of the 17th/21st Lancers. A cardboard box piled high with stale buns stood on his desk, over the top of which we could just see the skull and cross bones of his cap badge. He gave us a just and terrifying dressing down, reminded us of sailors drowning in the Atlantic Ocean bringing wheat from Canada and finally stressed how easy it was for him to return us all to our regiments to undertake menial tasks for the rest of the war. There was a long silence while he considered what sentence to give us, during which we bit our lips and our knees trembled:

"Regimental Sergeant Major, take these horrible men outside and see that they eat the lot," he said, pointing to the box on his desk.

I staggered out into the corridor, carrying the box with its fossilized contents where under the RSM's eagle eye and with a ghost of a smile he urged us to get on with it. Reluctantly we took a bite, but however hard we tried to demolish the stale buns they were now like rocks. We were saved by three Canadian cadets who began to slip the buns into their battle dress tunics. Thus I learnt another lesson, make the punishment fit the crime.

The Royal Military Academy at Sandhurst was divided into two wings, Tanks and Reconnaissance, each fully equipped with modern armoured fighting vehicles (AFVs) and staffed by battle-seasoned instructors. It was an excellent course and our teachers did not spare us for a moment, passing on every skill and battle procedure that they had learnt in combat. I hated the infantry part of the course, especially an exercise using live ammunition in Snowdonia. We criss-crossed those soggy hills, slipped on the shale, sank into peat bogs, cursed the endless rain and vowed never to visit Wales again. One night we camped just outside a small village called Penmaenmawr on the coast. I was accosted while on guard that night by Bronwyn whose lilting voice described why she loved Wales, urged me also to visit the Welsh valleys and alter my first opinion. Next day we were off again and this time I was given a Bren light machine gun to carry; my companion, a Canadian due to join the Manitoba Dragoons, carried the ammunition. We gave accurate covering fire in an attack on a deserted barn but then got bored waiting for a flank attack to develop. I scanned the opposite hillside and saw a bedraggled sheep perched on a cliff about a kilometre away. I took casual aim and accidentally squeezed the trigger a little too firmly; it was a very long shot and we were amazed to see the animal topple down the cliff. Unfortunately so did one of our instructors from another distant vantage point. I was placed under close arrest, made to retrieve the sheep which weighed more than the mortar bombs and Bren put together and was then locked up in a nice warm room at Capel Curig, while the rain continued to pour down on my comrades. Somehow I survived this disciplinary setback and I suspect that mutton must have made a welcome addition to the monotonous tinned rations.

Next we were taught how to drive Daimler and Humber armoured cars and initiated into the mysteries of the fluid flywheel. One day I stalled going up Guildford High Street, right opposite Woolworth's outside which there were lots of prams. A cheerful group of Canadian soldiers who had been surveying the scene swooped down and in a flash switched the babies between prams and melted away. The unsuspecting mothers leaving the emporium flung their shopping bags on to the prams and set off still chatting. Some had gone quite a way before they realized that Baby looked different. In no time the street resembled a scene from the "Massacre of the Innocents", with mothers running round in circles holding red-faced screaming children in their arms. It was a cruel prank but I am afraid we laughed and gave the Canadians full marks for originality.

Learning gunnery was a terribly dull business, as we learnt how to take cannons and machine guns to pieces and then reassemble them in the dark. In order to save ammunition we used an indoor range where we were taught how to hit an unseen target using a technique called 'bracketing'. A certain realism was achieved by 'Miss Puff' who pushed a trolley beneath a hessian cloth model on to which a pastoral landscape had been painted. Every time an officer cadet gave a 'fire order' she followed his instructions on a grid painted on the floor, and when he shouted "Fire", she squeezed a rubber bulb and a puff of white chalk came up through the hessian to mark where his shot had landed.

Miss Puff was in fact an ATS girl from Czechoslovakia, and I felt that my gunnery practice would be more successful if only I knew her better. We sat on raised benches behind a mock tank turret, and through a crack in the planks I could just see her neat khaki-clad ankles. I dropped down a note inviting her to meet me at the Duke of York's in Camberley. As I had only seen her ankles this was not going to be easy, but in the event she was the only girl to walk in at precisely ten to seven. We were both a long way from our families and our home countries, and, but for the tedious regulations of having to be back in our billets by 2359 hours, we could have spent all night among the rhododendrons beside Sandhurst lake where no target bracketing was necessary. A few months later she left for special training and possible operations in occupied territory. She was a brave girl and I have no idea whether she survived the war.

Finally we began to put all our specialist training together and learn the relatively new tactics which had been evolved for armoured car regiments. How could four vehicles drive down a road towards a hidden enemy without getting blown to bits? Each troop consisted of two scout cars and two armoured cars, ten men in all. It was continually stressed that these were officers' patrols and that all reports had to be accurate and verified by the troop leader personally.

The basic principle was stealth and speed, to see without being seen, and the ideal vehicle for this was the Daimler with its new fluid flywheel transmission. Time and time again, thanks to the silent approach and surprise, reconnaissance units avoided running head-on into enemy guns and sometimes caught the Germans unprepared. This was in complete contrast to our American Allies who to this day advertise their presence with bursts of gunfire at every bush in which an enemy might be hiding. All the skills they must have learnt from the Red Indians and put to good use against the British in the War of Independence seem to have been forgotten by their doctrine of reconnaissance by fire and reliance on massive superiority to solve every situation.

Our method of movement was the Snake Patrol, a scout car leading followed by the troop leader in an armoured car. We moved fast between bounds, but were very cautious going round corners or clearing crests, always keeping in visual contact with each other. Each car in turn remained stationary, ready to give accurate covering fire or to lay a smoke screen should one of the other cars be in trouble.

There were contact drills for every contingency; what to do if you spotted the enemy before he saw you, what action to take if he fired first and how to survive an ambush. Unless the mission was to protect the main route of an advance, we were expected to find a way round enemy positions and press on. We were taught how to seize and hold a bridge, how to move into observation posts, how to conduct a withdrawal, and many other tasks.

Our instructors, who all had battle experience, knew that their lessons might save our lives and so never spared us, day or night. We covered much of the British Isles, driving along the crests of the downs, along farm tracks and through fields and woods. Exercises were very realistic, sometimes taken to extremes as when Polish soldiers in Nottingham, ambushed an armoured car troop, destroyed the radios, removed the wheels and cast the crews into the local gaol.

At night we entered 'harbour' quite exhausted. Cars were reversed into bushes so that they could drive out in a hurry and gun turrets were traversed to cover likely enemy approaches. Then cars were refuelled, engines checked, ammunition replenished, maps and orders issued for the next day. Lastly we untied the bedrolls and cooked our food in square dixies on temperamental petrol cookers in the darkness. With only ten men in a troop everyone had to do his job properly. It was vital that all kit should be stowed back on to each car before we fell asleep, so that when we moved off before daybreak nothing was left behind and only bedrolls needed picking up. It was a tough routine to which we soon became accustomed.

Once this extensive and valuable training was completed we were given one week's leave before the Passing Out Parade. I wanted to go down to Devon but Uncle Jack was ill and Douglas had joined the Royal Navy. I had nowhere to go but found a bed at the Royal Armoured Corps club in Belgrave Square. London was a most exhilarating place. It now seemed certain we were going to win the war and the streets were full of men and women of many nationalities wearing every sort of uniform. Rumour had it that someone had actually worn a German uniform unchallenged among the crowds who gathered outside 'Rainbow Corner', the American Services club at Piccadily Circus.

After two days of aimless wandering I called on Miss Tomlinson who was delighted to see me. She told me that Mother's friends in Cairo had made an official application for her to join the Radio Monitoring Section as a translator from Romanian into English. This stratagem had worked and she and my sisters had left South Africa and arrived back in Cairo on 18 June 1944. Alas, my father who had been in Casablanca with the

French was now about to be sent to an interrogation centre for returning prisoners of war and refugees in Bari, Italy, so the family reunion in Cairo which they had both desired for so long was heartrendingly short-lived.

Meanwhile from Romania there was news that Ploesti had been under constant air attack by the Americans and RAF. On 24 August 1944 King Michael locked General Antonescu up in the royal vaults, having enticed him there to view the royal stamp collection. He then ordered the Romanians to rise up against the Germans. Some remarkable isolated battles took place and the Germans, already retreating before the Russians, were driven out.

The King wished to let the British know what was happening and chose an Englishman, Mr Gardyne de Chastelain, who had been a friend of my father's. He had been enlisted into SOE, probably by Eddie Boxshall, an expert in Romanian affairs, who sent him to Canada to recruit refugees who could speak Bulgar, Croat or Slovak. After being parachuted back into Romania he was captured, but luckily not handed over to the Germans. His Canadian son, General Alfred de Chastelain, Companion of Honour, became Co-Chairman the Northern Ireland talks in 1997. His father only got as far as Turkey where British diplomats placed endless difficulties in his way and prevented his onward journey to the West. This was because they knew that it had already been agreed by the Americans, Russians and, albeit reluctantly, by the British, that Romania was to be placed within the Soviet Union's sphere of influence after the war. Poor de Chastelain returned to Bucharest with no encouragement – proof, if any was needed, that once again in her hour of need Romania had been forsaken by Great Britain.

In Bucharest my grandmother recalled hearing the first sounds of shooting very early on 24 August. This was the start of an attack by the 2nd Cavalry Regiment, one-time Calarashi, on the German Air Force Headquarters which they succeeded in capturing after heavy fighting by midday. German reinforcements began to concentrate in the woods along the road to Ploesti and were bombed by the RAF. These woods now contain the British War Graves in which some of those airmen lie buried. Among the headstones is one to Captain Russell, Scots Guards, parachuted into Romania in 1943 and found murdered in a mountain hut. Allied intelligence officers arrived in Bucharest at the same time as American planes took out 1200 prisoners of war. Some Romanians, in the general euphoria of the occasion, welcomed the British and American officers as forerunners of an Allied military government and installed them in the Athene Palace Hotel.

The tiny Romanian Communist Party chose the moment to come out of obscurity and to ingratiate themselves with the Russians, claiming that it was they alone who had overthrown the Germans.

Gui wrote to my mother, "Mark my words, Micheline, we may have got rid of les sales Boches, taking half our country with them, but we are going to have far more to fear from these animals who have replaced them, and who this time may never leave our country."

The possibility of being able one day to return to the house at Doftana which he had built was my father's dearest wish, together with that of a family reunion. He had followed the conflicting reports of events in Romania with mounting excitement. He was placed at three days' notice to fly direct to Romania and given the task of checking lists of Romanians who had been named as providers of assistance to our prisoners and ensuring that they were to be rewarded. After many days' delay he flew in, only to be prevented from entering Romania, possibly because of mother's link with the Antonescu. He flew back to Bari and wrote:

"What a journey. What a failure. How disappointed I am. Poor Mother. Damn this war. Damn the Russians. Oh how I hate Bari!"

He cheered up a little when he found a letter in his mail confirming that I had been commissioned, but he did not write to my mother for ages, not knowing how to break it to her that there was no longer any hope of ever returning to Romania. There was now nothing left for them to look forward to and not even the bottle of *tuica* in his suitcase was going to provide the answer.

Back at Sandhurst we were warned not to do anything 'stupid' before the commissioning ceremony because we might still be held back. Evidently at another officers' school cadets on the night before a passing out parade had drilled a hole beneath a bronze equestrian statue, inserted a cork and poured buckets of blue dyed water into the stallion's open nostril through a funnel. As the climax of the parade approached, an accomplice jerked the string attached to the cork and the officer cadets, eyes turned smartly to the right, marched past the inspecting general on the saluting base, beside the rampant steed from which a thunderous jet of dark blue urine splashed onto the plinth and parade ground for at least five minutes.

The Passing Out Parade at Sandhurst took place on my 19th birthday, exactly one year after my halfpenny-size credentials had been accepted by the Army. It seemed I had come a long way from the numb shock and misery of those bleak drill sheds at the Guards Depot to the highly trained and independent person I considered I had now become. The form of parade has not changed much over the years and we Slow Marched off the square up the steps of The Old Building followed somewhat hesitantly by the Adjutant on a grey horse. We ran to our rooms and put on our beautifully cut uniforms made by Huntsman and Co in Savile Row, very much aware of the weight of the single Garter Star on our epaulettes.

On my first day back at the Household Cavalry Depot in Windsor I heard a stern voice exclaim, "One banger only today sir," followed by, "Goodness gracious, that's quite enough peas!"

Sergeant Beatrice Furse, ATS, ruled the officers' mess dining room with a rod of iron. She was a subaltern-slayer par excellence and newly commissioned Cornets of Horse, ie 2nd Lieutenants like myself, munched their lunchtime rations in abject fear, lest her eagle eye spotted a wasted piece of fat or gristle hidden beneath a lettuce leaf. Mercifully, a few days later I received a posting order to the 1st Household Cavalry Regiment (1HCR) who had just returned to England after five years in the Middle East. This was a disappointment because I had hoped to join 2HCR which had just completed a magnificent dash from the French frontier into Brussels and were in my opinion the finest reconnaissance regiment in the Army. On the other hand I had heard that 1HCR were a bunch of elderly pre-war soldiers who had lived in a different world and wished they still had horses. My information turned out to be very wrong.

At the outbreak of war The Life Guards and Royal Horse Guards, both under-strength, combined to form 1HCR at Hyde Park Barracks in Knightsbridge. Their service swords were sharpened on a grindstone in the farriers' yard and the horses were issued with special gas masks. Thus equipped for modern warfare, they travelled in cattle trucks from Olympia railway sidings to Marseilles and thence by ship to Palestine to join the 1st Cavalry Division.

They begged to be mechanized, but it was not till 1941 that horses were exchanged for ancient 'Guy' trucks and the regiment was designated a motor battalion. Three weeks later they were ordered to advance into Iraq; 60% of the drivers had less than ten hours' experience and the troopers accustomed to looking after horses imagined that life would be easy with no horses to groom or feed and hoped it would be a comfortable ride. They found themselves sitting eight to a truck with little suspension, pith helmets, shorts and puttees, setting off on what became an epic 6,500-mile journey across appalling desert and mountain tracks.

Their first action had been to rescue a besieged Royal Air Force base at Habbaniya in Iraq. Then they fought bitter battles against the Vichy French in Syria and finally invaded Persia (Iran) where they took part in a victory parade in Tehran with the Russians who had also invaded from the north. A few weeks later they drove all the way back to Palestine where they were at last given armoured cars. These were Marmon Harringtons made in South Africa with a Ford V8 engine, thin armour plate and only a light machine gun.

Whilst the regiment was retraining, a squadron was sent to drive dummy tanks in the Western Desert. These were made of canvas and rubber, designed to look like American Grant tanks and mounted on old Morris lorries. Their finest hour came when they advanced in battle formation towards an enemy strongpoint. An attempt by an astonished outpost of the Royal Dragoons to get Divisional Headquarters to verify their orders merely launched them further forward towards the enemy like the Charge of the Light Brigade at Balaclava. By the time it was re-alized that there was a mistake in the map reference and they were ordered to withdraw, which they did with boiling radiators at five miles an hour, two columns of Italian trucks had been seen to retreat from the position and Italian tanks which came out to cover this withdrawal were mistakenly attacked by German dive-bombers.

Retrained and re-equipped, 1HCR drove from Palestine to join the 8th Army in the desert. Kenneth Shennan had described this move in his lecture at Sherborne as "ships at sea with plumes of dust behind each armoured car billowing away in the wind and with pennants fluttering". Tied to the outside of each car were bed rolls, tentage, cooking pots, tow chains, unditching sand trays and chargol bags containing water which cooled by evaporation. The crews wore goggles, coloured neck scarves, all sorts of headgear and their faces were black with sweat and dust.

At the Battle of Alamein they were unleashed through immense mine-fields on to the enemy rear, spreading panic and destruction and capturing hundreds of prisoners. After the battle they were disappointed to be sent to watch the Turkish frontier in Syria. Then, in 1943, after a spell in Cyprus, 1HCR landed in Italy and was placed under command the 1st Polish Corps, whose 'Mermaid of Warsaw' they proudly wore on their sleeves. Once again different battle tactics had to be learnt. Every advance was slow and cautious, there were numerous rivers to cross and mountains to climb. Foot patrols wearing army-issue boots in the snow-covered Apennine mountains found themselves fighting German troops wearing skis; whilst down at sea level along the Adriatic coast armoured cars edged northwards.

In October 1944 these men, many of whom had not seen England for over four years, returned and their casual confident manner amazed the new highly trained and technical army that had been created in their absence. In hushed voices we were told that officers actually wore suede boots, coloured neck scarves, full-length shaggy sheepskin coats and had long hair. They still marched four abreast and used cavalry words of command such as "Sections Right, Walk March", and indeed continued to do so until the war ended. Drill instructors were sent from the Guards Depot to put things right, but they gave up in despair. It was evident too that 1HCR had not heard of the new much-vaunted Army Vehicle Maintenance System. It was as if a forgotten Roman Legion had at last returned from a distance province. They may not have been familiar with the new battle cries but nothing was ever going to replace their practical experience, versatility and exceptional team spirit.

I reported with ten other reinforcement officers to Beaumont Barracks in Aldershot, which, although it had once been a cavalry barracks, was a totally unsuitable place in which to station a fully equipped armoured car regiment. Contrary to our expectations, we were made most welcome by our brother officers, who actually spoke to us. I took over command of a troop of veterans from Lord Porchester, who suffered from a problem with his feet and was posted to the depot. Actually our arrival was just what the other officers wanted because quite naturally none had the slightest intention of spending a moment longer than was necessary examining the new Daimlers with which the regiment was being issued. They spent their time in London where business at places like 'Ma Feathers', who had an endless supply of girls, was brisk, whilst the new Cornets had to make do with the Variety Show at the Aldershot Theatre.

This show, which by any standards was pretty third-rate, nevertheless attracted a full house because of one redeeming act, a plump blonde who performed a tantalizing striptease. The climax came when she took cover behind a stand, on which a flock of white doves clustered hiding most of her body. She slowly removed her bra and hung it on the stand and then struggled out of her knickers which she hurled triumphantly into the air just before the curtain came down between her and the baying licentious soldiery. In 1944 nudity was only allowed in public provided it was a discreet 'tableau' and the performer remained absolutely still until the curtain descended. We went to the theatre once more in the hope of seeing what lay behind all those white feathers. As her performance came to a close there was a loud explosion from a small blank cartridge pistol in the front row of the stalls, which dispersed the doves and we saw all we could have wished for, and more, of the open-mouthed blonde. The curtain stuck coming down, the manager ran on with a dirty white raincoat to cover the girl who had run off stage and the doves deposited signs of their distress on to the heads of the audience. It was a sensational end to a simply ghastly show.

We each got a week's extra Orderly Officer duties which was much appreciated by our brother officers because it covered all duties over Christmas and into the New Year. It was also a little unfair because I had not been able to afford a good seat in the stalls, and so was sitting elsewhere, but it did not really matter because there was nowhere else I could have spent Christmas anyway.

Chapter Six

A WHIFF OF WAR

As General Montgomery's Second Army swept across Belgium towards Holland and the River Rhine, I became more and more anxious that the war was going to end before I had even seen an angry whiff of gunpowder smoke. I took my troop of armoured cars out into the countryside as often as possible and when we were not parked behind the Lupin Café at Bagshot we practised for every contingency we might meet in action.

We were equipped with one of the finest reconnaissance vehicles in the world, which remained in service for the next fifteen years. The Daimler armoured car and scout car could be driven backwards as fast as forwards. The armoured car actually had two steering wheels, one for the driver and the other, facing the rear, for the commander. He had to kneel down on the floor of the turret, open a tiny visor and shout orders over his shoulder to the driver, who then let go of his steering wheel but continued to work the pedals. If the driver was wounded, the commander was expected to use a rear handbrake, which was quite useless, and a hand throttle, which was unreliable. There were other hazards; vision through the rear visor could easily be blocked by a piece of loose bedding; worse still, if the gunner, sitting with his eye glued to a telescope facing in the opposite direction, suddenly traversed the turret to shoot at a new target, the commander was swept away from his steering wheel, which was fixed to the hull. In such an emergency the only thing to do, provided he could still reach it, was to press the 'dead man's button'. This stopped the engine but not the car! It was no more complicated or uncomfortable, I suppose, than trying to steer a midget submarine through a minefield!

Nobody envied the life of an armoured car crew. The infantry claimed that they were safer in their foxholes and tank crews preferred to sit behind thicker armour. Yet to me a reconnaissance troop seemed to be an ideal command, nine men, four armoured cars, operating far from the direct control of a superior headquarters and sometimes behind enemy lines, trying to see without being seen. Of course it could be terribly uncomfortable over rough ground and, with hatches open, wet and cold. If the car was 'closed down' for action it became claustrophobic, visibility was extremely limited through periscopes and thick blocks of bullet-proof glass. Some days the heat and smell of unwashed bodies, cordite and engine fumes made life very unpleasant for three tall men squeezed inside a 'sardine tin'. The perpetual 'mush' in our ears of a No 19 Set radio, the engine noise, the grind of four transmission shafts under the turret floor and occasional gunfire all added to our exhaustion.

Life was never dull for a troop leader. I had to anticipate where the enemy might be, tell Turner, the driver, where to go and Corporal Smith what target to be prepared to engage. I map-read, memorized the next few miles, listened on the radio to what was going on around me and controlled the movements of my other cars. Sometimes I pulled ammunition out of bins on the turret floor, loaded the 2-pounder gun and the Besa machine gun. If the guns stopped firing or the turret's rotation jammed I had to correct the fault. Above all I was expected to keep cool and send back accurate situation reports.

A new weapon had been invented and in conditions of great secrecy I was sent to the workshops in Aldershot to have a "Little John" adaptor fitted to the 2-pounder gun on my armoured car. This contraption made the gun barrel a foot longer and increased the velocity of a special armour-piercing shell so that it could make a tiny hole even in a German Tiger tank, which none of us would dream of shooting at anyway. However, it was no longer possible to fire high-explosive shells which we normally did at infantry and soft targets. Somewhat disillusioned, I returned to barracks with an elongated useless gun barrel wrapped in sacking to hide it from spies hiding in the bushes along Queen's Avenue.

Letters from Mother in Cairo now took less than a month. They were written on special airmail letter forms which after examination by the censor were put onto a micro film, flown to England, developed and posted again. My sisters, it seemed, had incurred the wrath of the Secretary of the famous Gezira Club, who wrote a stern letter to Mother complaining that his gardener had failed to catch two apple thieves, seen escaping over a wall, who closely resembled her daughters and threatened to withdraw their membership. This would have been a disaster because the club swimming pool was their great joy, so an abject apology was made and no more apples were taken.

At long last 1HCR was given an embarkation date for Europe and four days' leave in which to say our goodbyes. My 'Grandfather', FJN, gave me a splendid dinner alone at his house in Streatham, partridge and a 1935 Château-Margaux. I had never seen him in such good form and I wondered why I had always been so frightened of him. Dear Miss Tomlinson almost cried when I kissed her goodbye in that cold and cheerless Cannon Street office, seated behind a cumbersome Remington typewriter. Sadly it was to be the last time I ever saw her.

Our route to Tilbury docks took us all round London in a column of 350 vehicles which stretched for eight miles. Every two hours we halted for twenty minutes, as decreed in the Manual of Army Staff Duties, and, no matter where we happened to be, cups of tea appeared as if by magic from the nearest house. The welcome was amazing, waves and cheers in every village. It was exhilarating and had apparently been the pattern of events ever since troops moved down towards the ports of embarkation before the invasion of Normandy. Our Regimental Signals Officer, Henry Uxbridge, (now Marquess of Anglesey) deviated from the set route and took his huge eight-wheeled Armoured Command Vehicle right through the centre of London, down Piccadilly, conducting an imaginary philharmonic orchestra from the commander's hatch and stopping only to wave to the doorman at the Ritz.

We set sail in a small flotilla of tank-landing ships bound for Ostend which had only just been opened up after four years of German occupation. The senior officers of the regiment embarked on a somewhat better-appointed ship than ours which in due course ran aground on a sandbank in the Thames estuary. The crew had been heard to complain that the bosun was absent and the Captain drunk again. Meanwhile, we arrived leaderless in Ostend, so we parked our armoured cars in a Belgian barracks and spent two glorious days exploring the town, in my case with an enchanting Wren called Lib. She came from a naval family called Howard in Haslemere and for many months afterwards we exchanged letters.

We drove through Ghent and into the Dutch province of North Brabant, which extends up to the mouths of the River Rhine and River Maas, through Bergen-op-Zoom, famous for its oysters, before entering an incredibly flat countryside, enveloped in a strange beautiful translucent light. In the distance there was a shimmering wetness, broken now and again by tall church spires and windmills, many of which, suspected of being observation posts, had been damaged by shellfire. 1HCR had been ordered to take over about forty miles of the front line which followed the south bank of the River Maas, from the 11th Hussars, the "Cherrypickers", an armoured car regiment.

I found it exhilarating going forward towards the enemy for the first time and had no idea what to expect. I hung on grimly as my scout car followed the speeding Hussar guide through deserted villages until we got to the hamlet of Tonekreek, which lay between Willemstad and the ancient town of Breda.

"Don't worry," said Tony Hunter whose troop I was relieving, "it is really quiet here, the only bore are the Dutch SS who come over in silent electric canoes at night and shoot you up. They are a desperate bunch unloved by the Germans and of course hated by the Dutch." His parting advice was "Don't show yourselves too much by day because their artillery fire can be quite accurate, and do watch out for mines," a point made blatantly obvious by the bloated bodies of two cows in a nearby orchard.

In the event we were never shelled, because we kept our heads down and hid the armoured cars in the farmyard just behind a dyke which ran parallel to the river. The little window in the attic was just high enough to see over the top of the dyke and gave a clear view across the water meadows of the German positions on the far side of the river. One man sat in the attic all day with a map, compass, binoculars and field telephone, whilst at night two of us stood in a small trench dug into the top of the dyke. This routine also needed a person on the radio and telephone link to squadron headquarters, so with only ten men we were hard-pressed to maintain a 24-hour watch and to defend ourselves if attacked. A Dutch official arrived one morning on his bicycle and gave us a warning about digging into dykes. I assured him I knew about the little boy who had put his finger into the hole and promised to fill up the trench when we left.

At dusk I stretched a trip wire across every possible approach to the farm, tying one end to a hand grenade which I jammed into an empty tin can which had contained the ration of fifty cigarettes. When I was quite sure that the can was securely wedged, I pulled out the safety pin and only a gentle tug was needed to make the bomb fall out. Every morning, with some trepidation, I retraced my steps and put back the safety pins. Down by the water's edge we set up trip flares at possible landing sites; these were sometimes set off at night by wildfowl which would bring us running to our battle positions. The Germans meanwhile managed to lay little wooden Schuh mines in the footpaths which were impossible to locate with a metal detector. I lifted several, but not before Corporal Glover had lost his foot on one.

Occasionally there was a harsh roar as a German flying bomb, a V1, flew low overhead on its way to hit the docks in Antwerp. Silent but spectacular too were the V2 rockets launched against London, whose white vapour trail we watched climb steadily, like today's space rockets. We hurriedly took compass bearings on to the launch sites, but in spite of this information no attempt was ever made to strike these installations with aircraft or artillery.

It was perhaps an easy way for us to settle down to active service; the days were quiet enough but the nights became a strain as we peered into the mist and listened out for the grating of a boat's keel on the shore and the squelch of a boot in the mud. When an attack came it was very swift and as soon as the enemy had revealed their position our tracer bullets criss-crossed with theirs, lighting up the sky and starting an awful din among the duck and geese sleeping in the marshes.

After ten days we were withdrawn to Zevenbergen where I went to bed exhausted and did not wake up for thirty hours, by which time we were off once again to a position beside the Moerdyke Bridge, which the retreating Germans had partially destroyed. A stalwart company of Dutch Resistance men was placed under my command. They wore every sort of uniform, even German, and they were armed to the teeth. Their enthusiasm was tremendous, their ammunition expenditure prodigious and their discipline very different from the Guards Depot. I made friends with their commander, a young journalist who later became editor of *Die Telegraf* in Breda.

1HCR crossed the River Rhine into Germany on an immense floating bridge close behind the 1st British Corps Mobile Laundry and Bath Company, whom we caught up with near Osnabruck and were at last able to have hot showers and exchange our filthy underwear for new. We were then addressed on a hillside by our second in command who explained that about half the regiment should never have been sent abroad because they had spent less than the regulation entitlement of six months in the United Kingdom during the past three years, indeed for some it had been five years overseas. He then asked whether, as the war was nearly over, these men would be prepared to postpone their leave. Not unexpectedly all volunteered to remain with their comrades, and sadly some of these were to become casualties before the war ended.

We were then tasked to find a group of 20,000 German soldiers who had been cut off in an area of heathland between Celle and Luneburg, and if possible make them surrender. This area also contained many military establishments with instructors who knew the terrain well. The Americans had advanced across a similar tank-training area near Paderborn and lost many tanks from anti-tank guns manned by the school staff. I had hardly started my patrol when the leading scout car came reversing back to the scrub in which I had halted to tell me that there were enemy infantry on the far side of a gentle slope. I scanned the edge of a wood, spotted some figures and gave the order to Trooper Turner, "Driver advance, Co-ax (Machine gun) Traverse right". The car surged forward, the independent suspension hammering up and down. I hoped to catch them by surprise. I had just remembered to send a contact report to squadron headquarters telling them what I was about to do and received the reply, "Roger, good luck".

"For Christ sake slow down," shouted Corporal Smith. "I'll never hit them at this speed." We fired two short bursts and I was relieved to see white handkerchiefs waving in the distance, and shouted, "Cease fire, slow down". Luckily we had not hit anyone because they all turned out to be refugees; there was not a soldier among them! We continued to plunge ever deeper into the heath and forest on our allotted route; the going was terrible and at one moment every car was bogged down in the peat and I did not dare report the fact to my squadron leader. Making use of six prisoners whom we carried on our engine covers, we cut down trees, dug and eventually got through to firmer ground without being attacked.

A few miles to the south our friends the 11th Hussars had found the infamous concentration camp at Belsen. Today the place is called Hohne and the Federal Republic of Germany have erected a most emotive museum on the spot where for over forty years no birds sang. Beside a quarry near Soltau we found another small camp which was full of Germans who had committed political or 'black market' offences. They were in a pitiful condition and the camp smelt horrible. We were ordered to remain and to guard them for the night. As we settled down to cook a meal, a prisoner came up to the wire fence and in excellent English explained that he had been chef at the Hotel Bristol in Berlin and if we wished he would gladly cook our supper. We let him loose on the compo rations and he soon produced a wonderful dish which we enjoyed just as much as he did.

Inside every ten-man pack of compo rations there was a daily issue of five sheets of War Department lavatory paper per man. The paucity of this allowance was mitigated by the fact that the rations could be somewhat constipating. Nevertheless life had to continue in a regular fashion but the whole business of finding a shovel, digging a hole, squatting in the rain, avoiding stinging nettles and the attentions of mosquitoes was an awkward chore. I took care never to stray too far looking for privacy because an Irish Guards tank officer had been caught with his trousers down and had been strangled by a German in a forest.

German resistance to our advance may not have been well co-ordinated but when it occurred it was fierce. The road into the village of Witzendorf had been cratered by demolitions and in the fight to get through Corporal Wain, in a scout car, was hit in the stomach by a sniper. In the village there was a small prisoner of war camp which contained French and Italian officers, but it was not possible to risk spending the night there, so the officers were offered transportation back to our lines. The Italians accepted, but the French refused to leave, saying that they had to settle a few scores with the farmers who had used them as slave labour to pick potatoes for the past four years. Next morning, after a cautious advance, we re-entered the village from a different direction to find the French officers wearing threadbare but immaculate uniforms and clean boots, all lined up with small bundles of possessions ready to leave. There was not a sign of life in the village. Every window and door was broken, houses had been ransacked and the inhabitants possibly roughly handled. I suppose I was rather shocked, but now that old scores had been settled the French were ready to climb into trucks and drive south whilst we continued our patrol north towards Soltau.

I had not slept a wink the night before because of terrible toothache. I did not dare to report sick in case I was taken away from my troop, and, although I had taken several aspirins, the pain began once more as we edged our way into Soltau. The streets were littered with debris, some houses had been badly damaged and some were still smouldering, neither friend nor foe could be seen anywhere. On my right I noticed a brass plate outside a house enscribed "Zahnarzt" (dentist), so I halted the troop in a defensive position and with two men walked up to the house. The front door hung on one hinge; we entered and found the surgery deserted. We searched further and discovered the poor dentist and his whole family hiding in the air-raid shelter in the basement. They were terrified because we were the first British troops they had seen. I made them all come up to the surgery and explained in my elementary German what was wrong with my tooth and threatened dire consequences if he did me any harm. There were nine people in the surgery and I suspect they all were just as worried as I was. The dentist invited me to sit down and then with a great flourish extracted a tooth with a large abcess attached. The feeling of relief in that room was mutual and, thanking him warmly, we left the dentist wondering what other surprises the day might bring. Several weeks after the war ended I returned and repaid him with cigarettes and coffee, which may have been illegal but was very much appreciated.

We were given two days' rest and were told to guard a German Field Hospital just outside Soltau. The doctors and nurses were exhausted and had been working in terrible conditions with no drugs, soap, bed linen or bandages. The wards were full of wounded, many from the Russian front, the smell was awful and there was an air of utter hopelessness. I let the Commandant administer the place as best he could and we pitched our tents alongside our armoured cars in the hospital grounds. Once the maintenance on the cars was complete, the crews settled down to cook and read the mail which had caught up with us at last. Wandering around the grounds I was horrified to find an outhouse piled high with amputated limbs and unburied bodies whose white feet stacked on top of each other reached almost to the ceiling. I ordered the Commandant to get in touch with the town Burgermeister as soon as possible and get them buried the next day. The following afternoon as the bodies were being loaded onto a lorry I noticed two nurses who were watching the macabre scene, each holding two young children by the hand. Corporal of Horse Borman moved them away and I asked the grey-haired Commandant why he allowed such a thing. "It is perhaps wise that our young should witness such things and realize how terrible war can be," he replied and turned away. He may well have been right and I was glad to leave that melancholy scene.

That night a despatch rider brought written orders and it was with excitement that I learnt we were to move at first light to join the Guards Armoured Division and continue the advance alongside our sister regiment 2HCR. The CO, Lieutenant Colonel Eric Gooch, who had commanded 1HCR since the Western Desert, ended his message with the familiar words "Good Hunting, gentlemen. Push on."

As I got ready to leave that dreadful hospital I heard that Lieutenant Harvey Williams in 2HCR had been killed at Appensen in the region in which we were going to operate next. He had had an amazing adventure two weeks earlier in Holland. When turning off a main road he found himself in the middle of a stationary column of German guns, half-tracks and trucks. The 2HCR history continues, "He had no idea how many, in fact they stretched for over one mile. However, he decided to overtake them with his armoured car in front and the rest of his troop including a White Scout Car of assault troopers behind. It was impossible to miss, lorries burst into flames and exploded as ammunition and petrol scattered. It was not until they had gone 500 yards that the enemy thought of driving off or firing back.

"The faster the enemy drove the faster went the pursuing armoured cars. Both armoured-car turrets were kept traversed half-right with their guns blazing, the assault troopers lobbed hand grenades into all the open lorries they could overtake and everybody prayed that the road would not be blocked. A staff car got sandwiched between two armoured cars, they shot it up, it caught fire and had to be barged out of the way by the rear scout car. The Germans were by now lining the ditches with bazookas and 37mm anti-tank guns. Luckily they missed and sometimes hit their own vehicles, but things were getting much more difficult. A Corporal in the White Scout Car was hit in the lung, so troopers straddled his body and kept on firing. Then Harvey Williams's car was hit and crashed into a ditch. He and his operator climbed out and jumped onto the Corporal of Horse's car as it passed. Then his driver escaped by lying flat on the front tool bin of the rear scout car which accelerated out of trouble."

The now badly battered troop took up a defensive position in a small wood from where they beat off a German counter-attack before slipping away with less than a belt of ammunition left between them. No less than sixty-eight enemy vehicles including armoured cars and half-tracks were later counted destroyed on that stretch of road. The Regiment were furious when the Royal Air Force claimed the credit for this success.

It was now 30 April 1945 and we had received no news about what was going on elsewhere in the war. The Russians, assisted now by the Romanians, had crossed the River Tisa into Hungary and reached Budapest in February. Romanian armoured cars had fought their way through southern Czechoslovakia and were now roaming north of the Danube and approaching Austria. The Russians had overcome determined German resistance and were already within a few miles of Berlin. The German defenders were still holding on desperately in the hope that the Allies might soon capture Berlin from the west, which could easily have been achieved, because by 13 April the Americans were only fifty miles away, having crossed the last remaining obstacle, the River Elbe. However, they were ordered to halt and actually pulled back because, as has already been explained, it was the American intention to sacrifice Eastern Europe to the Soviet Union.

Advancing with a victorious army is very exciting for a young soldier. My father, who served under General Allenby in the final advance through Palestine in 1917/18, had a photograph album full of pictures of dead Turkish soldiers and their horses, overturned field guns and supply carts. Much has been written about the thrills of pursuit in war but nothing prepared us for the amount of carnage and destruction which we saw along the roadsides. Continually exhorted by our commanders to 'push on', a 2HCR officer wrote,

"There is no doubt that the chatter of machine guns, sudden head-on encounters, the cheering crowds of liberated towns, the orders and counter-orders all tended to build up a nervous exhilaration quite hard to define yet almost impossible to suppress." This of course was not quite the same after we entered Germany where the population was sullen and hostile.

We rejoined the squadron outside Soltau and set off in convoy to join the Guards Armoured Division which was located somewhere between Bremen and Hamburg. It took ten hours' driving in high winds and rain to reach our new deployment area. The rain beat into our eyes at any speed over ten miles an hour and there were many detours and unscheduled halts while convoys from other units crossed our route. It seemed as if the whole army was regrouping for the final thrust into Northern Germany. A heartening sight passed us going south, a column of troop-carrying trucks filled with cheering, recently liberated British prisoners of war. Eventually we reached our destination which was about five miles behind the front line and were guided into a muddy farmyard with pocket torches. We were absolutely exhausted and scarcely bothered to camouflage our cars because I was told we would have to spearhead the advance at first light next day, 1st May 1945. When I look back on it now I am amazed that we were expected to do so with only four hours' rest.

The drivers went off to collect jerry cans from the petrol truck and then, staggering and slipping under the weight, they returned to fill their empty tanks in the dark. Little petrol cookers were lit, bedding carried into a barn and faults reported to attentive mechanics. I set off to find Squadron Headquarters and get some orders, but could only find Guy Routledge, the second in command, who told me that Squadron Headquarters was in the next village and that detailed orders would be given at 4.30am next day. He told me the sad story of Robin Tudsbury whose armoured car had been blown up by a huge naval mine placed under a culvert in the road. Nothing much had been found of the crew or the vehicle; it had been an enormous explosion. The Germans were apparently using some sort of ratchet fuse set at, say, twenty clicks. Each vehicle that passed over pushed it down another click. Three Sherman tanks of the Coldstream Guards which were carrying infantry on their engine covers had driven over a similar mine, when the fourth tank which, as luck would have it, had no infantry on the back, was blown sky high, killing all the crew, and a jeep following close behind drove right into the crater. The driver's hair is said to have stood on end and he developed a pure white streak in his hair overnight. Bits of clothing hung from the trees, which were just coming into leaf, for many days afterwards.

I returned to my troop and gave them the sobering news as we ate the inevitable 'meat and vegetable' compo ration stew out of mess tins. We were lucky that we did not have to produce a guard that night or maintain a listening watch on the radio. My car, named Cavalier, had a nasty habit of stalling at critical moments, or maybe it was because Turner had difficulty in releasing the hand brake. The vehicle mechanics were still working on the twin carburettors when I fell asleep.

At 3.40 we were all awoken from a deep sleep, every engine was started and, after a quick shave, we rolled up our bedding and tied the bed rolls to the mudguards of the armoured cars using metal eyes which we had had welded on before we left England. Each commander checked his car to make sure none of the bedding was touching the hot exhaust or blocking the rear vision hatches which had to be clear if we ever had to reverse out of trouble in a hurry. Trooper Crabtree, who came from New Cross, produced a strong brew of tea and oatmeal biscuits which we ate while we checked that our maps were correctly folded. I don't know why it was that every patrol invariably had to cross two maps and it was very difficult to stop them separating. Squadron Corporal Major Offen looked in to say good morning and ask whether we had any letters to send home. Finally after a quick radio check we waved goodbye to the fitters and quartermaster's staff and set off. It was already 4.15am.

Major Gerard Leigh had moved his headquarters into the village of Fredenbeck, well forward, which in an advance was a sound move because it avoided the danger of losing contact on the radio with his patrols as they moved further away. We marked the battle situation onto our maps, or rather onto the transparent talc which covered them, before he gave his orders. This included the approximate front line and all the known German positions, and the route which each troop was to follow. My 'Mission' was to try to enter the town of Stade on the River Elbe from the north-west, whilst B Squadron would try to do so from the south. Somebody, we were told, had actually spoken to the Burgermeister of Stade who had agreed to surrender his town provided a sizeable force was assembled to break through his defences. However, as none of our troops numbered more than ten men it looked as if we were going to have difficulty persuading him to capitulate.

My second mission, if I could not get into Stade, was to turn north-west and seize and hold the bridge over the River Oste on the main road to Cuxhaven. This was, although I did not realize it at the time, the same road I had been driven down six years before on my way to spend summer holidays in Romania. I returned to my troop and the other car commanders, who gathered round to mark the relevant details on to their maps, including Report Lines and Bounds. We then wiped clean the lenses of our binoculars, loaded all the guns and started the engines.

If I had been a little nervous it disappeared as we moved off in the early morning drizzle and reached the so-called line of forward defended localities which ran along the edge of a wood. Either side of the road an infantry company stood in their slit trenches, looking pretty miserable with rain dripping off the edge of their helmets on to shiny ground sheets over their shoulders. They wished us luck and warned us that the enemy were not far away. Our silent approach once again caught the Germans by surprise and, after a couple of short bursts from Corporal Cross's machine gun, a small group surrendered. I called up the rear scout car and sent those unhappy unshaven prisoners back to the infantry we had just left.

Now I reckoned, for heavens sake let's move quickly before everybody realizes we are here. To my right I could see Michael Naylor-Leyland moving cautiously towards the main road from Bremen to Stade. We crossed the main road and followed a track alongside a field of beetroot which might take us round behind the city and to the main road from Cuxhaven in the north. It was all very tense and exhilarating; we were once more in 'Indian country'. The sky cleared and there was no dust to give away our approach, the track was easy going and we moved forward in bounds to scan the surrounding countryside carefully through binoculars before deciding it was safe to move again. I was moving fast across a stretch of open ground when Corporal of Horse Borman who was covering my move called up on the radio to report he could see what looked like an anti-tank gun on a hill to our right. The leading car had halted behind a clump of trees just short of where the Cuxhaven to Stade road crossed a small stream.

"Just check that the bridge is not set for demolition," I said to the scout car and pulled forward from behind an isolated house to cover him. "Keep your eyes on those chaps on the hill who may have an anti-tank gun. They may not have seen us yet," I ordered Corporal Smith.

Just as the scout car approached the main tarmac road the Germans blew the bridge. Even that close you can see the earth lift before you hear the sound. The gun on the hill opened fire on us. Corporal Smith fired a long burst from the machine gun and I fired a four-inch smoke canister to cover the withdrawal of the scout car. We hid our cars behind the house to take stock while Borman fired high-explosive shells from his position, which I could not do because my car was still fitted with a 'Little John' attachment and could only fire solid shot. I picked up the microphone and sent back a short contact report to Gerard Leigh. Our training had always stressed, "Once you have made contact with the enemy never lose sight of him," so I moved forward to see what was happening. The German soldiers on the hill were withdrawing so we fired a few more bursts up their backside. There was a very large crater in the road through which the stream flowed and which was now impassable. I sent a detailed report back about the size of the hole and its approaches which might be useful to the sappers when the main divisional forces got this far.

Frustrated in completing our first mission, we were ordered to carry on with the second which was the capture of the bridge over the River Oste at Hechthausen. This was not going to be easy because surely everybody now knew that we were loose behind Stade. The road to begin with ran dead straight through a small forest and all our training had been to move from corner to corner or hill crest to the next hilltop, but here was a road which was absolutely flat, dead straight and through dense pines.

"Move fast in bounds of about six hundred yards and I will be close behind," I told Corporal Farrance who had taken over the role of leading scout car. "Borman will cover us."

We darted down this dark corridor with a frantic look at the trees nearest to us every time we stopped, before scanning the road ahead. Nevertheless it still came as a surprise when I saw a startled elderly German in the wood just behind me holding a 'panzerfaust' anti-tank rocket launcher on his shoulder. There was no hope of getting Corporal Smith, with his eye glued to the telescope looking forward up the road, to traverse the turret by hand on to this chap behind me in time to prevent him firing first. I was paralysed with fear and hastily drew my Smith &

Wesson revolver which was strapped to my knee. I opened the nearest pistol port and fired wildly in his direction. He too must have been frightened because his rocket soared over my head to explode in the trees on the opposite side of the road before he fled into the darkness of the forest. I then noticed that I had put a couple of shots into my bed roll, which was secured to the rear mudguard.

As we approached the village of Dudenbuttel a military staff car entered from the far side, four German soldiers jumped out of it and disappeared as Corporal Smith fired a round of two-pounder armour-piercing which made a great flash as it hit the Mercedes. What a pity, I thought; that car might have made a useful runabout for us once the war ended. The village seemed to be deserted, it was as if everybody was holding their breath and hiding in cellars and cupboards. Just then a telephone rang in a house beside the crossroads. I called up Corporal Cross,

"Quick, they may warn the next village that we are coming."

We dashed into the house and tore the telephone wires away from the wall and the hands of a terrified old man.

"*Gibt es Deutsche Soldaten in diesem Haus?*" I asked.

"*Nein, Nein,*" he quavered in reply. We looked into a few rooms and decided it was best to get out of the place. We moved right through the village and took up a defensive position on the outskirts, which was one of the Bounds on which we had been ordered to stop, from where we could also observe the next village, Himmelforten. I reported that Düdenbüttel was not clear of enemy and requested permission to move out into more open country. I was told to consolidate and wait for the arrival of another troop commanded by Peter Sheldrick.

It was now mid-morning and we had already been on the go for about seven hours. I placed my car on a bend from where it could watch the main road and placed the others where they could watch the flanks and rear. There was still not a sign of life in the village, an eerie stillness which made us all feel uncomfortable. Taking three oatmeal biscuits from a tin which I kept on the turret ring in a clip normally used to retain the Wesco gun oil can, I spread some raspberry jam onto each before handing one to Smith and the other down to Turner, the driver. After thirty minutes I sent back a situation report and again asked for permission to resume our advance, but got the answer, "No. Stay where you are."

"Watch the front, Smith," I said. "I simply must get out and have a pee." I stood behind the car and with intense relief began to pee against the rear wheel. Just as I was finishing I heard two deafening explosions as 'Panzerfaust' rockets hit the car. I threw myself to the ground and caught a glimpse of Farrance's car speeding back to the village behind us, its flywheel screaming. Just then a machine gun opened fire on us. I looked up at my burning car and saw the top of Corporal Smith's head moving out of the turret. In two bounds I was on the engine cover and had my hands under his armpits. I dragged him with some difficulty up out of the smoking turret and down on to the engine cover when I felt a sharp pain and fell off. I got up, lifted him off the engine and carried him to the comparative shelter of a ditch. His legs looked shattered. Now for Turner, I thought. The side door to Cavalier had been blown clean away and I could see no sign of life from Turner. I grabbed two hand grenades, a Sten gun, two magazines and my map, and then I tried to disentangle Turner from his safety harness when the machine guns started again. Down on the ground once more, I rolled towards the ditch where I had left Smith. One last look at the car. Did I see Turner's hand move? That moment of doubt has always haunted me. Should I have gone back?

There was no sign of the rest of my troop, who must have all pulled back. Smith was too heavy to carry and in bad shape, so I made him comfortable and promised to be back soon with help. How was I to get back to the village, past the enemy who must have crept up behind me and would my troop still be there? Only then did all the uncomfortable lessons I had learnt in Fieldcraft during my early training begin to pay a dividend. I crawled, wriggled, rolled and ran back into Düdenbüttel, where Borman got the sharp end of my tongue for not protecting me. Peter's troop had arrived, so I used his radio to report what had happened and that I now intended going back to fetch Corporal Smith. I collected six assault troopers who had been in a White Scout car with Peter to accompany me and ordered Borman to give me covering fire if needed. I led the troopers back the way I had come, through fields and hedges, while Borman's car, driven by Trooper Clifford, a Green Line bus driver from Windsor, reversed cautiously parallel to us along the main road. Smith was still alive and so, while the others fanned out to cover me, I tried to put a morphia needle into his bleeding stump of a thigh, but could not bring myself to prick the skin. Corporal Cross, ever practical, did it in a flash.

Another look into my car; Turner was dead. Suddenly shots were fired at us from two directions and all hell seemed to break loose once more. Borman's gunner, Trooper Appleford, engaged the farm house whence some of the shots came and soon the tracer bullets set the thatched roofs on fire bringing terrified civilians running out of the cellars and barns. We laid Smith on the front tool bin of Farrance's car and sent him back with an escort to Squadron Headquarters. (He lived, after losing a leg, in Luton until he died in 1986.) I reported that there were signs of an enemy attack building up from Himmelforten and the weight of fire from that direction had increased. I asked permission to withdraw, which was granted, and we did so in short bounds leaving an awful trail of devastation behind us. Little did either side in this messy skirmish know that Adolf Hitler had already committed suicide in his bunker in Berlin and that Germany had lost the war. It was not until two days later that the bridge over the River Oste was captured and next day the Cease Fire was sounded for the third time since 1939 by trumpeters of 1HCR.

After a simply hideous journey in an ambulance, via every sort of dressing station, casualty clearing station and medical transit unit I arrived at two thirty in the morning at a Field Hospital outside Celle. It had been a very long day and a personal disaster because my precious icon, together with my bullet-holed bedding, had perished in the flames of my armoured car. I had had my whiff of war and did not ever want to smell it again.

It was not until sixteen days after I had been wounded that my father in Cairo received a telegram which drove him frantic searching fruitlessly for more information.

"GHQ regrets to inform you that War Office cable states your son Lieutenant Redgrave of RHG was wounded in North West Europe, date not reported." By which time I had returned to duty.

1. My grandfather, "a charming happy-go-lucky person and a versatile actor" (p.5) with my father, aged one, in 1898.

2. My mother's father, Mihail Capsa, "a pink-faced, gentle and conscientious man... who rose to the rank of General" (p.2).

3. Amateur theatricals in Kenya. My grandmother, Ellen Maud, with my step-grandfather, F.J. Nettlefold, at Juja in 1920 (see p.7).

4. "My uncle, Colonel Georges Capsa, considered it his duty to educate me in... the seduction of women and the joys of soldiering" (p. 17).

5. The flooded salt mine where my mother, "wearing a long bathing dress with blue and white hoops" (p.8) met my father.

6. My father at Juja shortly after he was demobilized.

7. My father at the wheel of his first motor car in Romania.

8. Oil wells at Ploesti.

9. With my sister
   Mary Maud at
   Doftana in about
   1930.

10. "Once, when we played Clifton College, I met my father's half-brother, Michael Redgrave" (p.47).

11. 306300 Trooper Redgrave, Royal Horse Guards, 1943.

12. Household Cavalry armoured car troop in Holland: 1. Trooper Turner; 2. RR; 3. Trooper Clifford; 4. Lance Corporal Farrance; 5. Lance Corporal Cross; 6. Trooper Appleford; 7. Trooper Crabtree; 8. Corporal of Horse Borman; 9. Corporal Smith.

13. "I still played rugby football whenever I could" (p. 134). Rhine Army v. France B, Paris, 1951.

14. "We were married at St Michael's Chester Square on St. Valentine's Day" (p. 139). On the left is Jane Wells, on the right Gilbert Lamb.

15. Four generations, 1956. I am standing between my father and my father-in-law. My wife, seated between Grandmothers Wellesley and Capsa, has our son Alexander on her lap. In the foreground are my mother and my mother-in-law.

16. My Headquarters car in Cyprus, 1958 (see Ch. 10).

17. Farewell dinner for Sir Richard Gale, SHAPE, 1960. Left to right: Major
    Pierre Roman, Chef d'Escadrons Michel Bion, General Wagner, General Gale,
    Colonel Erskine Tullock, RR.

18. Garmisch, 1962: General Fiertsh, General Spiedel, General Juin and General
    Sir Hugh Stockwell.

19. President Schell pays a surprise visit to the British Military Tattoo in Berlin.

20. The Queen's Birthday Parade, Berlin, 1976. Behind me are Brigadier Lennox Napier and Captain Hammon Massey, my ADC.

21. Valerie in 1976.

22. "A fairy-tale 'gingerbread' house called the Villa Lemm beside the Havel" (p. 194).

23. "An impressive ceremony then took place on the Glenike Bridge leading into Potsdam" (p. 206).

24. British Military Government, Berlin, 1977: front row from fourth left: Christian Adams, Tony Pielow, Francis McGuiness, RR, David Gladstone, Freddie Lockwood.

25. My arrival in Hong Kong, 1978. I am greeted by Captain Bob Molwand, RN, Group Captain Dan Honley, RAF, and Brigadier Derek Crabtree.

26. "The Governor, Sir Murray MacLehose, was a distinguished and much respected figure who literally towered above the Chinese" (p. 216).

27. Bob-a-Job week with the Hong Kong Scouts.

28. A boisterous welcome in the New Territories.

29. Vanessa, this time fully
    clothed! (see p. 190).

30. Lynn and her children
    visit us in Hong Kong.

31. With Papua New Guinea dancers: "How very kind of you, but I am afraid that all my grass skirts are made by Mr Gafoor, and, no, I can't stay for lunch...".

32. "A New Zealand mortar platoon came to Hong Kong..." (p. 221).

33. Valerie and I are garlanded on a visit to Nepal (see p. 231).

34. A Vietnamese refugee ship intercepted by the Royal Navy and the Royal Air
    Force (see pp. 224/5).

35. With some young residents of a Hong Kong Youth Hostel.

36. With the staff at Flagstaff House. On the outside left and right, standing, are Sergeant Lindsay and Captain Rupert Litherland.

Chapter Seven

WEREWOLVES

The war continued for three more days and there were more skirmishes and a few more unnecessary casualties as the Germans retreated. The Russians were already in Berlin, the Americans had reached the Elbe at Magdeburg and the British the Baltic Sea at Lübeck. Then suddenly on 5 May, after one final salvo was fired from hundreds of guns into open fields, the war in Europe was over at last.

After six days in hospital I must have recovered because I was bored to tears and had begun to find the nurses attractive. I resolved to discharge myself and get back to my squadron, but first I had to find my clothes. These I traced to a steel locker in a corridor which contained my tank suit and amazingly the holster and loaded pistol, less the two bullets which I had fired at the old man with a panzerfaust. Exchanging a pyjama jacket for my dirty shirt, stiff in places with dried blood, I thanked the nearest nurse for a pleasant stay and walked to the main road where I hitched a lift towards Hamburg.

The side of the road were lined with innumerable unit signs, as well as **"Beware Mines. Verges Not Swept"**. I soon spotted the ever-open eye, sign of the Guards Armoured Division, which reassured me that this was the main divisional supply route and when at last I saw a vehicle bearing our tactical sign, 44 on a diagonal red and blue background, I knew the search was over. The Quartermaster, Captain Nichols, whose truck it was, issued me with clean clothing, blankets and shaving tackle because I had lost all mine. The slogan "Don't clutter up your car with kit, you'll be sorry when it's hit" had been all too true. Luckily I had very few personal possessions with me when we were 'brewed up'.

It was wonderful to be back with my friends. The armoured cars had been cleaned and yellow pennants flew from every aerial mast. They were parked on the village green at Himmelforten, just beyond the bridge I had tried to reach. This had in fact been captured by Dickie Powle two days later and was partially blown up by the defenders as he crossed. Dickie had a charmed life. Seven months earlier he seized a small bridge with three men in Normandy, which then became a key route in the breakout from the invasion bridgehead. Two weeks later he was about to pick off with a rifle the crew of a German Tiger tank who were brewing coffee when he was wounded and taken prisoner by a German officer who had been using the same wood as a lavatory. The German is said to have chided him in good English with, "You must be a very foolish man if you think you can destroy a Tiger tank with just a rifle."

To which Dickie replied, "And you must be a most reckless tank commander if you really do not bother to keep a single man on guard when you might be in contact with the enemy."

They seemed to have developed a mutual respect for each other and it was agreed that, provided Dickie gave up his fur-lined flying boots and waited 30 minutes after the tank had driven off, he could walk back to wherever his troop were hidden and undoubtedly still observing what was going on.

Conversations with the Germans during combat were not unusual. Once in Italy the Regimental Intelligence Office (IO) driving a Jeep came round a corner to find himself looking straight up the gun barrel of a German Mark 4 tank. He rapidly reversed and in a panic took what was a wrong turning only to find himself the other side of the same tank. A head came out of the turret which shouted in English, "What the hell do you think you are doing? Do you want to get killed?" The IO made good his second escape.

Three days before the war ended our armoured cars were still trying to advance, but were held up by a German armoured train equipped with 88mm anti-aircraft guns which were being used with devastating effect in a ground role to halt any advance on two main roads. Eventually the British were able to speak to the German train commander using the railway telephone system and threatened, "Unless you withdraw your train in 30 minutes we shall attack you with Typhoon rocket firing aircraft."

The German officer was polite but firm. "You can do what you wish, but my orders are to stay here until seventeen hundred hours, then I will move."

The attack by RAF Typhoon aircraft was spectacular and the train, having been suitably forewarned, put up an equally impressive defence. When the dust finally settled the train was still there. At five o'clock, with a defiant hoot, it steamed off northwards and was found after the war in a railway siding in Cuxhaven.

I had hardly spread my blankets out on a bed in the local Gasthaus when I was told to take my troop to Stade where the airfield installations and personnel needed guarding. When the 11th Hussars were sent to the German naval barracks at Buxtehude, four hundred naval women, fearing the worst, barricaded themselves in their rooms for several days. We were unprepared for the sight that greeted us on Stade airfield. As we drove past the wreckage of fighter aircraft and bombed hangars, there, toiling on a vegetable patch, were fifty Luftwaffe girls in blue uniform skirts but without jackets or blouses. Stripped to the waist in the bright afternoon sunshine, with bronzed breasts and flaxen hair, they were, I sensed, going to make it very difficult to enforce the "No Fraternization" Order issued to all troops by the Allied High Command. In the next few days it became an impossible order to enforce and was ignored. The ice was invariably broken by children who were naturally curious and, like every other civilian, very hungry.

The other constant problem was caused by the thousands of "Displaced Persons" (DPs) who had been transported to Germany from practically every country in Europe. These slaves had been forced to work for the German war machine and were now roaming the countryside, looting and stealing, while they waited to be repatriated. Not all, however, wished to go home, as I wrote to my father, "Those DPs whose homes happen to be in Russian-occupied territory do not wish to return. I can not say I blame them, because I am darned sure what the Russians have in store for them is not much better than the conditions in which the Nazis kept them."

Our stay on the airfield was mercifully short because, when the sun failed to shine and the girls put on their shirts, Stade became a dismal grey place. We were now ordered to take over a sector from the Americans in the Harz Mountains. It was a long approach march, but the weather was fine and we were happy to leave the heathland and much-damaged northern cities for a beautiful virtually unspoilt region through which General Patton's "Hell on Wheels" Armoured Division had rolled without any heavy fighting, until they were halted on the River Elbe for political reasons beyond their comprehension at the time. We took over the delightful little town of Gandersheim and some excellent billets from a United States Cavalry squadron equipped with six-wheel Greyhound armoured cars and jeeps.

My duties were now to include intelligence and liaison with about one hundred DPs living in an old brewery. They came mainly from Poland, Ukraine and Yugoslavia, but there were also people of other nationalities, including their leader, a remarkable young lady from Carpatho-Ruthenia. This land, now annexed by the Soviet Union, was for a brief period in 1919 an independent republic. Subsequently it became the most eastern part of Czechoslovakia and touched the border of Romania. In November 1938, after Hitler had begun to annex parts of Czechoslovakia, the Hungarians seized Carpatho-Ruthenia and held it until it was overrun by the Russians in 1945.

Marijka came from a remote area called Verchovina which was peopled by a race called Boiki. She was in fact Romanian and was descended from a group of about ten thousand Romanians who had lived in Carpatho-Ruthenia for six hundred years, mainly around the Slatina salt mines. Until 1938 her parents had made a living smuggling tobacco, spirits and cattle past the Romanian and Czech border guards. Marijka claimed to have knocked out three German 'panzers' while fighting with Polish partisans and to have been twice wounded. She had been captured twice and escaped to walk westwards for many days until she reached the Harz Mountains where it seemed that bands of "Werewolves", fanatical Nazis pledged to continue the war against the Allies, were now hiding. I was prepared to believe almost anything after she had stripped off her blouse and lowered her skirt to expose her thigh, just to show me the scars of her wounds. She then offered to help find the "Werewolves", provided she was allowed to use a carving knife on them afterwards.

I reported this to Regimental Headquarters and was ordered to discover the whereabouts of these ex-SS soldiers and who was giving them succour. The next day I walked into the brewery where the refugees were housed. There was nobody to be seen as I crossed the cobbled courtyard and entered a grim grey building with green windows in which Marijka told me she lived. I climbed the stone stairs, knocked on a door which after an interminable wait Marijka opened. I stepped inside; then my senses quickened and my heart missed a beat as she quietly locked the door behind me and hung a rag over the keyhole. The furnishings were sparse, there was a huge wardrobe and an iron bedstead covered with some frayed grey blankets above which a tiny wooden icon and small cross hung. I spread my maps out on a table and handed her two bars of compo ration chocolate and some tinned food I had brought in a knapsack, which she hid away inside the cupboard. I asked her to look at the maps on the table which I hoped would indicate that I had come on business. She obviously had no idea how to read a map but drew her chair closer and gazed intently at them with her head resting in her hands. For the next hour I tried to match her account of wanderings through the

Harz Mountains with the map. Fortunately she remembered rivers, railway lines and reservoirs and I was thus able to narrow down the area in to which to conduct a search.

As soon as I had rolled up the maps she leapt to her feet and produced a bottle of what she called *tuica* from the wardrobe. She then indicated that she would like to put on something a little less formal, a little cocktail dress perhaps? She retired behind the open cupboard door. I watched her feet lift up and down until she reappeared and sat cross-legged on the bed wearing a one-piece black bathing costume. She pulled the cork out of the bottle with her teeth and poured out an evil-smelling white liquid which certainly was not *tuica*, and with a gracious sweep of her hand invited me to join her. Whereas she had been somewhat demure and puzzled by all the maps and planning, now she knew exactly what course to follow and, as her attack developed, I began to have serious doubts as to whether I was ever going to stand the pace. It was dark by the time she produced the door key which she had hidden and let me out into the unlit cobbled streets of Gandersheim.

The military plan was that I should be dropped off with my informant in the southern Harz Mountains disguised as a refugee and then picked up at a certain crossroads three days later. I did not disclose who my guide was to be except to my driver and radio operator who dropped us off on a dirt track outside a forest two nights later. With a sinking heart I watched the tail lights of the Jeep disappear down into the valley; my clothes were ill fitting and smelly but at least my shoes were comfortable. The bundle slung across my back contained a blanket, three days' rations for two, a few personal possessions and a P38 Luger pistol which was burning a hole in my pocket. We set off towards the lights of a distant village. Marijka was strangely silent and walked like a tigress stalking her prey. I had resolved to leave all the talking to her and soon adopted the dejected and hungry shuffle I had so often seen among refugees.

For the next two nights we moved stealthily around villages, looking and listening, and during the day we lay hidden deep inside cornfields or beneath the bushes which lined the edge of the forest. I preferred the open fields because then we could sunbathe and avoid the mosquitoes which thrived in the beech woods. As we lay on our backs watching the white clouds and the buzzards circling round, we talked of our childhood and of the gentle slopes beneath the Carpathian Mountains which we had both known. She described the streams which contained tiny specks of gold and semi-precious stones such as amber. Romanian amber was either pale clear yellow, like mother of pearl, or a beautiful cloudy brown or grey. She remembered the flocks of long-legged sheep passing through on their way to high pastures with a few donkeys carrying provisions in their midst, lots of shaggy dogs and shepherds in long sheepskin coats wearing tall black hats. For each of us it was pure escapism, every memory led to another, it was warm, sensual and not going to last.

When darkness fell we set off once more to explore a small village east of Seesen. Suddenly we could hear the sound of many feet and all the dogs started to bark wildly. Marijka, whose determination not to quit the hunt suddenly seemed vindicated, darted along a ditch in which we were hiding to discover where they went. We crouched behind a muck-spreader to watch nine men pass through the open door of a large farm house and into the warmth and light beyond. We hung around that farm for hours not daring to move in case the dogs started to bark again, until the men had left and disappeared into the forest whence they had come.

In retrospect there was no evidence that the men presented any military threat, but we had located three farms which definitely were supplying these wanderers with clandestine assistance. The old farmers were subsequently arrested, but released after a day, and the little bands of German soldiers were allowed to melt away back to their homes. I had I suppose had enough of Marijka and now wished to forget those very smelly clothes and the diet of corned beef and oatmeal biscuits, and decided to keep well clear of her. However, after a few days she was back with another request which we could not ignore.

It seemed that two days before the Americans entered the town the Nazis had taken two lorryloads of slave workers from her camp saying that there was a job for them to do in the neighbouring town of Goslar. When the trucks returned they were empty and now, three weeks later, there was no trace of the men.

"You must arrest the drivers. They were all big Nazis," she demanded, "and then allow my Liberation Committee to ask them what happened to our comrades."

Her fingers fiddled with an enormous .45 revolver and I made a mental note to remove it as soon as possible. She continued to speak with such passion and eloquence that I asked the civil police to track down the drivers. By the next morning it was clear that the DPs had been executed and that the drivers who had had nothing to do with the killing were indeed lucky to be in the hands of the Military Police and not Marijka's ruffians.

We agreed that the victims should be given a decent burial and so on Saturday, 9 June 1945 every citizen remotely connected with the Nazis in Gandersheim was rounded up. The Burgermeister had been directed to provide spades, coffins, gloves and transport. Early in the morning a column of DPs walked past our billet over the hill and out of sight.

"You had better drive down with your troop and just see that there is fair play," said Gerard Leigh, my squadron leader, "but remember it is all their own show, so don't interfere." Then as an afterthought he added, "And do be careful! These Eastern Europeans can get emotional and terribly touchy." As if I did not know!

I took my troop out of town and after a mile turned up a track towards the edge of a dark wood where I took over duties from Norman Hearson's. We parked alongside a seemingly endless line of farm carts all carrying empty hexagonal wooden coffins. Leaving four men to guard the cars and operate the radio, Corporal of Horse Borman and four crewmen followed me into the forest. "Blimey what a terrible stink!" exclaimed a trooper, words which barely described the intense and ghastly smell. We walked on towards a clearing surrounded by tall beech trees beyond which rows of young pine trees stretched into the distance. There was a large mound of red earth. How like Devonshire soil, I thought. Beyond it was a pit about half the size of a tennis court. Gathered on one side stood a miserable sullen group of elderly Germans, gathered on the principle that, although they had nothing to do with the crime, living nearby they can not have been totally ignorant of the fact. On the opposite side there was a wailing sobbing crowd of slave labourers from Gandersheim. Between these groups lay a pit about three metres deep in which four men were uncovering a treble line of bodies which had lain there about five weeks. The bodies of the men, who had probably dug their own grave, were fully clothed and must have been easily recognizable to their next of kin and friends, and, as the earth was brushed off each face, fresh screams rent the air. The men in the pit stoically placed each body into slings which were lifted out by other Germans, whilst the remainder watched unemotionally. The bodies were then placed in open coffins and a sprig of pine lain across each corpse.

As this macabre scene continued Marijka sat at a makeshift table among her comrades, importantly checking each name against her list. Every now and then she would rush to take another look at what was happening in the pit. It was on one of these sorties that she ordered all the men out of the pit and forced six German women to take their place, having first removed the gloves and spades.

"Didn't you see those filthy women spit at that body as it was lifted out?" she screamed at me.

I had done, but was unsure whether it was on to a body or on to the ground. It was an astonishing sight to see those women wearing high-heel shoes, working in that awful pit lifting out the remaining bodies with their bare hands. The stench was overpowering, yet the women worked steadily on and appeared to be unmoved by the cries and curses from above their heads. Eventually the last body rested in its coffin, the women were hauled out by their friends and a mournful silence descended around that vast red hole. The Germans bunched together. The DPs, emotionally exhausted, faced them, and my soldiers, somewhat shaken, stood in between. Then gradually a murmuring and whispering started which grew louder and more menacing. Marijka came flying towards me waving her lists. "The Committee have decided," she cried, "forty-one bodies came out of that hole, now forty-one German bodies must go back into it!" She put her hands on her hips and spat towards the other side of the pit. Her crowd then began to chant a slogan which I could not understand.

"Surely you do not want more blood and more dead men?" I asked. "Yes. of course I do you fool," she continued. "You never saw what the Germans did to the Resistance in Warsaw. You English, you did nothing. How can you ever understand?"

I told her that as far as I knew the Russians had deliberately halted thirty kilometres from Warsaw and allowed the Polish patriots to be crushed, whilst we British did at least fly bombers hundreds of kilometres from Britain with belated help. But it was no good, she had made up her mind.

"These Germans must die. My people all want it. You must give the order. You are an officer, you have the guns, the machine guns."

She turned and ran back to her people and climbed on to the table to address them. The hitherto unemotional Germans, still huddled together, lost no time in understanding what the implications were of the murmurs and chattering on the other side of the empty pit. If there was room for any other smell in that putrid air, it was the smell of fear. Cold sweat gathered on many brows while the passionate hostility of the chanting crowd was becoming quite frightening. I sent a trooper back to the armoured cars to radio for help and to fetch the light machine gun from a scout car, but it seemed that these measures might not be enough to stop another massacre.

"Wait Marijka!" I shouted. "I too have decided. I must also speak to your Committee."

Playing for time I walked slowly to where she had gathered her clan, about twenty yards from the pit, and climbed onto the table. Over the top of the crowd I caught Borman's eye and nodded. My emotional speech in very bad German was to the effect that we should not meet evil with evil; this was not what we had fought a war about. While this was being translated into Polish and Yugoslav, I noticed that the monstrous heap of red earth had nearly vanished. With a little encouragement from Borman the Germans had worked as if possessed with superhuman powers. Those without spades turned to face the pile and scooped the soil backwards between their legs with bare hands. Within a few minutes the pit was nearly full and the mud-stained party were being escorted out of the forest by the soldiers. There was a howl like that of a wounded wolf when Marijka noticed what had taken place behind her. She hurled herself at me, spitting, scratching and screaming with frustration, but was pulled off by some older members of her group who were relieved that the exhumation had been achieved without further bloodshed.

As we walked out into the sunlight, Borman said, "You certainly had them all taken in with your speech, sir. Was it Hamlet?" "I thought," he added, "that we had better finish the job while they were not looking. Anyway, it is nearly dinner time."

We drove slowly past the long line of farm carts laden with open coffins and sprigs of pine lain over each body. As we left the forest a dejected figure ran out of the bushes beside the track and waved us down. I stopped and bent down from the turret offering a hand. "All right, climb on. It's been a long day, Marijka."

A letter from my cousin Douglas who was in the Royal Navy told me that my one-armed Uncle Jack had died of cancer. He had somehow been able to attend a final voluntary disbandment parade of his beloved Cockwood Home Guard platoon outside the Anchor Inn. He wrote to my father afterwards, just before he died, "We have not met for more than three days in the last thirty years. It would be so nice to see you."

My mother in Cairo was very depressed with her family still scattered and wrote to my father, "For the time being it looks as if we shall have to make the best of it, keep our chins up and just wait and keep smiling. We can not afford to let ourselves feel blue."

Aware now that there was no chance to start life again in Romania, she did not know what to do.

"Darling mine, I cannot tell you how I long for peace to come and to be together again in a small place, and to feel secure. I dread this insecurity feeling so terribly, this feeling of not being wanted anywhere. . . . Cheer up my love. It just cannot go on much longer."

Events took a turn for the better when, three weeks after news of my being wounded, they received a long cheerful letter from me. The war was over in Europe and her father-in-law, FJN, had written to offer them a cottage in the grounds of Chelwood Vachery near Forest Row, provided my father could write through military channels to the War Office asking them to de-requisition the place! This he did and at the same time he explained that none of the family had any clothes warm enough for the English climate. FJN promptly sent £300, which was a handsome sum and my mother set about getting overcoats made out of dark grey army blankets. The other big worry was that they might have to pay for their passages to England. Mother, always resourceful, approached the British Consul requesting a Certificate confirming that she and her daughters were refugees, which in fact they were. This cost twelve shillings and sixpence and she noted, "If nothing else this should be useful for Customs clearance."

My grandmother, living in Bucharest, had managed to establish a link with the British Military Mission who forwarded her mail to Cairo. The Russians, however, were busy squeezing out the Western Allies. Romania was the first country to be "liberated" by the Red Army. It should have been a test of the good faith of the leadership of the Soviet Union to carry out the political promises they had made in Moscow in 1944 and at Yalta in February 1945. A pledge had been made by Russia, America and Britain, to "jointly assist the people of any European liberated state or former Axis satellite state, *to form interim governments representative of all democratic elements through free elections of governments responsible to the will of the people.*" Hardly a fortnight had passed after the signing of the "Declaration on Liberated Europe" when the Soviet leaders removed the constitutional Romanian government and set about establishing a "friendly government". The stage was being set for one-party rule in the name of the "Proletariat". All other political parties were suppressed and the way was opened for the complete Sovietization of Romania. Perhaps this was the start of the "Cold War"?

On 30 June 1945 I was sent through the Harz Mountains right up to the River Elbe near Magdeburg to participate in what seemed to us a most shameful operation. We had not been given the background to the Potsdam Agreement nor told why the Allied advance had been halted on the River Elbe instead of pushing on to capture Berlin, which could easily have been achieved. The decision to withdraw, in return for permission to occupy part of Berlin with an Allied force, was never explained to us. I was therefore horrified to be told over the radio by a Headquarters under whose command my troop was placed and whom I never saw that we were to be part of the rearguard of the British Army as it fell back before the advance of the Red Army, commencing the next day.

That evening I looked across that huge river just below "Friendship Bridge" which had been built by United States Army, at the low hillsides opposite which were aglow with camp fires lit by the Russian army. There were literally thousands of soldiers milling around and the whole scene resembled a huge antheap which had suddenly been disturbed and was on the move. Our orders were not to allow the Russians to cross until 9 am next morning, but by 6 am Rupert Watson and nine Household Cavalrymen on the western end of the bridge were faced by thousands of Russians, anxious to advance as soon as possible and get their hands on the loot that was surely awaiting them. They cheerfully accepted the delay, climbed down off their carts and tried their luck fishing off the side of the bridge and the river bank.

When we did begin the withdrawal it was through a series of ghost towns such as Quedlinburg. The population was terrified and had passed on the awful news "The Russians are coming", before going to ground in their shuttered homes. The engine covers of our armoured cars and a truck were soon carrying scores of wounded German soldiers from a hospital. They feared that if they fell into Russian hands they would be shipped back to prison camps in Siberia and face many years of internment. Fortunately the Red Army advanced on its feet or in horse-drawn transport and so we had time to clear the small hospital and run a ferry service to a railway station where a steam engine and eight wagons waited.

Just like the passage of Romanian gypsies through the Doftana valley, so thousands of Russians swept through these peaceful rural localities. It was as if the war, which had ended two months earlier, was still being waged, as if we were still in the heat of battle. We had just driven back into Hedersleben, a small village, to recover a scout car which had broken down when we heard and saw the terrible revenge for sufferings to their own families which the Russians now proceeded to take out on those German villagers. Doors and window shutters were smashed down, glass broken and the air was filled with the screams of terrified civilians as their possessions were looted and they were assaulted and in some cases raped. There was absolutely nothing we could do. We hitched a tow chain onto the scout car and withdrew towards the mountains with our tails between our legs.

After two days of constant movement and alertness reporting the extent of the Russian advance, I halted my tired men on the new border between the British and Russian Zone, high up in the Harz Mountains. It was an enchanting little village, filled that evening with the sound of cow bells as cattle returned from the mountain pastures, unattended, each to find its own way to its stall. We washed in the cool waters of a shallow stream and exchanged our tinned rations for eggs and fresh milk. We then erected a sky antenna and, using morse code, were able to re-establish contact with the 1st Household Cavalry Regiment who had moved their location.

I sat watching the sun set and thought about the behaviour of our Russian allies which I had witnessed. The clouds were darkening over the plains below in the east which we had just left and I wondered if the advent of the Red Army in Romania, which had been an unwilling ally of Germany for three years, had been as brutal. Had my grandmother and uncles survived? Was Doftana still standing? Would I ever get back to Romania or had too much happened to our lives? Indeed, what were my parents going to do? When would I see them again? It had been six eventful years and I now felt uneasy about remaining in the Army. After we had rejoined the squadron I was in despair to find that a suitcase containing the only plain clothes I possessed anywhere in the world had been 'stolen'. It had been entrusted to the keeping of a reinforcement officer from another regiment who, after a number of similar incidents had occurred, was tried and discharged from the army. It was to be two years before I accumulated enough clothing coupons to replace my wardrobe. Indeed, it is strange to reflect how much a blue-striped shirt as opposed to a khaki one meant to me. Clothes rationing continued in the United Kingdom until 1953, long after the Germans had lifted similar controls on their own people!

There were, sadly, a few British soldiers who chose to make a big profit from the Black Market, where the currency was cigarettes and coffee. Citizens of Hamburg complained that cigarettes which they had just received by barter were being found and confiscated by Military Police a few hours later. The culprit turned out to be a young infantry officer and his batman. Whenever he was Orderly Officer, whose duties included driving in a jeep to inspect certain installations, they would find time to wear Military Police caps and recover their cigarettes. They were caught when the Provost Marshal ordered all his men to remove the red covers to their caps and the culprits were soon identified.

We were unprepared to learn that the two regiments of Household Cavalry formed in 1939 were to be disbanded and reformed, 1HCR into The Life Guards and 2HCR into Royal Horse Guards. My troop was a mixture of both regiments and, having shared so many experiences together, we found it difficult to say goodbye. Those in The Life Guards remained in the Harz and were then sent to Palestine, whilst we drove westwards through the beautiful countryside of the Sauerland and joined 2HCR at Bruhl near Cologne.

My new squadron leader was Lord Amherst who had served for many years with Glubb Pasha's Arab Legion in Trans-Jordan. William was a delightful, kind man whose experience of armoured reconnaissance seemed to be very limited, but he ruled us with a light touch and allowed us to get on with the tasks we were given in our own way. The countryside around Cologne was still being terrorized by bands of Displaced Persons who were waiting to be transported back to their home countries. Meanwhile they considered it their right to wreak retribution on German farmers on whose land they may have worked. Some of these bandits had set up bases in the warren of underground forts that ringed Cologne. These were relics of past wars with the French, whose entrances were hidden by forest and undergrowth from which it proved very difficult to flush them out, and anyway none of us was particularly anxious to engage in a shootout in that labyrinth of dark tunnels.

We worked almost entirely at night, using patrols of two scout cars, just four men, and relied on our good communications and silent approach to make arrests or swoop in to relieve farmhouses under attack. One night we were free-wheeling silently into a village near Bad Godesberg when I heard shouts and screams from the upstairs windows of a large house. There were about twenty men outside removing the shutters and trying to get inside at three frightened girls upstairs. Shades of the Red Army I thought, but this time I am on home ground. It turned out that they were British soldiers from a Railway Construction unit and were all a little drunk. Feeling slightly foolhardy, I dismounted and advised them to pack it in and go home, while the corporal in the other scout car directed a spotlight on to the crowd. I was wearing a tank suit which carried no badges of rank and this may have induced one of the troublemakers to take a swing at me. He caught me a glancing blow and as I reeled back my corporal pushed me forward again and whispered, "Don't hit him sir, keep talking". I was able to persuade them that whatever my rank was in their eyes I was 'On Duty' and they were not, and furthermore I could call for considerable retribution on them over the radio unless they went home, which, thank heavens, they did. After that salutary lesson I always took care to wear my badges of rank.

Travelling along the short stretch of autobahn which had been built between Cologne and Bonn, I was overtaken at great speed by a Canadian Army Chevrolet truck. As the Canadian Army was either in Holland or on the way back across the Atlantic I pursued him, but although we reached 62 miles an hour in the Daimler scout car, he was faster, so I loaded the Very Cartridge Signal pistol and fired a shot beneath his back wheels. A red ball of fire ricochetted the length of the truck and rose from beneath the bonnet to hit the windscreen. I fired a green flare next and the very frightened driver drew up. He was a Canadian deserter trying to get to a girl in Koblenz.

The rather casual and independent manner in which we had been accustomed to work in 1HCR soon earned the disapproval of our remarkable commanding officer, Lieutenant Colonel Henry Abel Smith, who had forged 2HCR into such an efficient reconnaissance regiment. We were made to learn almost every 'tactical drill' again, to attend classes when we were not out on patrol and to go for lengthy runs every morning, which were supervised by the Colonel himself, much to the horror of poor William Amherst who had not endured such indignity since he left school. Colonel Henry's enthusiasm extended to everything he did. He once took a Dutch general for a ride in a Staghound armoured car, huge machines which we were trying to persuade the Dutch army to buy. They were cumbersome and under their weight the soft shoulders of neglected roads sometimes gave way. On such an occasion, with the car in a ditch, he continued to extol its qualities while the driver engaged emergency low gear and four-wheel drive, then revved the twin Cadillac engines so hard that the car leapt out of the ditch. This manoeuvre caught the Dutch general unprepared in the turret and practically castrated him. Ignoring his discomfort, Colonel Henry continued, "And there's power for you, didn't I tell you General!"

By the summer I was getting depressed. My parents had sailed from Egypt on the Cunard White Star *Britannic* on 10 July, with 5000 passengers. They reached Liverpool on the 20th when only the RAF were allowed to disembark; the Army families were kept a further 24 frustrating hours on board. I was still hoping to get leave and was becoming cynical about increasing military bureaucracy. I wrote to my father, "The Army still seems as ridiculous as ever. Only yesterday there were two startling bits of information on Orders, one to the effect that all vehicles will be properly painted, including a Yellow Gas Detector disc, the other was that too many men were losing their dentures being seasick while crossing the Channel, in future Disciplinary action will be taken etc!"

We continued to try to keep law and order but with less enthusiasm. One night I handed over a belligerent Pole, who was also hopelessly drunk, to two local German policemen. They were delighted to at last have a prisoner entrusted to their care and with great ceremony marched him off to the cell. Sadly the key to the cell door was broken, so the drunk was temporarily put in the police station office, whilst one of the policemen came out to tell me the problem. The Wachmeister who had been left behind to guard the Pole suddenly had a suggestion and rushed out to tell me, slamming the door behind him. No doubt he had the best intentions but he only succeeded in locking the drunk inside the police station and the whole police force out. It took them hours to get the prisoner to open the door for them.

Next day Valerian Douro told me I had been awarded the Military Cross for the action at Düdenbüttel and gave me his own ribbon to wear.

The Rhinelanders were a cultured people who showed no open resentment towards the British and had already had an occupation army stationed in their cities from 1919 until 1929. Ancient Austin armoured cars had then rolled across the Hohenzollern Bridge into Cologne just as our Daimlers did now. Emperor Claudius's wife Agrippina was born in the city which had been a Roman colony since 50 AD. It is one of the oldest cities in Christendom. The majestic Gothic cathedral, ruined by fire in 1248, had once more been practically destroyed by Allied bombers. Among the many other churches destroyed was the Church of Saint Cecilia, beneath which, according to legend, rest the bones of 11,000 English virgins massacred on a pilgrimage to Rome. No doubt history has added a few noughts to this unhappy incident.

The link between ourselves and the Rhinelanders was brought home to me in a curious manner. A young trooper in Julian Berry's squadron had fallen in love with a German cleaner girl who worked in his billet. He soon discovered that he had a great deal in common with her and asked his squadron leader whether it would ever be possible to marry a German girl. Julian played for time and said wait. At this stage he had never been into her home, but after a visit to meet her parents he returned to see Julian, a shaken and crestfallen man. It appears that sitting on a sofa going through a box of photographs, he was shown one of a British soldier wearing the puttees and uniform of the nineteen twenties. She told him that this was her real father, but that he had gone back to England and never returned to marry her mother, who eventually married a post office official. It was then that the trooper remembered that he had already seen exactly the same photograph in his father's album inscribed "In Koblenz 1923".

After a few weeks in Bruhl we were told to hand over our billets to the Belgian Army and move to proper barracks in Menden Westphalia. The British Military Government believed that the population of the desolate industrial cities of the Ruhr were getting restless and that a drive by four hundred military vehicles through the cobbled streets of Duisburg and Essen might have a salutary effect. We therefore followed a tortuous route through a dismal landscape of damaged buildings and empty factories. The impact of this show of force must have been somewhat marred when the dummy wooden gun, which had replaced the 37mm gun in Major Dick Wrottesley's Staghound armoured car, to make room for an extra radio, came flying out of the turret when his driver braked suddenly at a crossroads in Hamm. It was retrieved from the feet of two astonished elderly women shoppers.

Our new home in Menden was a former artillery barracks on a hill above the town. The officers' mess contained a Teutonic item of plumbing which was a standard fitting in the 'officers' house' of most German barracks. This was a 'vomitorium' usually to be found in the basement lavatory complete with head rest, two chrome-plated hand-grips and a push-button flush. In the small garden we were glad to find a fish pond and promptly sent a Jeep back to Bruhl to collect the gold-fish which we had left behind, only to discover that 'Les braves Belges' had already fried them.

One of the many duties of the Orderly Officer was to visit a women's prison at Hemer in which British prisoners of war had previously been held. The new inmates had the disconcerting habit of taking off their clothes in the light of the scout car's spotlight and dancing naked behind the barbed wire. Another dreadful task was being ordered to provide a firing squad to execute a murderer in Werl prison or, worse still, being ordered to witness an execution by guillotine in Wuppertal. This meant identifying two murderers, both DPs, as the same men who had been sentenced in a military court and then being obliged to stand in the same room, but behind a curtain, while the sentence was carried out within seconds of the man entering the room. The memory of the noise the blade made coming down and the hosing down of the floor with water after-wards made lunch with the North Irish Horse quite impossible to eat, but we did drink several glasses of brandy. I had no idea that the guillotine was used in Germany, but thirty years later I saw exactly the same execution room in Spandau prison in West Berlin where I used to visit Rudolf Hess.

I soon realized that the daily routine of an occupation army was going to be no fun at all. There were far too many parades and petty regulations, with countless inspections of vehicles, equipment and stores. Anything surplus to establishment was removed and this included three Jeeps, which we had bought for six bottles of whisky from our American Allies and were used by young officers as runabouts. On one such inspection the Technical Quartermaster, Sam Coles, had to take a convoy of surplus vehicles and stores which he had not yet had time to get rid of out of barracks and wait until nightfall before venturing back.

This was an unhappy time for me, because the officers' mess was dominated by a number of bored, hard-drinking, gambling officers who had personal incomes and pursuits very different from what the rest of us could afford. We resented their sarcasm and desire to return to what they imagined were the easy-going pre-war standards of soldiering, whilst they considered we were unnecessarily concerned with our military profession. This unfortunate division was made worse when we were all ordered to go through the riding school under two old-fashioned equitation instructors whose sadism made our lives a misery. Many of us preferred rugby football to equitation and had not joined the regiment to ride horses but to serve in armoured cars. Nevertheless the crunch obviously had to come one day because the decision to reform the ceremonial regiment in London meant that officers had to be prepared to serve there too, but it was nevertheless a most miserable course. Another problem was how to make ends meet, because a month's pay amounted to £12, barely enough to meet the mess bills which had risen to meet the extravagant demands for more magazines and better food from those with private incomes. Most of these problems were resolved by a new commanding officer, Sir Peter Grant-Lawson, who made a few judicious postings back to the depot and set about giving us a sense of purpose and the encouragement we needed.

Although I had not yet managed to get back to England, "Local Leave" could be taken in Brussels, whose inhabitants had given 2HCR and the Welsh Guards such a rapturous welcome in 1944. Being a junior officer and unable to use a staff car or a Jeep, my companion and I were told to use the squadron Bedford water cart, which had canvas doors and no windows. After many hours we reached the Guards Armoured Division's

"Eye Club", a requisitioned hotel in the centre of the city. Naturally, as soon as we had made ourselves presentable, we hurried to Madame 'B's establishment in the Rue Royale, which catered for the needs of young officers from 'respectable families and good regiments'.

She was the most terrible snob and could not resist revealing that certain well-known, titled senior officers had visited her house the last time they were on leave. She insisted, quite rightly, that everything should be conducted in a civilized and dignified manner; there was to be no sudden leaping into bed with her well-bred girls. So we sat in her drawing room sipping tea, surrounded by regimental prints and cabinets full of Limoges china, whilst from under a glass table top the cap badges of every regiment in the Guards Armoured Division sparkled beneath the light from a cut-glass chandelier. After half an hour of gossip, during which she probed into our backgrounds, we were introduced to those girls she considered were most suitable, but even then we were told to go away and come back at eight o'clock, by which time she had booked tables at a hideously expensive restaurant and juggled with the available accommodation. Thus it was that I met Françoise who had a great sense of humour and a simply terrible cold. We wined and dined far too well, after which I practically carried her back to the Rue Royale where she closed her eyes and passed out completely. She was a delightful person and I kept in touch until she married a banker and settled down to a more mundane life in Liège.

I had begun to wonder what I was going to do when I left the Army, because, having been commissioned, I was no longer obliged to complete a regular soldier's twelve-year engagement. I was much taken with the idea of joining Cooper, McDougall & Robertson who, among other products, made sheep dips in Berkhampstead. They had given me a diary whose foreword made the point that "the war will end with the flocks and herds of Europe slaughtered wholesale and with fields and farms pillaged, from Norway to the Mediterranean; there is therefore going to be a tremendous amount that this company can do to help to revitalise stock farming and improve harvests." Although this seemed a worthwhile career to follow, I also considered becoming a diplomat and using that as a means to get back into Romania, but above all I wanted to discover what my parents were going to do.

My father, still receiving only a Captain's pay, returned to England to await his demobilization. He stepped ashore into a country which he had only visited twice since 1921 and which was virtually unknown to his family. He was already 48 years old, he had no money, no home, no job and very few clothes until he was presented with an awful brown 'de-mob' suit, grey hat and a raincoat by a grateful Government for services rendered. Once again it was his step-father, F.J. Nettlefold, who came to the rescue and gave the family temporary accommodation over the stables at Chelwood Vachery in Sussex.

My chance to be reunited with them came when I volunteered to attend a short course in Tank Recognition at Lulworth Camp in Dorset. The war in Europe had been over for several months and there was no enthusiasm from anybody to attend a course which seemed so dull and such a complete waste of time. Having achieved my aim of getting to England, I now seriously considered leaving the army and arranged for an interview with the Foreign Office selectors as I passed through London. I rushed to Thomas's in Duke Street for a hair cut and then, wearing uniform, because I had no civilian clothes, to Burlington House where I was treated with the utmost kindness and understanding. The Board, however, were not prepared to consider my application unless I gave an undertaking to go back to college and study Greek and Latin. I explained in despair that I had had my fill of Latin and hated Classics, that I was quite good at modern languages and had plenty to offer them in other fields, but it was all to no avail.

The week at Lulworth passed all too slowly while we learnt to distin-guish friend from potential foe by some tiny feature such as the shape of a periscope. My mind was, however, set on the three days' leave I would get at the end of the course before returning to Germany. What a joy it would be to see my sisters again after six long years. Would I recognize them, had they changed? At least those lonely moments of doubt when I felt so lost and miserable were never going to happen again. The mental images of my mother and father which I had managed to sustain through a collection of countless air letter forms and old photographs were at last going to be confirmed and matched, or had the separation been too long for all of us? I took a taxi from Forest Row railway station the four miles to Chelwood Vachery where I found everybody in the sitting room above the archway into the stables. It was understandably an emotional and wonderful occasion; we all wept a little and talked a lot. My sisters were now teenagers, attractive and full of ideas and sparkle. My father was very moved and as kind and interested in what I had been doing as he always had been, but he clearly had many worries on his mind which he kept to himself. His diary records simply. "Roy came today, must be six years since we saw him." My mother had not changed. She wanted to know everything. Her vitality and urge to do something, to go places, had remained undiminished, but I was quite surprised to discover that I had forgotten how 'foreign' my mother was and out of place among the British institutions which for the past few years had smothered my life. I resented this and felt ashamed of myself, but on the other hand my mother refused to accept that I was anything but an overgrown schoolboy.

The truth was we had all changed. We were all that much older and we had each, at different times, been obliged to manage and to survive entirely on our own. Our wanderings may have ended, we may have been reunited but we had reached an emotional crossroads and I certainly had no idea what to do next. It was sad too that our great family reunion was incomplete, because grandmother, Gui, was still in Romania, as were many of our most treasured possessions.

After three days I said goodbye and took the train for Harwich, depressed and confused. The hopes which I had cherished for so many years now proved to be an illusion; I could never be content to live at home again, there would never be another Doftana, a transfer to the Foreign Office was impossible and the Army was rapidly losing its attraction. There was a five-hour delay before the British Military Train left the Hook of Holland for Germany, so I went for a walk along that bleak featureless Dutch seashore. It was high time, I thought, to forget the past, to cease being depressed and to look ahead and enjoy life. I should feel proud of my Romanian ancestry not uncomfortable. After all had not Dacian soldiers, the Aeolian cohort under command of Marcus Julius, Imperial Legate and Propraetor, once garrisoned Birdoswald, fifteen miles from Carlisle on Hadrian's Wall and helped to keep the Picts and Scots out of England? I sat down in that awful Transit Camp and wrote my mother a long and cheerful letter because I realized that she too must have been bitterly disappointed at our uneven relationship.

I had been advised to find a seat on the train as early as possible because there were few compartments which had a full set of seat cushions, light bulbs and unbroken windows. German rolling stock still suffered from war damage and the attentions of carefree British soldiers returning to England to be demobilized, fathers perhaps of the football hooligans of a later age. Travel on these trains was controlled by a Railway Transport Officer, RTO, who according to your destination in Germany directed passengers to board the Blue, Red or Green Train. When the 8th Hussars passed through the Hook of Holland on their way to Germany, the RTO decreed that all officers and non-commissioned officers should travel on the Red Train and all troopers on the Green Train. This edict horrified the commanding officer, George Butler, who tried to explain to the RTO that his men were not a bunch of gentle West Country farmers' boys but a lot of irrational Irishmen, whose behaviour without proper supervision would certainly cause even more damage to the coaches and that some might even decide to leave the train long before it got to its destination. The RTO remained adamant and so a few moments before loading was due to begin George ordered his adjutant to arrest the RTO and his staff and lock them in the station waiting room. He then loaded his regiment of Irishmen by squadrons into the two trains. Just as the train pulled out he gave the key of the waiting room to a highly amused Dutch railway official. Subsequently a blistering row with a 'higher authority' ensued which lasted for nearly two years, but this did not prevent George Butler becoming a Brigadier. Sadly he was killed in a helicopter crash near Bristol in 1966.

As there was no food provided on military trains, they took the unusual step of stopping for an hour in a siding near Krefeld, just inside Germany, where a tented transit mess had been set up. All passengers had to get off the train and queue to collect a mug of tea and a paper bag which contained two thick spam and cheese sandwiches, a slice of yellow seed cake and an apple. The next ten miles of railway track was lined with hungry German children who eagerly picked up the uneaten rations which the soldiers threw out of the windows and soon the fields were littered with brown paper bags. I fished around in my suitcase for a precious bar of chocolate and discovered a small flat parcel inside my pyjamas. I opened it carefully to find that mother had secretly replaced my lost Romanian icon with another. I took this as a happy omen and decided not to worry about the future. It was going to solve itself. Meanwhile I was going to enjoy every moment.

Chapter Eight

THE GREEN FRONTIER

There was a hole in the wire fence which surrounded the barracks at Menden, just behind the workshops. Everybody returning to barracks after midnight curfew used it, that is to say until Corporal of Horse Jarman, in charge of the Regimental Police, put his camp bed underneath it and caught Trooper Brown 22 and his friends as they stepped right onto him in the early hours of Sunday morning. Brown confided to me that things had taken a turn for the worst and that it was high time he moved on to fresh pastures. I agreed wholeheartedly and was able to give him the good news that I had been promoted to Captain, made Intelligence Officer and that I was off on detachment with a squadron to an isolated ex-Luftwaffe airfield at Wesendorf near the interzonal border, and that, if he wished, he could come along too.

This was a timely and most welcome change in my fortunes. The accommodation at Wesendorf was magnificent and the camp, which included the airfield, was spread across hundreds of acres of grass, heather and silver birches. We were commanded by a highly competent squadron leader, Major David Tabor. He had had some amazing adventures in northern France when with just two scout cars he captured five self-propelled guns and forty prisoners. My first task was to reconnoitre and map the frontier which had been established between the occupation zones after the war and our withdrawal from the River Elbe at Magdeburg. There were a few granite stones, inscribed KP or KH, which I took to be the ancient boundary markers between the Kingdom of Prussia and the Kingdom of Hanover. It could have just been historically possible that this was the eastern border of a British sovereign's domain in Europe, because King George I, whose statue stands outside Hanover railway station, was also King of England.

Wherever a road or track crossed the ancient boundary line the Russians had dug a ditch or felled a tree. At every such point I was soon able to spot the fresh earth which marked the slit trenches and foxholes dug by the Russians. The tops of the heads of those unfortunate soldiers were also visible because they had to remain there in all weathers ready to repel a British invasion or seize frontier crossers. If they ever got the excitement of a glimpse of a British armoured car, the switchboard at the Russian headquarters in Stendal was probably jammed with their reports. There was just one official border crossing point in our sector, at Oebisfelde, ten miles north of the tri-Allied crossing point at Helmstedt on the autobahn to Berlin. All road, rail and canal crossings were subjected to an amazing amount of delay, tortuous searches and bureaucratic procedures which continued for forty-five years until 1989. I got to know some of the Russian soldiers by sight and which of them would accept Western cigarettes or chocolate, which we offered only when the green-tabbed NKVD secret police were not present.

The little village of Zichere-Bochwitz had been cut in half by the new frontier and there was no contact between the villagers of East and West. One evening I went with the village policeman from Wesendorf, Wachmeister Wanneke, to negotiate a pass for an employee in our camp who wished to visit her sick mother in the other half of the village. My Sealyham puppy, Benjamin, who always travelled in the scout car, suddenly dashed across the ditch into the arms of the Russian sentry opposite. I thought I had lost him for ever but the good will I had built up paid off and Benjamin was returned by a smiling guard. Nevertheless troop leaders were always warned never to hazard their safety by crossing the frontier line; yet the day came when one of them just had to try.

One evening David Tabor and I were driving through the border villages to check on our patrols and give fresh orders when we saw four armoured cars parked outside a 'gasthaus' in Grafhorst. I asked the radio operator on duty in one of the turrets where the rest of his troop were and he said we would find them in the kitchen being served Bockwurst and potatoes by the innkeeper's buxom wife.

"Where is your troop leader, Cornet Sale?" I asked.

"Oh sir, the Russians got him about four hours ago!"

"Well why on earth did you not radio the information to head-quarters?" we asked, quite horrified.

They made several indifferent excuses but their complete lack of concern was an indication of the minimal impact this young officer had made on his men.

Evidently he had walked quite alone past the fallen tree which blocked the road east of Wittingen and was soon surrounded by Russian soldiers who removed him. As it was almost dark, there was nothing we could do and we realized that the impact of this news on Headquarters Rhine Army was going to be most unpleasant. We climbed into the Jeep and drove back to Wesendorf to consider what to do next and whether the awful truth could be hidden much longer from Headquarters. After all, he was our peppery Commanding Officer's son!

"It will take weeks to get him back if we follow the proper procedures and diplomatic channels," I said.

David agreed that the only thing the Russians might understand was a show of strength and determination on our part, which remains surely as true today as it did then, but with only one squadron and ninety-two men covering eighty miles of border, what immediate action could we possibly take? The solution of course just needed a little stage management as practised years ago by that gifted producer Fred Carno, who could conjure up imaginary armies of marching soldiers on a small stage.

Early next morning we returned to the border at Wittingen accompanied, albeit reluctantly, by a tall Yugoslav officer who was in charge of a Civilian Mixed Labour Unit repairing a railway line into Wesendorf camp and who was to be our interpreter. We walked towards the huge tree which had been felled across the road, plainly covered by the guns of two troops of armoured cars. We deliberately crossed the obstacle and continued resolutely into the Soviet Zone until our path was blocked by Russian soldiers, when we halted and demanded to speak to the Russian commander. A Senior Captain with four stars came running from a guardhouse buttoning up his jacket. We saluted and demanded the return of our young officer who had surely only being doing his duty trying to liaise with our glorious Russian allies when he had been kidnapped by somebody who perhaps could not recognize a British uniform.

A Russian major then joined us and a field telephone was cranked. "Ha," I noted, "no radios", and then more Russian troops were deployed. The pace quickened, our third troop arrived, while the Russians unlimbered two anti-tank guns. After a pregnant pause during which we each began privately to have our doubts as to the wisdom of our actions, several senior Russian staff officers arrived in a staff car and ordered us to withdraw, but we politely and firmly repeated our request. There was a lot more sabre-rattling as more Russian troops in Zis trucks entered the village. By now we had deployed all five 'sabre' troops and so it became the turn of the quartermaster's department to drive nine Bedford three-ton lorries round and round a dusty circuit between us and

Wittingen, signalling, we hoped, the arrival of a phantom infantry battalion. A second car with senior Russian officers arrived and the determination to press our protest was greatly helped by the timely arrival of our trump card. Two AEC Matador armoured cars with Churchill tank turrets drove right up to the tree, their 75mm guns then traversed slowly (because only the hand traverse worked) on to the Russian positions. The senior officers consulted with each other and agreed that they would release our young officer, but that as he was at their Headquarters it would take a few hours to deliver him. We saluted smartly and then walked back briskly, not daring to betray our relief. Having withdrawn all but one troop, we returned to a belated breakfast wondering if our intervention had indeed really worked.

Four hours later we signed a receipt for Richard Sale, his pistol, six rounds and a pair of binoculars. Headquarters Rhine Army were informed of his capture and subsequent recovery in the same signal, and were predictably angry that the correct procedures had not been strictly followed. Our swift, firm action had paid off and, no doubt because we had succeeded, the General Staff soon forgot that the rules had ever been broken.

After this eventful start I began to spend more and more nights in those little border villages talking to the dozens of people who crossed the border each way at night in order to visit relatives or to find work. I was especially interested in those returning to the West and endeavoured to build up a picture of what life was like in the Soviet Zone. There was a saying among these border crosses, who were known as 'Grenzgänger', which translated "One crosses from the scarlet East into the golden West on a black night across the green frontier." Alas, it did not stay green for long because, from a deserted sandy seashore alongside a crowded western beach on the Baltic, right down to the Czechoslovak frontier, the Russians and East Germans created in the next few years a great brown scar, 500 miles long and about 15 yards wide filled with anti-personnel mines, trip wires and barbed wire, and guarded by watch towers, searchlights, armoured vehicles and patrols who did not hesitate to shoot at illegal frontier crossers. There was also a prohibited zone within 25 miles of the border in which there were countless check points and controls. Few people ever got across unhurt except the occasional East German border guard who decided to escape to the West, but at the beginning in 1947 it was still possible to slip across without being caught.

One of the first incidents in the Cold War, which was just beginning, concerned currency. The Russians lodged a complaint with the Allied

Control Commission that the Western Allies were using their own currency in shops and clubs instead of Reichmarks, in our case British Armed Forces Vouchers (BAFVs). The Allies replied that it was the Russians who had been the first to insist that only US dollars, Swiss francs or pounds sterling would be accepted at the Leipzig Fair which they organized in 1947 in the Russian Zone.

The Reichsmark was almost worthless; vast quantities were held by individuals gained from 'black market' transactions. Some were held by unscrupulous Allied soldiers, including Russians, who had 'liberated' the money from German Army Paymasters. Most of the money was kept outside banks, under mattresses or in shoe boxes and, in order to avoid a repetition of the early 1920s when a loaf of bread cost 10,000 Reichmarks, the Western Allies decided to revalue the currency in their Zones of Occupation. The new 'Deutsche Mark' (DM) was printed in the utmost secrecy and news of the revaluation was not released until after the banks had closed on Saturday, 18 June 1948. We were given the task of escorting truckloads of the new money to banks all over Lower Saxony. The rules for the issue of the new currency were simple. The value of assets held in a bank or in securities was to be divided by ten, but only sixty DM would be exchanged in cash for sixty old Reichmarks, and so the small fortunes which had been hoarded became valueless overnight.

The reaction of the Soviet Union was swift and they used this as a pretext to walk out of the Allied Control Commission for Germany, while in Berlin the Russian Commandant walked out of the Allied Kommandantura. Until German reunification, a portrait of the last Russian General continued to hang in the conference room alongside those of the current French, American and British Commandants, and the start of each monthly meeting was delayed a minute just in case the Russians decided to reoccupy their chair. While the German civilian population in the West wondered if the new currency would restore their economy, instant changes took place along the 'green frontier'. Russian troop strength increased, every single official crossing point such as Helmstedt and Oebisfelde was closed, all road, rail and canal traffic to West Berlin was halted and a complete blockade of the city began. Many travellers were cut off and arrested trying to return to the West. Two weeks later we had to collect all the old bank notes for destruction by burning, an unforgettable sickly sweet smell of 'filthy lucre'.

With West Berlin now completely cut off and unprepared for such an eventuality, it was essential to get supplies into the city as soon as possible. The Allies set up the great air bridge or '*Luftbrücke*' which meant deploying hundreds of aircraft, mainly twin-engine Dakotas, on to airfields in the British Zone which offered the shortest flight to Berlin. These transport aircraft were able to fly up the centre of three air corridors which had been agreed at the Potsdam Conference in 1945 and were still used forty-five years later. An altitude limit of 10,000 feet was imposed within a narrow corridor ten miles wide, which may have been all right then but greatly increased the fuel consumption of modern jet planes which prefer to fly at three times that altitude. Only one airline from each Allied nation was allowed to fly into Berlin. In 1948 radio beacons were set up along the border to ensure that the transport aircraft entered the corridor precisely, because the Russians threatened to shoot down any who strayed off course.

The American base commander at Fassberg, an airfield near Celle, was married to a well-known cinema actress, Constance Bennett: he and his officers were frequent visitors to Wesendorf and they seemed to get particular enjoyment driving round the camp being saluted, and would remark, "Gee, there's plenty of courtesy around here". They came to a ball in the mess which had been beautifully decorated by the handful of wives who had been allowed to join their husbands, in particular David Smiley's wife Moy. It proved to be a wonderful party and the girls were danced off their feet. An American pilot saying goodbye to Ginny Grant-Lawson, our Colonel's wife and a fellow American, was heard to remark, "Why, Mam, I have not had so much fun with my clothes on for years!"

Very few officers were allowed to have their wives with them because War Office regulations decreed that unless an officer was over the age of 25 and a soldier over 21, no married allowance or accommodation was to be granted and they were deemed to be living in sin. However, there were lots of empty quarters at Wesendorf available for all ranks and so David Smiley decided that the wives of those legally married might employ the wives of those under 25 as 'Nannies', provided they were ready to take the risk of eviction and live in the empty houses. It took many months before this stratagem was discovered by Headquarters Rhine Army, by which time most of those concerned had already reached the magic age of 25 or 21.

As tension mounted on the border it was decided that we should carry out exercises with the Americans and French in order to show that our nations were determined to maintain the special status of Berlin and its access routes. The Blues sent a squadron of armoured cars to join the Black Watch who were going to act as 'enemy' to a US Division. The Black Watch were commanded by a remarkable officer, Bernard Fergusson, later to become Governor of New Zealand and Lord Ballantrae. He read with concern in the 'exercise instructions' that six of his men must be captured and thus test the intelligence staff of the American Division. He protested that men did not join his distinguished battalion just to be captured on the first night of an exercise and that anyway it would be very difficult to find any volunteers. The Chief Umpire said he fully appreciated and admired the gallant Colonel's point but there were more important things involved than the honour of the Black Watch, and so Bernard had a word with his men and that night six 'Jocks' were taken prisoner.

By noon the next day a serious international incident had developed and the Colonel was again summoned to Umpire Headquarters to be told that the Americans were much distressed because the 'prisoners of war' when interrogated spoke no known language and that the whole exercise was therefore being sabotaged. Bernard explained patiently, "My men are speaking their native tongue, Gaelic, and," he enquired politely, "how many of the divisional staff are there who can speak Russian, Polish or Czech, the armies you may be fighting?"

There was a long pause as the point sunk in and the reply was, "None". Bernard then ordered his men to revert to speaking English. The next three days went well but the exercise ended prematurely after another memorable confrontation. An American battalion had been cut off and was well and truly surrounded; even the umpires agreed it was an indisputable situation and that they should withdraw at least one mile. The US commander was, however, made of sterner stuff and decided to follow the gallant traditions of the US defenders of Bastogne who, when surrounded during the last great German offensive of the Second World War, said 'Nuts', and did not surrender. The armoured car crews, who were observing, prepared for a long wait and got out the tea-brewing pots and stoves. However, all this hanging about while umpires talked did not suit the men of the Black Watch who were lying hidden on the ground and had crawled much closer than the beleaguered US battalion realized. Their company commander ordered his highlanders to stand up in full view of the defenders and with a great deal of noisy parade ground drill cried, "C Company, The Black Watch, Will Fix Bayonets, Fix, Slow March". Then, with bagpipes playing, they advanced slowly and deliberately towards the somewhat mystified defenders who unfortunately contained among their ranks more than their fair share of conscripts from deprived sections of the community in the USA. They stood firm until, as their eyes began to roll, it dawned on them that these strange men wearing skirts were perhaps really out of their tiny minds and had hostile intentions. As I watched through binoculars a ripple of indecision soon became a well-defined retrogade movement which swept the battalion to better positions in the rear. Needless to say there was trouble about that too at the conference after the exercise, but the Black Watch made handsome amends and gave a splendid party for the Americans.

The increasing tension on the border made it all the more important that we should have some idea what was going on in the Soviet Zone of Germany and also discover which routes across the border were relatively safe for those who were still desperate enough to attempt the crossing. The Russians had begun to form an East Germany army which, to begin with, was deployed to assist them patrol the border. Many of these young soldiers chose to defect to the West until severe measures were taken by the East Germans against their families and comrades. However, it was going to take many months before these deterrent measures and frontier fortifications were to stem the flow of border crossers completely.

With the enthusiastic help of a National Service intelligence clerk, Trooper John Bellingham, an old Etonian, I tried to make sense of the many travellers' tales and rumours which came our way every night. It was all very low-grade information and covered a variety of subjects. Was it true that the inhabitants of the houses nearest the border in Bochwitz had been forcibly evicted and sent to Siberia? Well, moved, yes, but they were resettled on a communal farm nearby. Were female border crossers caught by the garrison in Oebisfelde now being stripped and brutally searched by a Russian police woman? Yes, but the searchers were East German prison wardresses. Had a Russian tank, using a new device like a snorkel, tried to cross the River Elbe under water, got lost and continued down river until the breathing apparatus was holed by a tree trunk and the crew drowned? Probably yes, but the Russians also demonstrated that they could build a floating pontoon bridge incredibly quickly. At last I was doing something which I found totally absorbing and worth while. I had forgotten about my parents looking for a house and my father job-hunting. I no longer seemed to find time to think about my grandmother and events in Romania. My life had become intensely complicated because of my concerns for the safety of some of the regular border crossers.

We received a request from some mysterious department of our intelligence services for samples of identity documents being issued by the Russians. I was taught how to use a simple device which was a box containing sheets of special paper on top of which I placed the documents to be copied and then put it twelve inches below an electric light bulb, which was to be switched on for one minute. A primitive photocopier, but it was still 1947 and this was magic!

My contact was a delightful eccentric called Edward Sniders who operated from a house in Hanover. He had been a bomber pilot, shot down and badly wounded and nevertheless managed to escape from two prisoner of war camps before being locked away again. Sometimes I had to handle his agents and help them to cross the border. Sometimes they never returned, betrayed by spies like Blake and Maclean. A few came back through West Berlin when I was there thirty years later. Edward asked me to meet a sinister character in a ruined mansion in Hanover. We drove to this dark shell of a building, with not a light to be seen. Entering with torches we followed the signs down to the air-raid shelter. An iron door opened into a candle-lit wine cellar which was full of people and we made our way to a table in a far corner. I noticed a man in a trench coat dancing with a brief case in one hand and a blond youth in the other. Then I realized that all the men were dancing together and so were the women. I told Edward that I had no intention of dancing with those guys. What should I do if one of them asks me to dance? He said I had to or it might blow our cover. Mercifully the man we had to meet arrived and I was spared.

There was one remote sector of border near Kaiserwinkel which ran across marshes, where there was no barbed wire, no mines and no checks on the approaches because they only led into a forest filled with wild boar and rabid foxes. The Russian soldiers positioned nearest to the forest were from Siberia, with sallow skins, high cheek bones and were young conscripts serving thousands of miles from home. They were allowed no leave during their two years' service in Germany and their free time was filled with political indoctrination. They seemed a sullen impassive lot unless we caught them away from their officers when they smiled and returned our waves. After the Berlin blockade began, security measures, even on that quiet corner, were intensified and frontier crossing in either direction became an uncomfortable and hazardous journey for girls like Giesela, who regularly crossed at this spot.

She was twenty-three years old, slim, with short black hair, and bright brown eyes. She had a sort of elfin quality and earned a living teaching music in a village near a huge Russian training area, the Letzlinger Heide. Several tank divisions were sometimes deployed within this vast heath-land which, lying west of the River Elbe, meant that if they wished to make a surprise attack, there were no major natural obstacles to cross before they reached cities like Hanover and Hamburg. Giesela was an articulate and observant girl whose hatred of Communism, and in par-ticular *"die Mongolische Soldaten"*, gave her a great sense of purpose. Her father had been an agent for a manufacturing company based in Hanover which began to export agricultural machinery and fertilizers to Eastern Europe soon after the First World War. Whilst he was working in Romania he married a Saxon girl from Brasov (Kronstadt) in Transylvania. He inherited his father's farm in the province of Magdeburg, which he worked until the beginning of the Second World War. He was then conscripted into the Wehrmacht, and was greatly relieved to become a pay clerk in an anti-aircraft unit. In due course his unit was sent to Romania to defend the Ploesti oil refineries, but during the final retreat he had been captured by the Romanians and handed over to the Russians. His mother lived in Peine near Hanover and it was to visit her grandmother that Giesela risked her neck every two months.

I had asked her several times in the year I had known her why she did not remain in the West, although her mother had also moved to Peine, but she was determined to wait for her father to be released from a pris-oner of war camp in Russia. I admired her courage and begged her to stay because the frontier crossing was getting so dangerous. She had by now changed her crossing point to a forest further south, which was safer, but she refused to stay. So it was with a feeling of foreboding that I watched from a clump of silver birches as she strode purposefully off into the darkness to cross a small stream and return to her village, with a bundle of food slung over her shoulder. Inevitably the day or rather night came when she failed to turn up at our rendezvous and after several more fruitless nights I eventually received news from another border crosser what had happened to her.

It appeared that her father had been released after five years in captivity and returned to the farm which his family had owned for many genera-tions. To his horror he discovered that, in the new German Democratic Republic, all farms had been taken over by the State in keeping with the Communist dogma of collectivization. In his village every cow, pig, chicken and horse had been pooled with those of other small farms, and his old farmhouse had become the administrative headquarters of the local farm commune. He lived with Giesela in what had been the hay loft above the stables and he had been directed to join the village work force as a labourer. He soon realized that he had returned from one form of bondage only to be thrust into another organized by his fellow country-men, an equally unpleasant tyranny to be endured without the comradeship of his fellow prisoners of war.

Sadly his freedom was to be short-lived because one night a convoy from a Russian Motor Rifle Regiment chose to stop in the village. Four drunken soldiers burst into their home and attempted to rape Giesela whom he tried desperately to protect, but he was savagely attacked by the four men who killed him with the wood chopper. Giesela escaped through a trap door into the stables and fled in terror to the woods. The next day she was found, arrested and charged with collaborating with a Fascist soldier in a monstrous assault on members of the Soviet Armed Forces. Not one of her neighbours or music pupils dared to testify in her favour and she was sent to prison in Stendal to await trial.

I felt bitter and utterly depressed at the news and frequently returned to the area to try to find more news of her. Two months later an elderly woman told me that Giesela had been badly beaten in prison because an informer in her cell had passed on to the authorities the fact that she had friends and relatives in the West. No one in her village, the old lady continued, imagined that they would ever see her again. The East German authorities, however, had no great love for their Soviet masters and, being well aware of what had really happened that night, secured her release on grounds of ill health. She was back in the village but had lost her job teaching music because she was now considered to be politi-cally unreliable. A few days later I received a message that she hoped to be strong enough to attempt another border crossing at the end of the month.

So it was that I found myself once more amongst the pools and marshes which separated the Soviet Zone from the British Zone, listening to the frogs which croaked incessantly until they took their cue from an alert sentinel and suddenly stopped croaking, because something had stirred in the forest. Trooper Brown and I were hidden on a small hill overlooking the stream which marked the interzonal border. Gradually the lights in the hamlet behind us went out and the dogs stopped barking until only the frogs in the water meadow again began their croaking chorus.

For a short while we watched every tree in turn cast a fleeting shadow as small clouds scudded past the moon. A West German Border Police Volkswagen car drove down into the valley and, after a brief halt, turned round and left without spotting my scout car hidden in the bushes with hessian sacking over the headlights and mirrors. I was fairly sure Giesela would choose this spot if she was going to attempt a crossing at all, but I realized she could not possibly be aware of the changes which had taken place while she was in prison.

"She is sure to walk straight into one of those East German patrols," I muttered. "Look, over there, Sir," whispered Brown, as a red signal light rose high in the sky followed by two illuminating flares which floated slowly down about a kilometre away. We heard a car engine and shortly afterwards saw the shaft of a small searchlight sweeping through the trees. A Russian BTR 60 armoured car came up to the barrier in the road three hundred metres away and swung the beam of its light into the British Zone. The frogs ceased their croaking and we lay absolutely still, our faces pressed down into the beech leaves. I was glad that we had hidden the scout car so carefully because if they saw it they might guess there was a reception committee waiting for someone and decide to hang around. "Hell, there are only three hours of darkness left," I mused, "I do wish they would go away." No sooner had I said it when the searchlight was extinguished and the armoured car reversed back the way it had come.

A few moments later we heard branches snap like whiplashes and the sound of running feet. Two people leapt into the stream and clambered out on our side, running on for a few hundred metres before throwing themselves, panting, to the ground just below where we were lying. "Just cover me," I said to Brown, "while I find out who they are." I got up and moved cautiously towards them, noting as I got closer that they wore some sort of uniform but carried no weapons. I asked them who they were and they explained that they were recently conscripted border police who had taken advantage of the distraction caused by another patrol pursuing a border crosser to escape themselves. They were very young and very frightened. I gave them a packet of cigarettes and pointed the way to the main road where I knew they would meet a West German Border Police patrol.

"I just hope it was not Giesela they were after," I said to Brown, who was looking cold and miserable. "Let's wait just a little longer, she might yet show up." The moon had long since disappeared and there was a gentle breeze, it was becoming damp and cool. Even the frogs seemed to have lessened their chatter as the first rays of daylight appeared above the thin belt of mist which followed the line of the stream. How many more nights can I afford to spend hanging around here, I wondered.

"They've stopped again, Sir," whispered Brown. "There is something moving down there, I'm sure."

We strained our eyes through the low belt of mist and caught a glimpse of a faltering figure before it disappeared. I rubbed my eyes. There must be something because the frogs were silent. There it was again, a small grey figure against the pale eastern sky, climbing out of the water then vanishing, perhaps to fall back into the stream or into the reeds.

"Be careful, Sir," said Brown as I got up, "they may be close behind."

I forgot all caution as I ran towards the stream past the notice boards saying "Grenze Ende – End of British Zone", and on towards where I thought I had seen the figure drop. A body lay face down on the moss with a knapsack on its back. I turned it over. It was a woman, still alive but incredibly thin with sunken eyes in dark sockets and wrists like matchsticks. I was still a little unsure who it was,

"*Sind Sie Giesela?*" I asked.

"*Ja, Ja, hast du mich vergessen?*" came the faint reply. "No, I never forgot you Giesela. What have they done to you?" I whispered, and carried her wet body up to where the scout car was hidden.

"Christ, she *is* in a bad way," gasped Brown. "Hang on while I untie my bedroll. She's like a ruddy skeleton."

He took out two blankets and wrapped them carefully round her and we lifted her over the side into the commander's seat.

"Let's get out of here quickly before it gets any lighter," I said and climbed on to the little seat above the engine cover.

We drove carefully through the woods back on to the main road and headed north towards Wesendorf. The camp was still asleep when we slipped in through the back gate and parked behind the Medical Centre. Five days later, when she had recovered from her exhaustion and malnutrition, we slipped her into an ambulance which did a weekly run to the British Military Hospital in Hanover, with Brown as co-driver, and instructions to go via Peine and drop her off at her grandmother's house. "Did you deliver her safely?" I asked Brown when he got back that evening.

"Oh yes Sir, but it was a little strange because the grandmother comes to the door, sees the girl and says something like '*Mutti ist tot*' and instead of being happy they both cried, so I gave the old lady your parcel of tea and slipped away."

Indeed, it was all too true. Her mother had only just died, possibly from a broken heart, having first heard that her husband had been killed so soon after his return from a Russian prison camp and then the awful possibility that she might never seen her only child again. Giesela, however, did recover and got a job teaching the piano at a high school in Hanover.

My commanding officer was uneasy at the success of our active patrolling and at the keen interest which higher formations took in our reports. Furthermore, he viewed some of my unorthodox activities, quite understandably, with the greatest suspicion and was keen we should get back to peacetime soldiering, whatever that meant, as soon as possible. It certainly came as a great surprise and a relief to both of us when the regiment received a signal from Headquarters Rhine Army ordering me to join them as a General Staff Officer Intelligence, Grade 3 (captain), as soon as possible. I was thrilled, but there remained one last task before I packed up my kit. The Russians had just suggested that it would be possible once again for the Western Allies to use the autobahn to West Berlin. It appeared that after eleven months the blockade was about to be lifted. After so much intransigence on their part and so many false hopes, the British authorities viewed this latest development with a little suspicion, but nevertheless ordered the Royal Horse Guards to send a convoy up the corridor to that beleaguered city.

It was left to us to decide what the test convoy should consist of and what cargo ought to be carried. We quickly agreed that one Jeep and three three-ton lorries would be sufficient to prove the point, but far more tricky was whom should we sacrifice if it turned out to be a one-way ticket to Siberia? A mere Cornet of Horse or Lieutenant was considered too junior a rank if a certain amount of discussion had to take place with the Soviet authorities on the way. On the other hand three clapped-out trucks which the Technical Quartermaster was only too happy to lose was hardly a Major's command, so a Captain was chosen, Alan Hutchinson. He was a quiet robust Scotsman who should never have remained in the Army once the war was over. He had studied to get into a medical school and hoped one day to become a General Practitioner in the Highlands. However, there was a delay in receiving his entrance exam results and so he joined up. Six months later he heard that he had been successful but declined to switch back to medicine. We now did our best to encourage him with tales of what a fantastic time he would have if he did get through to West Berlin and the hero's welcome he would receive.

There was much talk too about what stores should be carried by the convoy, something that the garrison really needed such as medical supplies, radios, ammunition, spare vehicle parts? Every suggestion we made was gratefully acknowledged by Headquarters British Sector Berlin, who replied that they had already received all they needed in the Allied airlift. Incidentally, during the blockade they adopted a unique shoulder flash, which was worn until 1990. This shows a black circle ringed with a red band and 'Berlin' inscribed above, known affectionately as 'The Flaming Arsehole". Eventually we heard that the two armoured car squadrons from The Blues which had been in the city during the blockade did have an urgent request: could we send some fodder for the polo ponies? So it was that the trucks were loaded to the brim with hay harvested off the disused airfield at Wesendorf.

I accompanied the convoy as far as Helmstedt where I was required to set up my radio next to the international autobahn control police post and monitor Alan's progress. We had first met in 1943 at the Guards Depot in Caterham, which I knew he had hated even more than I did. I wished him good luck and gave him a large bottle of whisky. The red and white barrier was raised and, as I watched his jeep and the trucks, with little bits of hay blowing off, drive towards the Russian check point I realized that the bottle might have been a mistake.

The mandatory time allowed to drive from Helmstedt (Check Point Alpha) to Berlin (Check Point Bravo) was two hours, which ensured that Allied vehicles did not break the speed limit, deviate or stop. On this special occasion I am sure there were Generals and Ambassadors sitting beside their telephones in Bonn, Paris, London and Washington anxiously following that plucky convoy's progress. Was the blockade of Berlin over at last? Had the Cold War eased a little? Could the Allies now end the incredibly costly airlift? But radio contact with the convoy was lost when they reported that they were twenty miles east of Magdeburg and two hours later neither we in Helmstedt nor West Berlin could speak to them on the radio. The Russians were most upset when we asked them to explain what they had done with our men. Their concern was genuine and they agreed to accompany an Allied Military Police patrol to find them. It did not take long to locate them, because there in a lay-by stood three unattended British trucks – after all who wants to steal a load of hay? – and just beyond them were five Russian lorries. Sitting on a grassy bank in the sunshine was a happy band of warriors who had obviously been comparing the merits of Ukrainian vodka and Scotch whisky.

I thought it was a good omen and it increased my faith in human nature, but, sadly, just like when British and German soldiers fraternized between shell-torn trenches in Flanders in 1914, the Higher Command on both sides of the Iron Curtain took a deplorably unimaginative view of this delay in the arrival of the first convoy up the corridor since the blockade.

Chapter Nine

SPORTING CHANCES

Headquarters British Army of the Rhine was located in Bad Oeynhausen, a small Spa town quite close to where the River Weser cuts through the hills at Minden. As there were no barracks in the town or suitable buildings in which to house the officers and men of the headquarters, a wire fence had been erected around the centre of the town when the war ended and the inhabitants were told that their property had been requisitioned, but that a rent would be paid. The Spa Hotel became the actual headquarters building, in which the main staff branches were comfortably installed in bridal suites and ornate bedrooms. The rest of the offices were scattered around town and we were billeted in private houses.

I was to be a member of number 11 Mess, which was run by a delightful White Russian gourmet, Captain George Hartman, whose father had commanded the Imperial Russian Horse Guards. George had a splendid supporting cast of individualists who all worked as I did in G (Intelligence) and gave the mess its character. Among them was an elderly White Russian, also Intelligence Corps, called Alex Soldatentov, who impressed me with his address book which was not in alphabetical order but in which his girl friends were listed by the cities they lived in and their specialities. Alex had also driven a racing car at Monte Carlo in 1907 and treasured a fading photograph of himself cradling a silver cup and two girls. I shared number 49 Porta Strasse with the two Russians, who, when they became melancholy, which was at least once a month, sang sad Russian songs with moist eyes. Alex was always hard up and spent hours one night trying to sell me a battered lead tobacco tin which contained two shark's bladder contraceptive sheaths made in 1907. Their provenance, it seemed, was quite remarkable and for purely historical reasons I wish I had written it down and bought them, but I was too short of money. The difference between number 11 Mess and the regimental one I had just left was unbelievable and I loved it.

To begin with work naturally centred around my intimate knowledge of the interzonal frontier and I welcomed the chance to visit a small intelligence detachment at the Friedland Transit Camp near Göttingen, just south of the Harz Mountains. My visit coincided with the arrival of a 'transport', as the trains were called which brought returning prisoners of war from the Soviet Union. I could see the plume of smoke from the steam engine in the distance as it negotiated the last of the Russian frontier controls and entered West Germany. There were hundreds of gaunt grey faces staring out of the train windows, hidden now and then by billowing clouds of smoke. Their eyes shone bright with expectation as they searched the platforms for a face they might recognize, but as usual there were none because nobody had the slightest idea, let alone the Russians, until the last moment that a 'transport' was due from the East, and certainly not the names of those prisoners due to be released from the depths of the Soviet Union that month.

All German and Italian prisoners of war who had been captured by the Western Allies had been released within a year or so of the war ending, in accordance with the Geneva Convention, but this was certainly not so in the case of those imprisoned in the Soviet Union. German prisoners had been forgotten in remote camps in the Siberian tundra or retained to work in factories for up to eleven years after the war ended. Naturally we took a keen interest in these men who had worked in Russian industry in remote cities. Their recent experience and detailed knowledge of living conditions revealed an extraordinary state of affairs, of incompetence and sheer unmitigated misery. In fact I felt very much more sorry for the average Russian factory worker or peasant farmer than I ever did for the German prisoners, who did at least have some hope of attaining a better standard of living if they were ever released, whereas the Russian workers had been condemned by their Socialist State to endure permanent shortages of housing and every-day essentials such as food right up to this day.

The German Red Cross carried out a major operation at Friedland in sheds alongside the railway sidings. Every new arrival was checked against his old records which contained the last known address of his relatives. If these happened to live in West Germany it was easy to contact them, but at least one-third of the men's families no longer lived in the same home as they had done in 1940, and so tracing them became a painstaking process. On the walls of the transit sheds were lists naming thousands of men whose whereabouts were still unknown and photographs of smiling young soldiers taken years earlier, but which nevertheless might be sufficient to prompt recognition. Every returning man was asked to tell all he knew about the comrades he had left behind in Russia and in this way it was subsequently possible to present lists to the Russian authorities and urge them into releasing men of whose whereabouts they may well have lost track.

The reception camp was full of pallid people in threadbare clothes. There was an all-pervading smell of poor nutrition and sanitation which lingered around these unfortunate men for several days, even after they had been bathed, fed and reclothed by the Red Cross. When the highly efficient organization failed to trace their families the men were sent to Resettlement Centres elsewhere in West Germany. A totally different problem was caused by the trainloads of entire civilian German communities which had lived for centuries in Eastern Europe and were now being evicted by the Russians. They came from that part of Germany, lying east of the Rivers Oder and Neisse, which had been handed to Poland, and from East Prussia which had been split between Russia and Poland. Small groups also arrived from ancient Teutonic settlements in the Ukraine near the River Don, from the old Hansa trading ports in the Baltic States absorbed by Russia and Saxons from Transylvania. The forceful deportation of these people may have avoided a minority problem in years to come but it was a heart-rending exodus to watch. Not only were Germans expelled but there was also a group of French who had settled near Banat in Romania and were temporally resettled in a deserted mountain village near Cavaillon in Provence. This Communist expulsion of unwanted minorities even extended to China, whence Germans who had lived there for three generations were expelled to West Germany.

On a subsequent visit to Friedland on a dull autumn afternoon I watched yet another train steam slowly into the siding, packed with prisoners of war. They were leaning out of the windows of every carriage except one, whose occupants sat motionless trying to understand an incomprehensible situation. Their grey wooden faces, vacant looks and subdued attitude set them quite apart from the others. They had to be encouraged to get out, they did not wear uniforms but a shapeless grey prison garb and they seemed to be somewhat older that the others. These were men who had lost all hope of ever seeing their homeland again and whose families had received no evidence that they might be still alive. They were German merchant seamen who had had the misfortune to be the crew of a ship loading timber in the Russian port of Murmansk at the beginning of the Spanish Civil War in 1936. Germany under Hitler had given active support to General Franco whilst the Soviet Union under Stalin supported the Communists, so the German seamen were immediately interned, although their countries were not at war with each other. The extraordinary thing is that not even after the so called Treaty of Friendship between Germany and Russia in 1939 were they released. They had already been forgotten and in due course even their families gave up all hope of discovering their fate.

By the middle of 1948 the Communists had already virtually destroyed all trace of the so-called ruling classes in Eastern Europe. My mother was horrified at the news coming out of Romania, especially as many of her elderly relatives were still there. My father had got a temporary job as a Technical Officer in the petroleum branch of the Ministry of Fuel and Power in London at a salary of £700 a year, plus £60 War Bonus. He simply hated being a civil servant, but an income, however small, was essential, because he could no longer expect his stepfather to support him. My grandmother was still living in the Calea Victoriei in Bucharest and trying hard to leave the country.

"How can I possibly get permits to leave from the Ministry of Foreign Affairs and from the Russians who will certainly make the most difficulties?" she wrote. "It seems, however, that because of my age they might be more helpful."

Her letters always mentioned food. "I am lacking supplies because I do not have permission to eat," which referred to the denial of a proper ration card. She had been trying for two years to sell our home at Doftana which had been damaged by the earthquake. Eventually in the summer of 1946 she had to virtually give it away, including most of its contents. The furniture went to a museum in Ploesti. The proceeds were only just enough to pay for the cost of shipping several crates of personal possessions on the SS *Transylvania* to England. This was thanks to the endeavours of the British Military Mission, which had been told by the Communists to leave Romania.

I soon learnt that dealings with the Russians required a lot of patience and hours of waiting for nothing much to happen. It could be a very trying experience, especially if a Russian soldier had deserted into the British Zone or been arrested because he accidentally strayed over the border. Such incidents were rare, but continued to happen until the Russians withdrew all their soldiers from the interzonal border and its temptation. Nevertheless the British and Russians each had the right to interview their soldiers and persuade them to return. Very few Russians ever elected to go back because they had often committed a minor crime and feared double retribution. The Russian penalty for desertion was execution and continues to be so to this day. In the 1970s a Russian sergeant was believed to have been shot for desertion near West Berlin and a Russian destroyer in the Baltic was bombed by Soviet aircraft for trying to escape after a mutiny.

Those British who fell into Russian hands usually did so as a result of their bad map-reading and stupidity or, in the case of an ENSA concert party, which included the late Dame Gracie Fields, their inability to read the signposts on the autobahn to Berlin. Old habits die hard as in the case of an Irish Guardsman, who, when he was based in the New Territories, Hong Kong, got lost and drove his truck over the border into mainland China, causing much diplomatic panic. Ten years later, by now a sergeant major stationed in Berlin, he strayed off the autobahn with his truck and drove deep into East Germany before being arrested and returned to us.

However, one day we were surprised to be told by the Russians that they were holding a British deserter in Leipzig. He had gone absent from his unit while it was in the Rhineland and, after a few weeks, had made his way east, crossed the border in the Harz Mountains and had given himself up to the Russians. The British accepted the Russian offer to interview him and our party spent the night at the Helmstedt Check Point before setting off at the crack of dawn with a Russian escort for Leipzig. After a four-hour drive the staff cars pulled up in a cobbled courtyard surrounded on three sides by an imposing yellow building which seemed to be a military headquarters. The British officers had arrived forty minutes before the meeting was due to begin and were ushered into a sparsely furnished waiting room, heavy with the smell of stale tobacco and boiled cabbage. The Russian liaison officer disappeared and it was nearly two hours before he returned accompanied by an evil-tempered Major in the NKVD (Security Services), who cursed the British for keeping him waiting and causing him so much work. Having made his attitude clear and elicited from the bored British a patronising "Oh, you poor fellow, you must have had a simply terrible morning," they followed him into a court room where a grey-haired Colonel sat behind a wide table flanked by a stern-faced female Major in the uniform of the Legal Service and another officer. The British soldier was brought in wearing civilian clothes and looking well fed.

"Why did you leave your battalion?" asked the British Major.

"I was frightened what my mates would do to me when they discovered I had been stealing from their lockers," he replied. "Nobody, it seemed, wanted to know my problems." Further questioning revealed that he had made no attempt to talk about his worries with any of his non-commissioned officers, nor with his platoon commander or the Padre. He agreed that there had been a German girl involved when he first went absent, but that she had left him when he decided to join the Russians in East Germany. The British party then suggested he should think about his mother and his friends in England. Had he considered his long-term future? But whatever point was made to him he seemed convinced that he would be better off if he remained in East Germany.

Every word was written down and translated for the benefit of the Russian officers present in the court room. When it became clear that he was determined to stay, the British Major pointed out in measured terms, "You realize that the Russian Army has no higher regard for deserters than the British." Russian heads nodded in agreement. "And now that you have confirmed that you are also a thief, do not expect any favours from the Russians or East Germans. Finally I warn you not to expect any diplomatic assistance from the British in years to come."

The British party thanked the Russians for their cooperation and took their leave. As they were crossing the courtyard, escorted by the unfriendly NKVD Major, a young Russian Lieutenant ran up and asked the Major, "Tell me please, Sir, will he now be going back with them?"

Major Serge Albert Frosell, RE, who understood Russian, was astonished to hear the Russian Major reply, "No, the bloody fool!"

A nice glimpse of the Major's pragmatism. It was to be another twenty-three years before that same deserter entered West Berlin through Check Point Charlie and asked to be returned to his home town, Darlington. After being officially discharged from the Army and receiving a suspended sentence for desertion, his wish was granted.

Soon after going to Leipzig, Frosell, who worked in Technical Intelligence, spotted in the ruins of East Berlin close to the border a Russian 155mm gun barrel which we had not yet examined in the West. He got a recovery vehicle from the workshops and drove it up as close to the border as he possibly could. He then unwound the steel cable from the winch, pulled it into the Russian Sector and hitched it around the gun barrel and had begun to drag it when two East German policemen arrived and asked what was going on. He expressed astonishment that they had not been informed what was happening by the Kommandantur, especially as their police chief had been present, and so on. By the time they had shaken hands and accepted 100 cigarettes the gun was safely in our Brigade Workshops.

I still played rugby football whenever I could and was aware that, in spite of the differences such as language and culture which set Romania apart from other nations, she was the only country in Eastern Europe to play the game. I had grown up to love the game and was now training hard to gain a place as a wing threequarter in the Rhine Army XV. This would enable me to get out of Germany to play against teams at Klagenfurt in Austria and Trieste in Italy, but most memorable of all the tours were those we made to France.

The first time we went to Paris we were met by a dozen friendly young men who declared that they were members of the France B XV, known as *"Les Espoirs de France"*, whom we were to play the next day. The French authorities had arranged a small *'vin d'honneur'* for us and afterwards our young hosts suggested we should glimpse the night life of Montmartre. When we declined and said we were going to bed they reminded us that they too would be playing next day and surely we could at least have one last drink together. I awoke next day in our hotel near the Gare du Nord feeling a little jaded, but drew some comfort that the opposition might also be suffering. We ran on to the pitch and lined up to face each other as the National Anthems were played. I looked hard at the French team. I could not believe it. There was not a single face we had ever seen before! They ran us off our feet and won by nine points.

A year later we returned to Paris that much wiser about the temptations and hazards of that great city. Our manager insisted that we all wore uniform for the traditional *'vin d'honneur'* and after a singularly dreary evening I walked back towards my hotel feeling very conspicuous. I longed for the match to be over so that I could explore this fabulous city before returning to those gloomy garrison towns of northern Germany. Then I realized I was being followed. I quickened my pace and turned into La Place Madeleine, but the footsteps quickened too. I had already hurried past a great many seductive ladies offering hospitality from various doorways but I was determined to get back to bed unscathed. The footsteps behind me broke into a run and a moment later my smart red and blue dress cap was whisked off my head and I was overtaken by a trim little backside which disappeared into the darkness. Astonished and angry I was soon in hot pursuit of a pair of the fastest-moving ankles I had ever seen. After a couple of hundred metres and two sharp turns she was at bay in a doorway near l'Opera, her breasts heaving as she tried to regain her breath and holding my hat firmly behind her back.

"Will you please be so kind as to give me back 'mon kepi', Mademoiselle?" I asked as calmly as possible.

"Mais non Monsieur, why dont you first spend a little time with me?" she pouted and squeezed her bottom even further into my cap. I took a second look at her, I had only seen her tight undulating dress from behind and now that she looked me straight in the eye I realized that she was very attractive and confoundedly sure of herself.

"Mademoiselle, I am very sorry but I just can not join you tonight. *Pour l'honneur de l'Armée Britannique du Rhin*, I have to play in an important rugby match tomorrow at Stade Baudouin." Then after a moments reflection I added, "Perhaps we can meet tomorrow evening?"

She looked at me kindly as if she was really trying to understand what on earth it was that I was worried about, and still held onto my cap. "*Mais Monsieur, ça vous fera beaucoup plus souple!*"

She had a point, but nevertheless it was not good enough. After further discussion I did retrieve my cap. It was an exciting match and we only just lost and of course I had dinner with Jacqueline afterwards.

As a sports writer wrote in *France Dimanche* afterwards, "In spite of the sang froid of Redgrave etc *les Britanniques* could not achieve much against the aggressive youth of *les Espoirs de France*". My goodness, were we all so old already? I was twenty-five and all I had to show was a shoe box full of medallions and a few broken bones. There were, however, still those precious seconds in each match when everything seemed to be under perfect control, when anticipation, a hand-off, a side-step or change of pace and a perfectly timed pass all combined to open a fleeting gap in the opposition, to cut through and score. Perhaps that is all I shall ever remember.

Ever since I revolted against compulsory cricket at Sherborne School I had taken up athletics. This took up far less time than a cricket match and suited my rugby training. After a successful season I was selected to run the 400 metres for Rhine Army against North-West Germany in Hamburg. Although we won the afternoon's contest, the Germans achieved moral superiority early on by entering a one-legged war veteran for the high jump. He approached on crutches and stood facing the bar, until a stunning blonde came to remove them, then hopping on one foot and swinging his stump he cleared every jump except the last and came a worthy second.

Our next meeting was in Stuttgart in Southern Germany, where we had to compete against the French and American Army teams. The *Stars and Stripes* newspaper predicted that this would be an easy victory for the lithe American athletes whose pictures covered the sports page. My first warm-up sprint was the night before out of the Graf Zeppelin Hotel where a homosexual made a determined attempt to pick me up in the bar. The Tri-Allied Track Meet turned out to be a sensational success for the British who won 15 out of 18 events.

The following year, 1952, the "Allied Cinder Teams" clashed in Hanover and it was evident that the Americans were determined to avenge their defeat, because their team now contained some remarkable talent whom we discovered had only just been posted from the USA to European Command. These "stand-out stars of the cinder empire" won many events that afternoon by a clear and distinct margin. However, we just managed to hold our own in the long distance races and some field events, so that by the time the last race, the 400 metres relay, was due to be run, we were absolutely equal with the United States, with the French in third place.

The American 400-metre team were all tall muscular black men who warmed up with short sprints, leaps into the air and rapid toe touching. We had warmed up earlier and were taking a brief rest to allow nervous energy to build up. I put on a new pair of spiked running shoes, removed my blue track suit and placed a small precious denture inside my gym shoes beside my clothes on the running track. The race, whose first leg was to be run in lanes, was about to start and the stadium fell silent. The three Allied Commanders-in-Chief sat in the box of honour in a crowded stand. We had tried to think what tactic might win us this race and decided to put our fastest runner, aptly named Sergeant Speed, in as first leg, running in lanes, instead of running last. The Americans had a faster team on paper, having already won the 400-metre individual event, but if Speed were able to give us a commanding lead over their slower runner, we might get them worried and use our wits to remain in front when running out of lanes.

The starter's pistol fired and we were off. Sergeant Speed gave us the precious lead and then Mickey Farmer held it until the last few metres when he gave the baton to Derek Brierley. He made a magnificent recovery and came out of the last bend just ahead of the American. When his baton hit the palm of my hand, I knew that unless I got to the bend first and took the inside track, it would be impossible to beat the last American. I drew on all my nervous energy and set off as if I was doing the 60-metre dash at prep school and beat him to the corner. I then shortened my stride and slowed down a little; he tried to overtake on the bend but I just lengthened my stride. Just before the end of the back straight he tried once more but I anticipated his sprint and entered the last bend still in front. He tried once more but possibly my change of pace had upset his natural rhythm. Unknown to me the crowd was on its feet and in uproar, I was about to collapse but fixed my eyes on a spot three metres beyond the tape, thrust forward with my arms, reached further with my toes and crossed the line just in front. To spectators it was an unexpected victory but to the relay team it was a splendid climax to the hard training we had done together. As we lined up for our medals, the loudspeakers announced, "A denture has been found on the track. Will the owner please claim it." This and a medal were presented to me by a highly amused French general.

I had spent long enough in Germany, nearly seven years, and very much looked forward to rejoining my regiment which was due to return to England. During that time I had had ample opportunity to judge for myself the results of the tragedy which was being played out in Eastern Europe, the misery and turmoil which the compulsory exodus brought to thousands of people who had no wish to leave their native lands. It was ironic too that there were also many people who wished to escape the gloomy hardships of life under a Communist government but were forbidden to leave. Such was the price in human suffering which the Western Allies scarcely thought about when they agreed at the Yalta Conference to let Joseph Stalin have his own way throughout Eastern Europe, except in Greece.

In Romania, Anna Pauker, a coarse uneducated Russian protégée, had managed to swell the ranks of the Communist Party by offering jobs and promotion to her friends and to a great many uncouth opportunists. My sister Ioana, who visited Romania as part of Lord Thompson's entourage, brought back a story about a State banquet in Bucharest in honour of a visiting foreign dignitary. Anna Pauker turned towards one of her recently appointed ministers and said, "Dimitri, your feet smell. Leave the table, go out and change your socks." He left the dining room discreetly and after five minutes returned to his seat. However, it became all too apparent that the smell still lingered around him, so she turned on him again and said, "Dimitri, I told you to go out and change your socks."

Bitterly hurt that his ability to carry out her request had been doubted, he turned towards her and cried, "But that is just what I have done. Look!" and he put a grubby hand into his pocket and held up the offending pair of socks.

Uncle George Capsa, the old cavalry General, was still alive. He had been kicked out of his house in the Calea Victoriei by the Communists but was allowed to continue living in the stables which were alongside the courtyard. He had access to a cold water tap and was allowed to share a kitchen stove with three other families to whom his house had been allotted. He eked out an existence on short rations and received no pension until somebody remembered that in his youth he had fought for his country's independence against the Turks.

My mother had asked a friend to take an overcoat for George out to Romania. On arrival in Bucharest he sent a message to George inviting him to the Athene Palace Hotel to have a drink and collect the parcel. When poor George, in his threadbare clothes and worn-out shoes, reached the entrance to the hotel he was abused by the doorman and the policeman on duty outside who prevented this 'enemy of the people' from entering the hotel in which he had spent so many happy hours during the past fifty years. His humiliation was sad news to us. I never discovered if the coat was ever delivered, but learnt that Uncle George had died of flu a few months later.

My grandmother, Gui, at last received permission to leave Bucharest and she rejoined her family in Rye, Sussex, where we were overjoyed to see her again. It is, however, open to question whether old people, who have lived a lifetime in one country, should ever be transported into an alien culture, whose language is almost incomprehensible to them, just in order to be able to live with their children. However awful conditions under the Communists might have become, I wonder if she might not have been happier had she stayed amongst her old friends and familiar surroundings. At any rate by the end of 1952 we were all for the first time since 1939 living in the same country.

In those days it was still necessary and indeed good manners to ask your Commanding Officer for permission to get married. It was therefore with some trepidation that I approached Lieutenant Colonel David Smiley with my request. He immediately expressed his delight. Quite a different reaction, I would imagine, from that of the Commanding Officer of the South Lancashire Regiment (I believe) in the late 1930s who questioned a young officer about his bride to be. Would she fit in with the Regiment, did she understand about being an army wife, would she understand her duties and so on? Exasperated by the young fellow's terse replies he asked, "Might I know who this young lady might be?"

"Yes, Sir," the subaltern replied, "It is your wife!"

Needless to say the young man had to change regiments, but it did not spoil his career. He became a full General and a Commander-in-Chief.

Living with my regiment at Windsor I was happy to be allowed to join the Harlequin Rugby Football Club and to play for one of their many teams. However, early in 1953 I broke my nose and got two black eyes which suggested that perhaps my concentration on the game had been wavering. It was ten days before my wedding to Valerie Wellesley, whom I met in Bad Oeynhausen and whose father and grandfather were both soldiers and indeed among their ancestors was the Duke of Wellington. I could see her house from mine in Porta Strasse and watch her in the riding school opposite. Her father was then posted to Bermuda, as a reward for being the only officer in the Headquarters who did not pester the authorities about his next posting. I had just managed to ask her to marry me, in Green Park, before she sailed to Bermuda. We were married at St Michael's Chester Square on Saint Valentine's Day and stood in a snow flurry beneath the swords of Regimental Corporal Major Sallis and a Guard of Honour from the Blues.

There was scarcely time to get used to my new circumstances when I was unexpectedly caught up in one of the great pageants of State Ceremonial this century. Six Admirals, twenty Air Marshals and twenty-six Generals were warned that they would be required to ride in the Procession for the Coronation of Her Majesty Queen Elizabeth II on 2 June 1953 in Westminster Abbey. As many of these officers had not been near a horse for many years there was a fair chance that there might be some entertaining moments for the crowds, unless they and their mounts were properly prepared. With this in mind it was decided to create a special camp in Hyde Park where all the horses taking part in the parade would be stabled and trained.

Headquarters London District were no doubt at their wits end trying to find the staff to run this and the many other establishments needed to marshal the 5396 people who were to take part in the procession. The Royal Horse Guards, an armoured car regiment, at Windsor were ordered to find an officer, a Corporal Major and two clerks to run Hyde Park Horse Camp. It was with utter disbelief that I was told, just before my wedding, that I had been nominated Camp Commandant with the acting unpaid rank of Major. I went to the motor transport office to tell Corporal of Horse Ted Mantell, who knew even less about horses than I did, that he had been nominated my acting Corporal Major.

"How on earth," I asked him, "are we ever going to get through the next five months without losing our names many times over? We know so little about equitation!"

"Don't worry, Sir," he said, pointing to his desk covered in Work Tickets, Oil and Petrol Consumption States, Vehicle Inspection Reports and Accident Reports in quadruplicate, "it will be wonderful to get away from all this bloody paper work, and," he added hopefully, "I am sure there must be somebody at Hyde Park Barracks who can tell us how much to feed the brutes."

But in the event the officers of the Household Cavalry Regiment were all far too busy to give us much help. The Horse Camp was to be erected opposite the barracks on a narrow strip of grass between the South Carriage Way and the Serpentine lake. It had been the site of the original Crystal Palace designed by Sir Joseph Paxton for the Great Exhibition of 1851. Just one reminder of that great occasion remained, a gnarled oak tree surrounded by a low iron fence. The Crystal Palace had been built over the tree and it seems that sparrows and pigeons continued to roost in it and their droppings fell on the exhibits. When Queen Victoria and Prince Albert visited the exhibition, accompanied by the Duke of Wellington, he allayed their fears that shooting the birds might break the glass by offering an alternative effective measure, "Hawks, Ma'am."

A bowler-hatted staff officer from Headquarters London District met me the first day and indicated with sweeps of his umbrella over the wet grass the bounds of the camp site. He informed me that six truck-loads of tentage, poles, ropes, pegs and duck boards would arrive in two days' time, together with a 'working party' and that temporary stabling for ninety horses would follow. We pitched the fourteen tents, in which the grooms were to sleep, on the highest ground and then struggled to erect six marquees. We were feeling rather pleased with ourselves when the same staff officer, accompanied by an official from the Royal Parks, arrived and observed, rather testily, that the outside row of tent pegs encroached by fourteen inches on the precise area of grass that I had been allotted. Had I not read the Manual of Administration section on erection of tents? This, it seemed, contained exact instructions on how much space a six-man tent should take up. As it was still early days and we might well need their help before the adventure was over, we did it all over again, without telling them what we thought about this display of petty bumbledom.

The arrival of such palatial accommodation in Hyde Park was viewed by the Knightsbridge prostitutes to be a timely humanitarian gesture by the authorities to help them cater for increased demand. Certainly the troop of tarts who marched down the South Carriage Way at noon and six pm each day, halting every twenty yards to drop off one of their number, thought that the tents were a great improvement on the amenities that they could offer their clients. It soon became quite a problem keeping the girls out of the camp until the iron fence, intended to keep the horses in, was completed. Even then, working alongside, metaphorically speaking, these dedicated ladies did create problems and some very noisy scenes.

Apart from six men from the Household Cavalry, I was given thirty men from the Royal Army Veterinary Corps and forty Royal Air Force dog handlers, who, as soon as they understood the basic differences between dogs and horses, quickly settled down. Most of these cheerful adaptable young men had never been to London before and found that the rich tapestry of big city vice on the sidewalk right beside the camp was more entertaining than any football match they had ever watched. As soon as a prospective customer in a white Jaguar car pulled alongside a girl, there was always an airman or soldier who would shout, "Watch it, Sir, you're the fifth today and you should have seen the pox-marked guy she had at dinner time!"

The girls too received unsolicited advice, which infuriated potential clients, "For gawd's sake dont fall off, Vera, he's much too fat for you."

The inevitable posse from the bowler-hat brigade arrived in their staff cars and I was ordered to stop all banter between my men and the prostitutes, because it upset the genteel decorum of a Royal Park.

However, with typical British hypocrisy, the girls were allowed to continue to seek custom, which they did with success, all except for one, "old copper nob". This veteran with flaming red hair was to be seen still sitting on a bench long after the last of her colleagues had found a client. The Canadian Defence Liaison Staff, then in Ennismore Gardens, took pity on her and placed a red and white sentry box on the bar in their mess for loose change. Eventually, after one of their "thank God it's Friday parties", they all walked up to the park and found this lonely creature still on her bench. After a number of eloquent speeches, they presented her with a very big cheque and a plea for heaven's sake to find herself a bedsit and a telephone, because they just could not bear to enjoy themselves in the bar knowing she was outside sitting in the rain.

Once the marquees were ready to take the saddlery, forage and farriers, loose boxes were quickly built to take ninety horses which came from all over the country and from riding clubs in Rhine Army. The Riding Master was Captain Bill Ritchie of the Royal Army Veterinary Corps. His wide experience in stable management and tactful equitation instruction made him an ideal choice to give the Admirals, Air Marshals and Generals the confidence they might require. Many had ridden as young officers but the sailors lacked recent experience, except the First Sea Lord who rode with his stirrups as short as possible, like a jockey, and wore a pork pie hat back to front. The officers were not supposed to let their mounts go out of a walk, but as their confidence increased, some of the very senior ones could not resist a canter. Those junior ones who felt their promotion prospects might depend on it tried to keep up and there were a few falls which included the Director of Movements at the War Office.

The horses too had to be taught to ignore the clamour and distractions which would certainly occur on the great day and so we constructed a sort of noise training tunnel on the tan alongside the camp which was festooned with flags, bunting and tin cans all flapping around in the breeze. The Royal Signals fixed six loudspeakers to the trees and provided a turntable on which we played scratched records of martial music which could be heard as far away as Hyde Park Corner. Each day I invited children from local schools to cheer, wave flags, beat dustbin lids and twirl gas alarm rattles whilst the horses grew more and more bored with the whole business. The horses were always exercised in exactly the same grouping as they would be in the procession. After the only full rehearsal an Air Marshal said to me, "It was a perfect sortie, old boy. Just one moment of flap when my horse decided to pee in Oxford street, outside Selfridge's. I did exactly what you told me and stood up in my stirrups and let him get on with it, but I had no idea how I was ever going to rejoin my flight, which was disappearing fast. Would you believe it, as soon as I sat down, off he went with absolutely no guidance from me and rejoined exactly in the right place!"

This was good news, but there were still three horses who had not settled down and I made the mistake of mentioning this in an aside to the Press. For the next few days the most amazing offers came in from the public to calm these horses: herbs, black boxes, vibrations and faith healers. Bill Ritchie chose to give the latter a chance because they were less likely to cause any physical damage and under his careful supervision the nervous horses were cured.

We were not the only ones to have troubles because Pompey, the drum horse which was to have led the Band of the Royal Horse Guards in the procession, died on the journey back to London after the Queen's State

Visit to Scotland. He was 19 years old, sixteen hands and weighed sixteen hundredweight, having joined the Blues in 1938 and spent the war years at Melton Mowbray. He carried the two George II silver kettle drums which weigh one hundredweight each, with as his groom said, "bags of swank". After his death his hooves were fashioned into silver inkwells with silver shoes. They became a much sought-after collectors' item and five or six are said to have been sold!

The camp really began to hum with activity when the Royal Canadian Mounted Police arrived with another forty-eight horses. I had persuaded the War Department nurseries at Aldershot to send me a lorry load of potted trees and shrubs to decorate the camp entrance and the Ministry of Works to provide nine flag poles and the services of a signwriter. In no time the camp became a colourful and interesting attraction to Londoners and was referred to by newspapers as a "Canvas City with all the trappings of an old-time cavalry corral, gleaming saddlery, horse troughs and sweating farriers."

Each Commonwealth Head was to have an escort of four riders behind their carriage, except Mr Nehru and Mrs Gandhi, who possibly considered that it might damage their 'peace-loving' image. There were men from the Australian Hunter River Lancers, the Canadian Horse Artillery, New Zealanders, South Africans and Pakistanis. British Mounted Military Police were tasked to escort the heads of many Colonial territories. We admired the courage of the Maltese and Nigerian escorts who were probably riding for the first time and did surprisingly well. Mr Winston Churchill had his own personal escort from the 4th Hussars with whom he had served as a young man. All this galaxy of talent and colour ensured that there were never any dull moments for the public or camp staff.

The Admirals were worried that their slender ceremonial swords might flap against the flanks of their mounts and encourage them to trot. A man from Gieves was summoned, who arrived within the hour dressed in a black coat and pinstripe trousers carrying a small black leather Gladstone bag. An Admiral in full dress mounted his horse and was paraded in front of a worried group of senior officers who tried to visualize what this last-minute hazard could possibly be. The man from Gieves took a tape measure out of his bag and did his sums, he then introduced a modification which maybe exists to this day in Royal Navy Dress Regulations: "Twelve inches of stout black thread will secure the tip of an Admiral's scabbard to the girth of his horse". The trials were successful and we were given six pieces of thread for emergencies, which

143

we forgot to use in the final rush to get ready on Coronation Day.

Final Parade Orders began to flow from Horse Guards; nothing was going to be left to chance; every aspect had been considered, which, of course, is the only way perfect ceremonial can be achieved. These included such details as:

"0915 hrs Field Marshal Montgomery's horse holder will conform with orders from Field Marshal Ironside's horse holder, but lead his horse from Wellington Barracks to Great Smith Street."

"1715 hrs RAF Fly Past, all horse holders must take particular care at this time."

Administration was to be kept simple and included some helpful caveats,

"Plans must ensure that there is a quick issue of haversack rations and that no one receives more than one ration."

"There are latrines in Royal Parks, but men must be encouraged to make maximum use of latrines in camps beforehand."

Communications, security, traffic control and first aid posts, even for horses, had all been carefully considered. Reveille in Hyde Park Horse Camp on Coronation Day was at 4.15 am. Any horse that was liable to prove troublesome was well exercised and then they were, according to the Press, "groomed to Hollywood Glamour Queen standards". There was almost a carnival atmosphere as the riders began to appear in full dress, Canadian Mounted Police in red tunics and Baden Powell hats, Pakistan Lancers in turbans, Australians in bush hats and Nigerians in tropical uniform, just to mention a few. As soon as the last of the distinguished senior officers had mounted and been sent on their way, I was able to join the marching contingent from the armoured car regiments of the Household Cavalry who had halted at Hyde Park Corner. We were 400 men dressed in blue with tight overall trousers with red stripes, boots and spurs and all carried swords at the slope. Half an hour later the rain began, but in spite of the constant showers and the eleven-mile march in soaking uniforms over which white pipe clay began to run, it was an occasion which nobody who took part will ever forget.

Of the many stories recounted is that of a beaming larger-than-life Queen of Tonga sharing her open carriage in the pouring rain with an unknown, wet and miserable small Indian gentleman. Someone asked who he was, and Nöel Coward is said to have replied, "He is her lunch". There is also the tale of an unhappy Admiral, sitting well back on his horse during the long halt while the Coronation Service was taking place in Westminster Abbey, his hand gripping the pommel of his saddle. A Cockney voice from the crowd, recalling a recent popular war film, called out, "Wot price The Cruel Sea nah, Guv?" The Admiral is said to have smiled, faintly. However, there were no disasters and all riders and horses returned safely to the Hyde Park Horse Camp. It had been a very long day and as I walked back towards Holland Road where my wife and I had set up our first home, in a miserable, dingy bedsitter, it was still raining. There sitting on a park bench, ever hopeful was poor old 'copper nob'. We exchanged greetings and, as I moved on, she added in a husky voice, "Don't worry about me tonight, dearie. Now that that parade is over, I reckon I am in with a sporting chance!"

I suppose that 1953 marked the end of any remaining links we might have had with Romania, because grandmother was once again living with us and all mother's half-brothers and aunts had by then died in Romania. It was most unlikely that any of us would ever see Doftana again and now that I was married, my life too was going to be different. The Coronation heralded a new Elizabethan era in which many people in the Commonwealth were granted their rightful independence and were free to conduct their own affairs. For Romania the year marked a hundred years since the first steps were taken towards creating the union of Moldavia and Wallachia and winning their independence from Turkish rule. Sadly, by 1953 the aspirations and achievements of that brave new nation had totally disappeared. Romania had once again become a vassal state, dominated by the Soviet Union and was still ruled by a tyrannical Communist dictator, Ceaucescu. There was every indication that the situation would get far, far worse.

When the tents and horses had been removed I was sent for four months to run a Territorial Army camp near Weymouth, before returning to Windsor and a gloomy bungalow in Datchet. My wife, after three home moves in seven months, was beginning to get the feel of being an army wife. Soldiering at Windsor was going to be very boring indeed so I applied to be allowed to study for the Staff College Exam. This was considered a bit unusual at the time and showed that I did not have the right attitude towards regimental soldiering, but David Tabor had succeeded and I was determined to follow him. In the event I passed by a narrow margin and was posted to the Canadian Army Staff College in Kingston, Ontario. We were lucky to do the course with Nigel and Rosemary Grove White and were the first British students allowed to bring their wives. We had to borrow hundreds of dollars from our empty bank accounts in order to buy cars before we could find a place to live. We were eternally grateful to Bill Heald, the British exchange instructor at the college, and his wife Jean for all their help.

We saw *Salad Days* the night before we sailed on Christmas Eve 1954 on the Cunard RMS *Saxonia* for New York, which we reached on New Year's Eve. With a few hours to spare before catching the night train to Montreal we went to the top of the Empire State Building and cut a ribald message on to a 78rpm record in a booth to Valerie's parents, Arthur and Margaret Wellesley.

Kingston was the first capital of Canada, a beautiful and historic city on Lake Ontario with fine buildings, three well-preserved Martello Towers and a magnificent fortress guarding the exit from Lake Ontario into the St Lawrence River, old Fort Henry, built to resist the Americans in the War of 1812. The Staff College was located in Fort Frontenac on the water front and among the students were twelve foreigners from NATO countries and Australia. The course, which lasted a year, was extremely well managed by some exceptional instructors with battle experience who worked us hard.

It was much easier to be a foreigner in somebody else's college. There was not quite so much competition as in one's own country and we were expected to offer some original solutions to the problems we were set. A special effort was made to show us how vast and varied Canada is, and the fascination of the first trip into the High Arctic encouraged me to travel in those inhospitable regions many times since.

We lived about ten miles from Kingston in a log cabin at Collins Bay beneath a small bluff close to the lake. It was incredibly primitive by Canadian standards, but we felt like pioneers, with chipmunks, raccoons and skunks sharing the woods with us. Valerie was expecting our first child, Alexander, who was born in Kingston and received a little bunch of flowers with a card "Welcome to our fair city, little stranger". In an attempt to make lots of money we hoped to take a skunk, which had had its evil-smelling glands removed, back to England and sell it to Harrods pet shop. After months of searching I found one, but its arrival coincided with another trip to the Arctic and by the time I returned it had set up home under the bath and frightened everybody except the baby. We sold it to a Canadian, Colonel Mike Webber, for $15 and I understand both lived happily together in Ottawa for many years.

Before leaving Canada I offered to produce a pantomime, the first ever staged at the Staff College. I relied on the old formula of short skits with even shorter ones between, which either made fun of the 'system' or gave talented individuals a chance to shine. There was no problem getting the audience in the right mood by offering a drink beforehand but it was essential to keep the cast sober until afterwards. It was a happy ending to what had been a fascinating year that had seen the start of many friendships which endure to this day.

Chapter Ten

TERROR IN CYPRUS

We exchanged the log cabin beside a lake in Canada for a brand new red-brick army quarter on the edge of Windsor. The lush black topsoil had all been removed by the contractor and the house stood on a bare patch of clay. After sustained complaints we were given green turf which extended for ten feet round the house; the rest stayed bare. Every electric bar heater inside was matched by the issue of a coal scuttle, brass poker, shovel, tongs, hearth brush and folding fire guard. We were 'marched in', pages of inventory were read aloud: 'Brushes hand scrubbing, brushes long handle soft, brushes crumb, brushes flue, brushes water closet' and so on.

A strange thing happened just after we moved in. It was the evening before Easter 1956 and I was most surprised to see my sister, Mary Maud, in the dining room, which had French windows opening on to the garden. She had made quite a name for herself as a fashion model and often featured in the popular newspapers. She was quick-witted and very attractive, but had made an unhappy marriage to Sir Dudley Cunliffe Owen, a heavy drinker and an unlucky gambler.

A moment later she disappeared and I went to tell Valerie what I had seen because my sister lived miles away in Dorset and had never been to the house. Naturally we thought it was just my imagination. An hour later there was a knock on the door and a police officer gave us the news that she had died in a car near Tetbury. She was only twenty-eight. She had been out hunting all day and was on the way to stay with my cousin Dorothy Balean (previously Nettlefold). The car had left the road and travelled a long way along the grass verge before coming to rest against a tree. No brakes had been applied. There was not a mark on her body except a blue mark on her skull. It seems she died of a burst blood vessel while driving. Needless to say it was estimated to have been at much the same hour as she came to say goodbye.

My first staff appointment was at Headquarters London District in the Horse Guards, which meant a hideous daily journey by bus, changing trains, changing underground and a walk in each direction. I simply hated it, especially always having to wear a dark suit, a stiff white collar and carry a bowler hat and a rolled umbrella. The dingy office was shared with a delightful companion, Philip Ward, who had been to the Staff College in Camberley and knew much more than I did about the job. Every day we stood up and said "good morning" in unison to our colonel, Raoul Lemprière-Robin, as he passed through to his magnificent office overlooking St James's Park. He seldom spoke to us until after midday, by which time he had placed his bets and arranged the rest of his day. He was fun to work for and left us to get on with the job.

After two uneventful years in London I rejoined the Royal Horse Guards in Cyprus.

Great clouds of dust from the armoured cars in front swirled around us, making it impossible to hurry. There were countless sharp bends, crumbling shoulders above precipitous valleys and the ever-present danger of an ambush, which all demanded a high degree of skill and alertness from the crews, such as I had not experienced since 1945. The northern slopes of the Troodos Mountains were supposed to hide a gang of terrorists who had always managed to elude capture, however swift or silent our operations had been.

Suddenly it was as if some sort of delayed-action fuse had set off an explosion in my head, when it dawned on me that I had just seen a feather. I had only caught a glimpse of it among the many small rocks which lined the edge of the mountain track. What could a feather possibly be doing under a stone?

"Stop, reverse," I cried to Corporal Veale, my driver. "I think I have seen something most unusual."

So, after warning the car in front that we had stopped, we began to reverse, back and back, until I began to worry whether I had in fact seen anything at all. Suddenly there it was, a brown and white hoopoe feather lying quite definitely beneath a round yellow stone. I got out and examined it carefully. I crossed to the other side of the track and looked up at the mountain side. The feather pointed to a saddle between two small peaks.

"Let Headquarters know where we have stopped and then come with me," I ordered my radio operator. We climbed steadily through the pine trees towards the crest. Although I knew what I was looking for, I

149

was still surprised and excited when, as we traversed an outcrop of rocks, I noticed the tiny scratches made by hobnails in a boot. Every now and again there were similar telltale signs as we climbed towards the top; broken twigs on the steepest parts, signs that men had slipped and slithered, all helped to lead us into a small circle of rocks where the ground had been flattened. There were no cigarette ends or evidence of its use except what looked like rabbit droppings which turned out to be eleven olive stones. Far below I could still see the track and our two vehicles. I stood up behind one of the rocks and looked over at the other side of the mountain. There across the valley stood Makheras Monastery, beautiful and solitary among a profusion of trees and shrubs which thrived around a spring rising just above the 12th century monastery.

Through my binoculars I could just pick out the tops of the aerial masts of my squadron headquarters, which I had established on the turning circle outside the monastery. Clearly visible on the opposite side of the monastery to my headquarters vehicles there was a large blue and white Greek flag hanging from an upstairs window.

"Go back down to the cars and tell Headquarters that I want them to pack up and move out of sight of the monks," I said. "If I don't join you in 30 minutes come back."

I watched him disappear down the slope and realized what a fool I was to remain there alone. If I could see the window then I too could be seen, so I moved to one side into a clump of bushes and waited. It did not take long. I saw the two Saracen Command Vehicles and landrovers drive off out of sight. I then settled down to watch the monastery, wondering if there might be any link with terrorists. I focused my glasses once again, but there was no change or movement. Then, when I was not looking, it happened. The flag disappeared. That's enough, I reckoned, and hurried back down to the track.

"Let's get going. I think we have found an ideal place to put an ambush." Two weeks later, after a skilful and protracted operation, two EOKA men were captured on that trail and the follow-up operation led to the death in a nearby hideout of Gregoris Afxentiou, second-in-command to Colonel Grivas, the EOKA leader.

I was thrilled to be back with soldiers and especially to command a squadron of armoured cars on active service. Cyprus in 1957 was in the midst of an 'Emergency'. Once again a small number of politically motivated terrorists had shown how, with an apathetic population and some legitimate grouses against an insensitive irresolute government, it is easy to cause havoc. We received no indoctrination as to the reason for our presence on the island, a British possession since 1878. There was no talk of preparing the Cypriot people for Independence. We were there 'in support of the Civil Power' and, although I had studied the appropriate manual carefully before leaving England, it made little sense in the circumstances. The terrorists, EOKA, had a slogan 'Enosis', which meant Union with Greece. This was difficult for us to accept, since the island had never belonged to Greece and was quite unacceptable to the Turkish minority whose parent country was traditionally hostile to Greece. Nevertheless, there is no doubt that Cyprus flourished during the Bronze Age, and that the first Greek settlers from the Aegean began to arrive after the fall of Troy in 1270 BC. The rivers, dry much of the year, take their names, as they do all over the world, from the earliest inhabitants eg Mavrokolymhos, Vasilikos and Xeropotamos. The names of towns and mountains may change with the times, but rivers' names never change.

The plentiful supply of copper and timber made Cyprus a highly prized island. The timber was used to build ships and thus enhance the sea power of whatever nation wished to be top dog in the Eastern Mediterranean. The real prize was to be able to control the trade which flowed between the Orient and Southern Europe. The island changed hands many times, usually between the Egyptians and Persians. The Roman Empire took over in 58 BC. The Jews did much to make it flourish until Hadrian expelled them in 117 AD after they had revolted at Salamis and massacred thousands of Greek Cypriots. When the Roman Empire split, Cyprus went to Greek Orthodox Constantinople and 796 years of Byzantine rule began. Initially Cyprus continued to prosper under Byzantine Emperors until AD 644 when the Prophet's nurse fell off her donkey in a fracas outside Larnaca. This gave the Moslems an excuse and the first of many Arab invasions began. These pirate attacks continued for about two hundred years until the Byzantines hired Basil the Armenian, a General with a ferocious reputation. He once returned thousands of prisoners to Bulgaria after putting out their eyes and leaving one man in ten with one eye to lead the others home.

It was not until Richard Coeur de Lion and his Crusaders arrived, quite by accident, blown by a storm in 1191, that Cypriot fortunes improved. Richard, who only stayed five weeks on the island, sold it to the Knights Templar, but after one year they begged Richard to buy it back because it was too much to control. He took it back and sold it to Guy de Lusignan, a Roman Catholic, who founded a dynasty which ruled for 372 years. They were ousted by the Venetians, until another warlike

Moslem nation, the Ottomans, invaded in 1570. After a seige lasting forty-five days, they captured Nicosia and slew 20,000 inhabitants before going off to do the same to the brave defenders of Famagusta, after an epic nine-month seige. In 1571 the Ottoman army was disbanded and the soldiers were given little parcels of land in Cyprus, thus becoming the first Turkish settlers among the Greek Orthodox Cypriots.

For the next three hundred years trade with the rest of the world virtually ceased as Cyprus languished under Turkish rule. When the Ottoman Empire in Europe began to crumble Russia seized the opportunity to invade Turkey in 1877 and, aided by the Romanians and nationalists in Bulgaria, advanced almost unchecked towards Constantinople. A foreign military observer with that Turkish retreat who witnessed the Battle of Plevna was Colonel Fred Burnaby of the Blues. Attacking with the Romanians was my grandfather, Mihail Capsa.

The British, who until then had been strictly neutral, dispatched the Royal Navy to the Bosphorous. The Russians took the hint and, fearing also an attack on their rear from the Austrians, withdrew. At the Congress of Berlin in June 1878 Turkey assigned to England the island of Cyprus on the understanding that we would use it as a base to defend her Asiatic territories and would return Cyprus to her if the Russians ever returned certain territories to them.

The British Channel Fleet landed at Larnaca on the south of the island on 4 July 1878 under the command of Admiral Lord John Hay. A party of exhausted sailors and marines marched from Larnaca to Nicosia and raised the Union flag outside a Turkish Barracks. Admiral Hay travelled in a wagonette followed by two mules carrying sacks of shiny new silver sixpences with which to pay the Turkish officials who had been unpaid for weeks. Subsequent British units, including the Black Watch, marched by a devious route slowly towards Nicosia, suffering casualties, but only from disease, probably malaria and heatstroke. I was surprised to find a tiny military cemetery on the south side of the road to Lythrodhonda with tombstones of that date.

The area given to my Squadron to patrol stretched from the Kyrenia mountain range in the north to about the middle of the Troodos Mountains in the south. In the west we operated from Morphou Bay to about half-way across the Mesaoria Plain towards Famagusta, some 1200 square miles. The task given to our commanding officer, Valerian Douro, was to keep the peace in the vast rural areas, while infantry battalions looked after the cities. The other two armoured car squadrons were initially based at Famagusta and Limassol.

Although each squadron was only one hundred and fifteen men strong, we did have some excellent new equipment, the Ferret scout car. This worthy successor to the Daimler was still in service twenty-five years later with the United Nations Forces in Cyprus. The armour could just about keep out bullets or bomb splinters but car commanders were ordered never to sit on the back of the turrets, where they were easy targets. The Ferret weighed around four tons and, if the side of a track or hillside crumbled, they could easily roll over. Unless the Commander was well down in his turret, and hanging on tight, he was likely to be thrown out and crushed. The Browning machine-gun mount was pretty crude and accurate sighting practically non-existent. The writer Auberon Waugh, while doing his National Service with the Blues, was seriously wounded by the machine gun on his own scout car. Due to a mechanical fault the gun accidentally fired about nine bullets into him as he stood in front of the car. His life was subsequently saved by the skill of an army surgeon.

Each squadron consisted of five troops of four scout cars and a support troop of infantry carried in five Saracens, as well as a workshop and echelon. The Saracens were also brand new, six-wheeled armoured personnel carriers with a command vehicle version. They had trouble initially from overheating until our regimental workshops designed a deflector plate to alter the air flow through the engine. They had another unexpected feature which we only discovered after two village buses each lost a wheel in close encounters on narrow lanes. The Saracen drivers judged the width of their vehicle by using the tips of their mudguards as guides but did not realize that their wheel hubs, which contained complicated epicyclic gears, were two inches wider than the mudguards above them.

Camp Elizabeth was 'home' to the Blues for three years and I do not believe they have ever had to call such a dreadful place 'home' for so long. It was a tented camp on a solid rock plateau three miles west of Nicosia, where every tent peg had to have a hole drilled for it in the rock and the latrine pits were blasted out with explosives. When it rained, pools of water lay on the surface until evaporated by the sun. When the dry winds blew, every bed was soon covered in a fine red dust, and if the tent sides were rolled down the heat inside became unbearable. Only the mess rooms were built of corrugated tin and timber. In spite of this, we were a very happy regiment, incredibly busy and professionally very competent. It was, I suppose, typically British that we should live in such conditions, spend days and nights out in the wilds trying to arrest terrorists and their helpers, only to discover that they were then placed into accommodation which was infinitely superior to ours. Not only did they live with a roof over their heads and with proper sanitation and washing facilities but were paid sums of money greatly in excess of what they could possibly earn as, say, shepherds. I doubt whether any other nation in the world took such trouble over the welfare of people held without trial. Sir Hugh Foot was determined not to offend the Greeks.

Whenever a soldier was murdered we were all shaken, especially so when our popular Medical Officer, Gordon Wilson, was shot at point-blank range after attending to a Greek patient in her home. We were stunned during one particularly hectic and prolonged operation to hear that Stephen Fox-Strangways had been shot in the back. He died with a young trooper, Proctor, inside a Greek grocer's shop buying food for the messes in Famagusta. He had just managed to fire one shot before dying. There was a risk that the fury felt by all that afternoon might be vented on the nearest Greek Cypriot and we were ordered to keep tight control.

EOKA now began killing British civilians. Mrs Cutliffe and Mrs Robinson, both German and wives of Royal Artillery sergeants, were shot in the back, and Sergeant Hamond, who was holding his two-year-old son's hand, was also shot in the back.

A few days later an infantry battalion played a friendly football match against Lefkoniko village not far from Famagusta. After the game, which the local team won, the soldiers were invited to quench their thirst at a well alongside the pitch. When they were gathered round the bucket a bomb went off, causing terrible casualties. The regiment, which was not always noted for its observance of the Queensberry Rules, returned to the village that night and literally took it to pieces with their bare hands. There was never any 'trouble' again from the villagers and, although the 'Authorities' huffed and puffed, they probably privately thought that retribution had been swift and fair.

In spite of the shots fired at us during those years, I do not recollect a single terrorist having been killed by us. Of course we fired back, with the intention of at least pinning them down until we could move in closer and make an arrest. A Corporal of Horse who had been fired on from the top of a church tower reported that his tracer bullets were making a different noise on the church bells than his ball ammunition. He then arrested the two men at the bottom of the ladder but had to climb up to collect their weapons.

When Nicos Sampson was captured in a room by a trooper, he reached for a gun under the bed and should perhaps have been killed there and then, but was only wounded in the leg. Sampson had murdered at least fifteen soldiers and civilians. It was his attempted assassination in 1974 of Archbishop Makarios and the subsequent slaughter of hundreds of Makarios supporters that precipitated the Turkish occupation which sadly continues to divide the island.

The task of trying to keep control of events in the rural areas could never have been done without the mobility and excellent communications of a wheeled reconnaissance squadron. As soon as an incident was reported by the Police or other units, or indeed if we were ambushed, it was possible to redeploy the squadron so that within minutes every road leading away from the incident was blocked. Then our own support troops or nearest infantry unit could start to hunt the terrorists. In order to avoid being blown up on mines, our resourceful REME Workshops Officer designed a mine-roller contraption which could be bolted on to a Ferret. The snag was that the wheels came off water-cart trailers and soon demand exceeded the total stocks held on the island.

As the opposition became more cautious of making daylight attacks they switched to twilight, making use of approaching darkness to escape. We received dog handlers and tracker dogs, but in the heat of the day they had difficulty in finding any scent to follow. However, when we set them on to a trail after dark, they soon proved their value. The regimental workshops fitted spotlights to every car and a gun-mount on to the bonnet of my Champ, a sort of luxury Jeep. We were still pretty blind unless it was a perfect moonlight night, and needed better illumination. I asked whether we could fit a two-inch mortar to one car in each troop and then fire illuminating flares. This proved a great success. As soon as a bomb exploded, a troop could fire illuminating flares, pin down the attackers with fire from the Brownings and get the tracker dog out of the Saracen personnel carrier at the rear of the patrol. As the dismounted troopers approached the spot the firing would have to stop. This was the moment the attackers would run if they had not done so already. The wires leading to the explosive device would be found and followed to the spot where the men had been lying. Then the hunt began with the hound straining at the leash, and our soldiers trying to keep up in the dark, with the ever-present danger of running into another ambush. We had several successes with this technique. Bill Legge-Bourke managed to catch three men in bed with their boots still on and coils of the wire hidden under the bed. With the remote detonating devices which now exist, we would not have stood much chance of achieving a capture. Armoured cars should not move around at night in a hostile environment and, although we were winning every encounter, we were wisely ordered to take no more risks.

Our daily life became easier with the arrival in Camp Elizabeth of the squadron which had been stationed in Limassol and we could now spend some time on the beaches. I had rented a little house from Mr Georgardies in Kyrenia on the road towards Bellapais. There were orange and lemon trees almost constantly in fruit, a hedge of tall prickly pomegranates and a beautifully scented tangerine tree outside the bathroom. One of the few objects we had brought from England was a large icon of Saint Nicholas which made a most favourable impression with our landlord. Every day when I was not already on an operation or on standby in camp I drove over the mountains to Nicosia, leaving my wife to fend for herself with a revolver in the oven. She and Inès Wilson had stones thrown at their car in a village near Famagustsa. A few weeks later cars were set alight outside officers' homes in Kyrenia, but she never allowed her anxiety to show. Ben Wilson, my second in command, had married Inès, the daughter of the Belgian Ambassador to Turkey, in Istanbul. When he was asked by Julian Berry what wedding presents he would like from his brother officers, he replied a saddle, and had to be reminded that the present was for both of them. Ben's reluctance to realize the duality of marriage was evident at Istanbul Airport as they prepared to leave on their honeymoon and he remembered that he had only bought one flight ticket.

The tension gave us all a great zest for living, and we really did have some marvellous times. A little further out of Kyrenia we built a rest camp for the squadron on a deserted beach where we were able to let one troop at a time have a holiday. I loved the Kyrenia Mountains and the Crusader castles of Saint Hilarion, Buffavento and Kantara. From the top one could sometimes see the snow-covered Taurus Mountains in Turkey and marvel at the contrast between the barren plain around Nicosia and the abundant lush vegetation on the Kyrenia side. Huge vultures glided in graceful patterns below, looking for dead sheep among the olive trees. Sadly, these birds had by 1990 ceased to exist due to misuse of poison bait to kill dogs, which they then scavenged.

The most popular haven for any visitor to Kyrenia was the Harbour Club run by Roy and Judy Findlay. It was perched up above the port next to the 13th century castle. The food and service were superb, there was a wonderful atmosphere and it just bubbled with activity. How Roy managed to deter EOKA from blowing the place up was quite remarkable, an indication of how much he and Judy were loved by everyone. We were sometimes invited to Sunday lunches with our Greek friends under a vine which covered their courtyard. The potatoes had to be fetched from the bakery down the road whose ovens were used by many families as they cooled down. On these occasions I could not bring myself to wear a pistol, which we were obliged to do. A photographer from *Paris Match*, seeing young officers at the Harbour Club in jeans and beach shirts with guns belts, remarked, *"C'est très Far West"*. The big difference was that if a cowboy lost his gun he did not get tried by court martial and severely punished. The possibility of this all added to the tension. Indeed, when this did happened to Ben Wilson, a Turkish entrepreneur, Sabri, was approached, who, with deep regret, said he could have supplied any pistol except a Browning 9mm automatic. Ben survived the furore.

The threat of bombs or bullets was never far away and one Sunday morning a sharp sentry caught the NAAFI cook coming into camp with a bomb in his suitcase. He was made to sit on it in the car park and sweated for a long time until the bomb disposal team arrived. The Officers' Mess caught fire one night and, as the bar stock began to burn, it was said the Crême de Menthe bottles exploded with a green fireball. One officer ran into the flames with great gallantry, it was thought to rescue valuable mess property, but he emerged clutching the Bridge Book which recorded that he was owed a substantial sum of money by his brother officers.

Another sad loss was that of a pet raven which sat on a perch outside Joe Laycock's tent. This bird was devoted to him and followed him around the camp. If his troop left on patrol, the raven travelled on top of the Ferret turret. As time went by the bird began to cut things fine and spent more time asleep on his perch. He could not bear to hang around while preparations for a move took place, such as loading ammunition, maps and radio checks. He would wait until Joe's scout car was pulling out onto the main road, swoop over the barbed-wire fence and land on the turret lid. One day he made a mistake, awoke in a panic and landed on a Ferret belonging to the Grenadier Guards which happened to be passing and we never saw him again.

Counter-terrorism can only be successful if there is a flow of good intelligence. In default of this we had to rely on instant reaction and quick follow-up of every incident. We also tried to have an unpredictable pattern of patrolling and observation posts. Every gun-runner or courier worth his salt knew where a roadblock was within an hour of it being set up. We carried out snap roadblocks which seldom lasted more than twenty minutes. Observers were hidden about 300 metres before the block to spot the vehicles which turned round on seeing the block or jettisoned packages. This proved very successful, yet we were still hampered by not being allowed to search women without a police-woman, and it seemed impossible to entice a woman police searcher away from duties in Nicosia. An infantry battalion from Ulster, convinced that arms were being smuggled into their area by women, dressed an officer up as a Turkish woman to search bus passengers in a tent beside the highway. Thank heavens for that. The results were dramatic arms finds among the local buses. They were forbidden to ever do such a thing again, but afterwards the High Command were a lot more willing to provide women to help us and we received some from the Women's Royal Army Corps.

EOKA men nearly always carried photographs of themselves draped in bandoliers of ammunition and brandishing a weapon. Intelligence officers had built up such a collection of pictures that a little pocket book was produced, *Wanted men in Cyprus*, which was carried by every patrol. Crossing those out who had been arrested was a little like collecting Sunday School stamps.

It was very difficult to enter a village at night without being given away by the sound of our engines or marching feet. Johnnie Watson, who commanded the squadron in Famagusta, decided to hire donkeys and a patrol under command of Patrick Beresford achieved complete surprise. In summer families slept on the flat roofs of their houses and we were expected to climb up, lift the blankets and compare faces with the Wanted Men book by torchlight. Hardly a task for soldiers, as was made clear to the Police by Jim Eyre, the Regimental Intelligence Officer.

Just as in war, complete surprise can achieve results. A platoon of Irish Guards operating in the foothills south-west of Nicosia reported that they had been attacked and a prodigious amount of ammunition had been fired at invisible targets. The news reached their Commanding Officer, Colonel Will Berridge, who was dining with Julian Berry, at about eleven o'clock. In the time it takes to finish a decanter of port a plan had been made and both regiments had been awoken and were on the move. At first light, when the two colonels, still wearing their dinner jackets, joined their troops, a tight cordon had been established and Henry Hugh-Smith captured some much-wanted EOKA men who probably had nothing to do with the incident, and indeed probably considered themselves to be in a safe area.

By coincidence there were three officers in the Household Division on active service in Cyprus with Romanian parentage, John Ghika,

Irish Guards, Guy Ellerington, Grenadier Guards, and myself.

Whenever a Cordon and Search operation took place, my squadron would try to seal the village off with an outer cordon before the infantry arrived in their trucks. This type of action should not be confused with the American version used later in Vietnam, Search and Destroy, which achieved even less than ours towards winning the hearts and minds of the people. I certainly felt uncomfortable when a hooded informer was put into the driving seat of my Saracen whilst men of the village were each in turn brought face to face with him. Nevertheless, by the time three strangers and one local man had been arrested, their hidden explosives found and our cordon lifted, the whole village seemed to give a sigh of relief and life returned to normal. We had mended the village well, fixed the football posts and repaired two tractors before leaving; it had only lasted five hours, but there was no satisfaction or pride in rootling through a poor family's few precious possessions.

I had never considered the moral issue of how much mental or physical pressure should be put on a suspect to get him to talk. Interrogation methods used by German SS officers during the War of Allied agents and Resistance members were, I considered, despicable. Yet here we were trying to prevent our friends and innocent civilians being shot or blown to pieces. Usually if terrorists were caught red-handed, so to speak, they were so scared they might be shot that they volunteered a lot of information. If the police could act upon this within the hour it often resulted in another arms find and arrest.

One evening I was asked to provide an escort for a police Landrover which was bringing a prisoner to an orange grove near to where I had set up my headquarters. For some days we had heard rumours that there was a huge arms dump near Nicosia and here was a possible breakthrough. I watched the suspect climb out, a well-dressed young man who seemed confident and at ease. The British police sergeant led him to a small rise in the ground and asked him where was the arms cache he had told them about. The young man said it was not in this orange grove, that he had made it up, and that he now refused to co-operate any more. A Turkish constable took him aside, asked him again and then hit him hard with a rifle butt. As he was threatening to do so again, the man pointed to the corner nearest the track. We started to dig and soon recovered boxes of weapons and over 500 pounds of explosives. It took two trucks to shift the stuff. I felt much the same as I did when, as a child in Romania, I had watched the Gendarmes beat our driver, but as the munitions were unearthed I reluctantly conceded that the tough line was acceptable.

To have sent him back to comfortable detention just because he had changed his mind would have allowed his murderous friends to use this huge stockpile of war material.

Sir Hugh Foot in due course replaced Field Marshal Sir John Harding as Governor and a somewhat more liberal line was being taken towards the Greeks, no doubt with a view towards paving the way to Independence. There were days when, only knowing one side of the story, we would bitterly criticize the latest concession made towards the Greeks by the new Governor. By chance he appeared one morning in the mess for breakfast where his charm and persuasive arguments soon had us understanding the aim of his policy.

There was, however, one occasion when we began to wonder whether our orders to eliminate terrorists and their equipment really was the sincere wish of the colonial government. An EOKA gang had been cornered in the village of Kythrea against the Kyrenia Mountain range. We were maintaining a protracted cordon around the village and, as the interrogators progressed, more and more information came out and our soldiers were busy digging up numerous arms caches. The prisoners were being held in a 'cage' at the top of the village beside a flour mill guarded by some men from an infantry battalion. This unit was suddenly withdrawn to stand by to fly to Jordan, together with the rest of the 3rd Infantry Division, which had recently arrived from England. A Captain who had visited his soldiers guarding the cage had a farewell dinner with a senior government official in Nicosia at which he expressed his suspicion that the prisoners were being tortured. How otherwise could the interrogation officers have been achieving so much success? His host said that the Governor should immediately be informed, even though he too was giving a dinner party for the Director of Operations, Major General Kenneth Darling. The Governor decided they should visit Kythrea immediately. The General said he wanted to put on uniform and the Governor insisted he would accompany him to his house to ensure no warning was given. I was sitting on a ration box in a field opposite the school in Kythrea, with Ben Wilson and the rest of my Headquarters, cooking a chicken on an aerial rod over a fire when suddenly we heard the sound of Ferrets in the distance and, knowing where all ours were, guessed it must be the Governor's Escort Troop. My instinct also told me that he could only be interested in the police interrogation centre and sent Ben up the hill to ensure the ten soldiers I had up there were alert. The convoy arrived and the party, accompanied by Brigadier Victor FitzGeorge-Balfour who commanded 1st Guards Brigade, entered the school house which was being used by Headquarters of the Suffolk Regiment. The Governor said that he had received reports that violence and torture was being used on the prisoners. The astonished acting CO denied this, but the Governor said he wished to see for himself. He drove up through the village to the interrogation centre, where he confronted the Special Branch civilian interrogator with the accusation that he was using 'ice torture'. His face fell in astonishment and all he could say was, "No ice up here, Sir".

Then the Governor had every single suspect in the cage brought before him, made to remove his shirt and examined for signs of maltreatment. They were asked if they had any complaints to make and none were made. The effect of this extraordinary intervention was that the operation dried up there and then; the police interrogators felt that they no longer had the support or confidence of Government House. The line between mental torture and clever interrogation or bluff is narrow, but numerous arms and explosives had been found. No doubt others remained hidden to be used later against ourselves, Turks and fellow Greeks. We were slowly having our hands tied behind our backs.

All the concessions made by the Governor to meet the aspirations of the Greek Cypriot population now began to upset the Turks who thought that perhaps the British were actually considering union with Greece. They staged some spectacular riots which became quite exciting. Being inside an armoured car when the rocks start flying is like pulling an eiderdown over your head while a thunderstorm rages outside. Charles Booth Jones did not have time to get under cover and suffered a cut face. The only thing the British Army is allowed to throw back in this sort of situation is a tear-gas bomb, but even these were being picked up and thrown back. Captain Wheeler REME, our resourceful workshops officer, modified the smoke dischargers on the front of the Ferrets to fire a tear-gas grenade. This could drop 150 yards away, by then far too hot to pick up and too far to throw back. He also electrified the armoured cars so that, provided the engine was running, rioters on the ground received an electric shock if they touched the car. I saw a yellow mongrel cheekily cock his leg against the wheel of my car and get a terrible shock when he least expected it. The Turkish rioting, having made their point, was soon over. The Greeks then began to turn on the Turkish minority and at the start of June 1958 we found ourselves in a new situation.

The first indications came when our patrols in the rural areas discovered that small Turkish hamlets, 'chifliks', had been destroyed and their occupants were either dead or had disappeared. Groups of Greeks would descend on any Turkish community, whom they greatly out-numbered, and cause havoc. By the end of the first week in June 1958 we were answering calls for help all over the Nicosia Plain. At midnight on 10 June a Turkish Muktar in the village of Skylloura said he felt sure he was going to be attacked. There was a population of 500 Greeks and 300 Turks in the village. A search revealed that about a quarter of a mile outside, crouching in a dried-up stream, there were 175 Greeks armed with sticks, knives, clubs and pitchforks. They had come from neigh-bouring villages and, parked outside the village, we discovered nine buses with their lights switched off. The Greeks were disarmed, arrested and then released. Ethnic cleansing had begun.

At 5.30 am a few days later we heard that the Turks in the mixed village of Ayios Vasilios (436 Greeks and 94 Turks) were going to be attacked. As the scout cars approached, they saw two buses turn round and speed away. After a 'cops and robbers' chase, they stopped five vehicles in all which contained 250 Greeks from other villages, all armed with some sort of weapon. They were disarmed and, because we already had other calls for help, they were told to walk back to their village across the fields, and their vehicles to be driven off ahead. This pattern of events continued all day and, as no end seemed in sight, I had to make sure some of my troops got a moment's rest and cars and radios serviced. The Regiment was motoring over 6000 miles each day trying to keep things under control. There is no way that the subsequent Army policy of issuing tracked vehicles instead of armoured cars to reconnaissance squadrons could have possibly coped with a similar situation.

Towards noon of the following day, 12 June, which had been particu-larly exhausting, a troop went to assist a police sergeant and an RAF Squadron Leader who had found thirty-five Greeks hiding in a ravine on the edge of the Turkish quarter of Skylloura. Their weapons were removed and we were ordered to deliver the men in their bus to the central police station in Nicosia. The situation in the joint operations room had been hectic for days and on this occasion was made worse because a riot was developing outside the central police station. We got a message, "On no account bring the prisoners here", because it would aggravate the situation, but by then the convoy was already on the city ring road and there was no time to lose. I told them to take the next turning away from the town centre, which happened to be the road to Kyrenia, to go beyond Geunyeli, a Turkish village, until the Greeks could see their own village on the south side of the Kyrenia Mountains, and then make them all walk home. Fortunately Peter Baring's troop was already in the area, together with a platoon of Grenadier Guards, and they reported that all was quiet.

The prisoners set out with a group of Grenadiers, while the scout cars kept an eye on Geunyeli to the south. After about half a mile the Greeks were left on their own and the troops watched them disappear over the brow of a small hill. A few moments later a great column of smoke was seen as a dry field of 'bearded wheat' was deliberately set on fire either by Greeks or Turks, probably the latter. The troop rushed to the scene just in time to intercept a huge crowd of Turks coming up from Geunyeli armed to the teeth with clubs and knives. The Greeks had been attacked by a party of Turks who were working in the fields with the utmost savagery. Four were cut to bits on the spot, four died in hospital and five were severely wounded. A Greek survivor said, "If it had not been for the armoured cars, we would all have been slaughtered".

The troop managed to arrest two Turks on a motorcycle with blood-stained weapons and a few others, but they disappeared as suddenly as they had appeared and the soldiers had their hands full looking after the wounded.

A little while later I got reports of hundreds of Greeks pouring out of every village west of Nicosia and heading towards the Turkish villages of Geunyeli and Orta Keuy. Although we had the invaluable support of a spotter plane, it was a hair-raising job, blocking every column before it could make trouble over such a wide area, and only our mobility and excellent communications made it possible. At the height of the action Ben Wilson was heard to say, "Do you know this is better than a day's hunting in Leicestershire?" We were getting very tired indeed, there was no let-up in sight and the Greeks accused us of plotting the whole incident in advance with the Turks. The Governor ordered the Chief Justice of Cyprus to carry out an inquiry. So, while we continued day and night to protect each community from each other, we also had to appear before the commission and give evidence, being cross-questioned by no less than eight Greeks, three of them QCs. Our Counsel was the Deputy Director of Army Legal Services at GHQ, Middle East Land Forces, in the British Sovereign Base on the opposite side of the island and totally out of touch with events.

In the end British troops were cleared of wilfully exposing Greek Cypriots to a Turkish mob and the *Daily Telegraph* quoted the Chief Justice as saying, "There can be no doubt that were it not for the magnificent work carried out by the Royal Horse Guards, events in the Nicosia district would have been very dire indeed". Nevertheless, we were very bitter that it took until December for such a statement to be made and that at no time were the constant murders and attacks made by the Greeks on the Turks ever condemned by Sir Hugh Foot or by the Government. Morale among the soldiers was not much helped by the MP Barbara Castle who visited the island. She appeared generous in her praise for Greeks and seemed to criticize the Army, which greatly upset the Gordon Highlanders who had suffered many deaths in a forest fire which had been deliberately lit around them by EOKA.

Meanwhile we were now well aware that the word of any Greek was initially going to be considered more credible by our political masters than anything said by the Security Forces, so we carried out our duties in support of the Civil Power with much less enthusiasm.

If there is one thing at which the British excel that is the use of minimum force to accomplish their many strange duties in Aid of a Civil Power. I was ordered by a Brigadier to take my squadron and "teach a certain village a sharp lesson" because its women had thrown rocks at a Royal Artillery convoy. I hesitated, which annoyed the Brigadier, but there really is nothing in any training manual as to how this should be accomplished. So I decided on a show of force and some restriction of movement in and out of the village. Ben Wilson suggested he could handle the problem alone, and so, having encircled the village, I sent him in alone in a Landrover. He dismissed the car and sat down outside the coffee house in a deserted square. No doubt from behind every shuttered window a pair of eyes was watching him and eventually the coffee house owner came out. Ben lit a cigar and asked whether he might have the pleasure of the company of the priest, the school master and village headman. When they arrived, he ordered coffee and a glass of brandy for each of them and they sat around in silence for a while. Ben then, using the schoolmaster as an interpreter, began to tease them about their inability to control the women. Did they realize the ridicule this had brought upon them throughout the island? Were these men so impotent? After another brandy they were the best of friends and we were able to report that yet another punitive expedition had been successful.

Another example of the use of minimum force happened when women in a tiny village in the Troodos Mountains brought a column of trucks carrying Scottish soldiers to a halt by lying in the road. There must have been at least forty Greek girls, watched by an equal number of small children and old ladies dressed in black. There was not a man to be seen. The young platoon commander sized up the situation and consulted with his sergeant, while the Jocks, all wearing kilts, gathered round and no doubt made their own assessment. Clearly it was not going to be possible to drive over the women and to lift them out of the way might provoke a serious disturbance. There was nowhere to turn around and anyway that would lose British 'face'. Finally, to go back involved making a detour of at least thirty miles. Once again there was no military solution, but Sandhurst had encouraged him to use his initiative and consider every option. An old Jock with a somewhat depraved look about him and lots of ginger hair whispered to the rather shocked young officer what he reckoned those lassies needed and put forward his solution. Clutching at a straw, the platoon commander gave him strict orders not to touch a single one and sent him forward into the sea of prone women. He then began to perform a sort of sword dance over their prone bodies, leaving them in no doubt that he was deficient of one pair of underpants. He made great play of choosing the most attractive girl and, after dusting the ground beside her with his grubby handkerchief, he lay down beside her. There was a moment of complete silence, then a great wail from the women who were instantly on their feet and running back to their homes. The Jocks climbed aboard and moved on. Each side had made their point and once again minimum force had been used.

A little persuasion and shock tactics had to be used to get the villagers of Paliometacho to remove slogans from the walls after persistently refusing police requests to do so. We were ordered to mount an operation as soon as possible in order to re-establish the authority of the police in the village. I went to look at the offending slogans which were daubed on about six different walls. It really did not look the sort of task we should ever undertake and there was a very real danger that any action we took could quickly develop into a very different situation. However, I was told to think up a plan and get on with it. The key solution, I decided, was to get the job done before the village knew what was happening, but how on earth could we round up enough men to do the work without alerting the whole place? I had collected enough fire buckets, brushes and a runny tar substance to deal with each wall simultaneously and organized troops and police accordingly. We swooped in silently on a Saturday night right up to the village cinema, where as the local paper quoted "the Hero was just about to get his girl". Instead, the Security Forces got their men, sixty-two of them, and gave the order 'start scrubbing'. The projectionist was trapped because soldiers took his ladder to reach the higher slogans and one man was left half-shaved as the village barber was given a tar brush instead of a shaving brush. Ten minutes later we had finished and were withdrawing fast as the church bells were beginning to ring and the village became an angry hornets' nest. There were no more slogans and the Government seemed satisfied, but I really thought it was not necessary to misuse the army and risk confrontation over a few unpopular slogans.

The Blues were about to spend their third Christmas on the island and, as our return to England was in sight, I was prevailed upon to produce another pantomime. In fact, I loved doing so because it always was a good opportunity to make fun of the system, but not individuals. My first show had been in 1947, an Edwardian Music Hall in the canteen at Bovington Camp in Dorset. While we were at Wesendorf in Germany in 1949 I was helped by an excellent script writer, Corporal of Horse Fritz Freason. The production was "Robin Hood: A fearful tale of ye Sheriff of Wittingen's ceaseless struggle against ye couldn't care less outlaws of Shoneworde Forest". This really reflected the problems which the Regimental Provost NCO experienced with National Service young soldiers.

At the Staff College in Canada I produced "Off the Cuff", their first ever pantomime, in a magnificent new theatre. Three of the script writers became generals in the Canadian, Australian and United States' armies. Now I once again had the indispensable Fritz Freason in my squadron and we settled down to write a revue called "Watch Your Backs", because, with gunmen now free to travel around at will, thanks to the Governor's liberal attitude, we spent our time looking behind us. Among the skits was one called "It's all happened before" and showed a bunch of elderly Crusaders from St Hilarion Castle carrying out a roadblock on the Kyrenia road. Nothing was sacred among the acts, least of all three Corporal Majors as black-bearded Orthodox Priests who sang "Where will it be? Where will the Bishop's time-bomb be?", to the tune of "Where will the baby's dimple be?", they all looked like Archbishop Makarios with weapons under their black cassocks. Using the words and music of "We don't need this ole house no longer" two troopers discussed what to do with the twelve-seater latrine when we left the island, one of them, Trooper Lawson, became Regimental Corporal Major of the Household Cavalry Regiment in London before he retired in 1983. We gave a performance in Famagusta and were all set for our final performance on Boxing Day when a summons came to appear before the Governor at Government House on Christmas Eve. He had heard about the pantomime; it was much too late to tone down the script. We were horrified

166

at what sort of a reception we might get. In the event, it was a delightful evening and we were all made most welcome by Sir Hugh and Lady Foot.

On 18 May 1959, our son's fourth birthday, the Blues, after three years' active service in Cyprus, sailed into Southampton Water on the troop-ship *Devonshire*. Literally dozens of people came out in small boats to greet us as we entered the Solent. The quayside was lined with so many people, bands and no doubt HM Customs officers. It was such an emotional experience, exceeded only by our welcome at Windsor where the Pipes and Drums of our old friends the Irish Guards met the train. Then, headed by our Band and Julian Berry, Nicholas Nuttall and RCM Jock Neill, we marched through crowded streets with suntanned faces and our pride bursting through our battle dress. We turned down Peascod Street opposite the statue of Queen Victoria, whose life had been saved on Castle Hill by an Eton schoolboy G.S. Wilson, later to be killed commanding the Blues in 1914. We passed familiar landmarks and finally marched into Combermere Barracks. Did I really feel any different from when I first walked through those iron gates to enlist in 1943? True, I did now know the ropes, but I had no idea whether I still wished to remain a soldier. Everything would be so dull after Cyprus. Soldiering in England was certain to be frustrating and the possibility of Public Duties in London was to be avoided at all costs.

I had barely drunk my first gin and tonic in the Mess when I was asked if I would like to go back to Cyprus on the staff and be Brigade Major of an infantry brigade in Cyprus under Basil Eugster whom I greatly admired. Even if I had not had to consider Valerie's feelings, faced with that stark choice and the memories of the past few months, I had no wish to go back for a very long time, so I refused, firmly. There was no way in which I was ever going back to a situation in which military common-sense would continually have to be reconciled with political expediency. How naive I was; little did I realize that I would eventually spend the last five years of my military career in West Berlin and Hong Kong endeavouring to carry out precisely that delicate task.

Chapter Eleven

STICKS AND CARROTS

As the bronze ash tray, presented by the "Commando Brigata Alpina", crashed into the door behind me, I drew comfort from the fact that General Sir Richard Gale, Deputy Supreme Commander Allied Forces Europe (DSACEUR) was just peeved with the system which did not allow him to always travel in an RAF Comet and not with me personally. In 1960, as a major, I had been posted to be his Military Assistant at Supreme Headquarters Allied Powers Europe (SHAPE) which was then still located just north of Versailles outside Paris. There were several occasions when I had considered leaving the Army, but somehow I had always been offered, albeit unwittingly, a carrot of promotion or an interesting appointment such as this one, which encouraged me to soldier on.

'Windy' Gale was recalled from retirement when he was aged sixty-two, in order to take over from Field Marshal Montgomery. SHAPE had been activated on 2 April 1951 by General Dwight Eisenhower and the single-story building with eighteen wings had been constructed in eighteen months. When I arrived in November 1959 there were about 220 officers and slightly fewer soldiers, sailors and airmen from fourteen different nations. Only Iceland did not have a representative.

Windy Gale's arrival was welcomed because it brought to an end our isolation from the rest of the multi-national staff, which Montgomery had caused by placing only British officers in his office. Consequently, much of the work in SHAPE by-passed DSACEUR's office. Nobody dared to show the Field Marshal any new plan or proposal because he could not resist fiddling with it and changing it. Indeed the only major task his office was encouraged to carry out was to organize once a year a huge high-level tactical exercise without troops called SHAPEX. As the venerable and distinguished Generals gathered in the SHAPE lecture hall, and some of the Dutch and Danish ones were very old indeed, Monty would address them most sternly and recommend that if they wished to cough they should endeavour to get it over before his speech and the tactical presentations began. He then urged them to help themselves liberally to the efficacious cough sweets which his staff was about to pass around the hall.

Quite clearly his advice and salesmanship had either failed or not been appreciated. I found store cupboards full of revolting sticky throat pastilles. I cleared them all out with the rubbish, which I did not realize would automatically have to be put through the office secrets shredding machine and the Chief Clerk only just averted a mechanical disaster. Monty's other great disappointment was that he had failed to persuade the Officers' Restaurant to include cottage pie and rice pudding on the menu. It was generally acknowledged that it had been madness, when SHAPE was formed, to give management of finances to the French and of the restaurant to the British.

Windy Gale was a very different sort of person; on D Day in 1944 he had parachuted into Normandy in order to capture a vital bridge over the River Orne. He loved the French and enjoyed good wine, which had been an anathema to Monty. He was relaxed and gregarious and his office soon became multi-national and a port of call for anyone of any rank passing his door. He got on extremely well with SACEUR, United States Air Force General Larry Norstadt, a remarkable man of Norwegian descent who was much respected by the entire Headquarters. He decided that DSACEUR should be his proper deputy and not just concerned with Army matters and issued a clear directive to this effect. This brought DSACEUR's office into the main stream of events and made my work much more interesting.

Windy Gale worked in close harmony with the Naval Deputy, Admiral Barjot, who had commanded the French fleet in the Suez operation in 1956, and with the Air Deputy, General Leon Johnson, holder of the Congressional Medal of Honour, who had led the only wing of United States Flying Fortress bombers successfully to reach their targets in the famous raid on the Ploesti oil refineries in Romania in 1943.

Both Generals Norstadt and Gale lived in little châteaux in a leafy suburb of Paris at Marnes la Coquette. Their personal staff occasionally had to search for them through the gardens at weekends, when crises always seemed to occur. Baron Jan de Smeth, a Dutch Aide to a previous SACEUR, asked General Norstadt's wife whether she knew where her husband might be, because Washington wanted him to call urgently. She had no idea where he was, so Jan, trying to help, asked, "Might he perhaps, Madame, be in your bedroom?" to which the Southern lady drawled, "Well you can go and look, sonny, but he ain't been there for twenty years."

Most of the work at SHAPE was concerned with the threat which the numerically superior Warsaw Pact countries posed. What should the NATO strategy be, what forces should each country contribute and how on earth was it all going to be paid for? Even if an attack in central Europe could be held, it was the countries on the flanks who felt vulnerable, Denmark and Norway in the north and Turkey and Greece in the south.

Sir Richard Gale proposed an Allied Mobile Force (AMF), which could be flown quickly to the flanks of NATO, composed of many nations and known by some as 'Gale Force'. I pointed out that the smaller the force the greater the need for accurate intelligence and that the AMF needed an air-portable reconnaissance squadron such as only my regiment at Windsor could provide at the time. Such a unit was soon added to the AMF and suddenly the dull routine of being stationed at Windsor was made more exciting with a worthwhile overseas role.

Having declared an interest in NATO's remote flanks, I was able to arrange some fascinating tours for DSACEUR. In Turkey protocol dictated that, while in Ankara, we should lay a wreath at the tomb of Kemal Ataturk. I was told not to worry about the wreath because the British Military Attaché would provide it. The next morning there was no wreath at the hotel so the cavalcade of white-helmeted Turkish Military Police in Jeeps and motor cycles set off ahead of our staff car for the mausoleum, where again, to my dismay, there was no wreath. The General played for time and chatted to every soldier while I picked a few wild flowers from the verges. Eventually the Turkish officers suggested we moved on. I whispered reassuringly to the General, "Don't worry sir, I have picked a small bunch of flowers. After all it's the thought that counts."

He grunted and we passed slowly between lines of men from the three services, all Presenting Arms. As we walked up the steps to the President's tomb which also contained his huge Mercedes car, two Military Policemen came running up behind us carrying an immense wreath. I took it from them and thrust my flowers into it, before handing it to the General who muttered, "In the nick of time, or born on the vestry steps!"

Sitting on a red velvet sofa without safety belts, in an old Turkish Dakota transport plane, I looked down on the turgid waters of the Upper Euphrates and on the town of Erzurum which had once been the most eastern fortress of the Byzantine Empire. It was now headquarters of the

Third Turkish Army and guarding the south-eastern borders between NATO and the Soviet Union. Our aircraft was the first to land since winter had closed the airfield. As we taxied along the bumpy runway towards an immense reception committee the plane came to a sudden halt because the ground caved in and we ended up at a tilt 400 yards short. Undaunted, the Guard of Honour, Band, senior officers and red carpet all doubled a quarter of a mile to line up opposite our puddle and the welcome began with the Janissary Band in full cry. Windy Gale caught sight of a peculiar instrument in the band, a jingling Johnnie or glockenspiel, which reminded him to rush back into the plane to spend a penny before facing the music.

A demonstration of fire power and battle skills by the 26th Infantry Division had been arranged to take place in a mountain valley outside the city. What made it unusual was that citizens of Erzurum had decided to travel three miles on foot or in carts and trucks to watch the show with us. They listened intently to a briefing over loudspeakers about the battle plan, the effects of an atomic strike and a blunt address to the enemy in their mother tongue (Russian) to the effect that if they did not surrender quickly they would be skewered on the bayonets of the brave Turkish infantry.

Clutching glasses of hot goat's milk and cinnamon, Michel Bion, the French ADC, and I left the VIP tent and wandered around crowds who pulled our sleeves and pointed out every new event. Tanks attacked one behind the other along a narrow ridge, the infantry doubled up the next mountain and the artillery lifted to fire a couple of air bursts in the shape of a Turkish crescent. Thus the battle was won and, amid cheers and back-slapping, we retired to the warmth of the officers' club.

Chef des Escadrons Michel Bion was a cavalry officer and at the age of fifty-one he believed he was the oldest ADC in the world. In 1940 as a young officer during the retreat through the north of France, he had caught a German tank squadron refuelling from petrol bowsers, with their trousers down so to speak. It only took a moment for his Panhard armoured cars to set them alight before beating a hasty retreat. Sadly he then had to spend the next four years in a prisoner of war camp in Germany. We both agreed that Eastern Turkey was one of the few places in Europe where only a horseman using mark one eyeballs could carry out effective reconnaissance. Unfortunately American advisors, who only stayed a few months, insisted that US organizations should be followed to the letter and so Turkish cavalry regiments were disbanded. The sheer logistical problems of supporting just one 26-ton US tank on a mountain track were immense, let alone an armoured reconnaissance regiment. Turkish cavalry, fed on 2½ pounds of barley a day, had been able to carry out deep reconnaissance penetrations in 1916 which could never be achieved by US tanks. Indeed, the immobility conferred on the Turks by being obliged to accept tanks for this task has only been mitigated by the sheer physical fitness and determination of the Turkish conscript.

Four days by train from the austerity of Erzurum was the paradise of Istanbul and Headquarters of the 1st Turkish Army. The exits from the Black Sea have often been threatened in the past five hundred years by the Russians. When I went there a second time in 1961 with a different DSACEUR, General Sir Hugh Stockwell, we were shown an enormous coastal artillery gun on railway lines. It had been pushed out of its cave and sixteen men with numbers on their shirts were lined up beside the gun to explain their tasks. The General inspected the men, then took a careful look at the breech. "Krupps 1903," he snorted. "Why, that is the same year that I was born. We are both far too old for the next war. Push it into the sea." Fortunately only the Turkish General heard and he agreed with a hearty laugh.

On 16 September 1961 General Sir Richard Gale retired from the Army for a second time and bade us an emotional farewell at Villacoublay military airfield outside Paris. A few days before leaving he had paid a farewell call on the President of France, General de Gaulle. Windy Gale had just re-read the President's memoirs and was well aware of his determination to make France a great power again and to be acknowledged as such by the rest of NATO. The President hinted at a complete French withdrawal from the Alliance. He objected strongly to the American influence on NATO and rejected any idea of integration.

Sir Richard asked him what solution he proposed and he said that there should be only three major powers in NATO who would decide NATO policy in a worldwide context. When it was pointed out that this would be much resented by the other smaller nations who all had equal status in deciding NATO policy and were quite prepared to be integrated in order to fulfil the strategy, the President replied curtly, "You already know my views."

As we drove back to SHAPE through heavy Paris traffic he told me to make careful notes of the interview before he forgot. Within two years of that meeting France had withdrawn from NATO and SHAPE had been moved out of France into a disused coalmine at Mons in Belgium.

We were living at this time in a delightful old farmhouse in the village of Crespières about ten miles west of Versailles. We made lots of friends, including Philippe and Colette Daniel Dreyfus who lived in a small château in St Nom la Breteche. My son, Alexander, went to l'Ecole Communale in the village where all his written work was done on a slate. Every six months General Sir Hugh Stockwell, who had taken over as DSACEUR, gave a dinner party for the senior generals and members of the NATO Council. I had taken advantage of these occasions to form a dining club for all the aides de camp. Monsieur Bertholet, who was patron of L'Auberge qui Chante, the village restaurant, would excel himself with whole roast pigeons in pastry and his own selection of Burgundy wines. The international significance of the event was not lost on the villagers who trooped in to inspect the table setting with its many flags and red, white and blue flowers. The 'Garde Champêtre', who normally settled grazing disputes, would put on his police 'kepi', his only item of uniform, and supervise the car parking in the village street. Although we were only twenty-five miles from the centre of Paris, there were still old people in the village who had never been into Paris and some very simple girls. There was panic one morning before the dinner when the only waitress was seen walking through the village carrying a newborn babe still joined by the umbilical cord. She had been picking potatoes with her brothers when this unexpected event occurred and they fled leaving her to walk back.

We were made very welcome by the village and even the garbage collectors left a smart card: "*Les Eboueurs de Crespières vous presentent leurs meilleurs voeux pour la nouvelle année.*" Woe betide us if we had forgotten the tip or to open a bottle of Calvados.

Whenever I got the chance I tried to accompany DSACEUR on his travels around Europe even though it meant a lot of work writing up the notes afterwards. In Germany one of the current problems was what sort of hair-net to issue to longhaired youths conscripted into the Bundeswehr. In Belgium it was the language issue, how to establish equal career opportunities between the French-speaking Walloons and the Flemish. I was surprised to discover that there were not just two languages spoken in the Belgian Army, but three, because the Chasseurs Ardennais had two companies of German-speakers.

In the Grand Duchy of Luxembourg the whole army was on parade in their barracks at Diekirch, a fine battalion whose predecessors had put up a brief but brave resistance to the German panzer divisions in 1940. Many men had Korean War decorations, having fought as part of the Belgian battalion with the United Nations. Before leaving we called on the Grand Duke who was also Colonel of the Irish Guards. The palace grand staircase was smothered in the most beautiful azaleas in bloom presented by the public in celebration of his birthday.

In Northern Italy we spent a week with the Tridentina Alpini soldiers whose techniques of rock-climbing and fighting in those high mountains were quite new to me. I had no idea how much longer it took to cover small distances. There was a particular problem in that all Italy's northern borders faced neutral countries whose ability to withstand sudden aggression by the Warsaw Pact countries was uncertain and whose neutrality precluded any exchange of ideas between them and NATO commanders. The Savoia Cavalry Regiment in Bressanone had the task of providing a covering force, but their equipment was already twenty-five years old. They had carried out one of the last cavalry charges in history when they escaped through Russian forces which had encircled them near Stalingrad in 1943. A scrapbook in their museum showed lines of horsemen in a dried-up river bed wearing steel helmets with sabres drawn, just before the final charge. I was glad to see that the 2nd Mountain Artillery regiment still had a number of pack horses and mules which carried their collapsible mountain guns.

Visits to SHAPE by international leaders such as Chancellor Konrad Adenauer brought home to me the intricacies of protocol which years later seemed to impinge even on the simplest ceremonies in my life. The Head of Protocol was an Italian Admiral, Longanesi Catani, a charming and courteous gentleman who had thrice been awarded Italy's highest decoration for bravery. His most notable exploit was to penetrate the defences of Alexandria harbour in a midget submarine and sink a British battleship at anchor. Among the younger visitors to SHAPE was Edward Kennedy, younger brother of the President of the United States, who had just been to Warsaw. Unfortunately his behaviour and the statements he made gave the impression that he was still a trifle immature. He revealed, incidentally, that he had once been a military policeman, a "snowdrop" on duty at the main gate to SHAPE.

When Vice President Lyndon Johnson came in 1962 I went with DSACEUR to the airport to meet him. General Sir Hugh Stockwell then accompanied him for the rest of the day and to lunch in the officers' restaurant. As he walked out of the dining room afterwards with Sir Hugh beside him, two American security men closed in on the Vice President and inexplicably decided to manhandle DSACEUR aside. Sir Hugh, who was in uniform, was furious and swung a punch into the nearest man's tummy who bent double and whose pistol fell out of its shoulder holster, saying, "Don't you ever dare to handle a British officer in uniform like that again." The Vice President appeared unconcerned, but the CIA men, I am sure, understood and kept well back.

Sir Hugh was anxious to employ some British Military Policewomen at SHAPE and in particular at his special entrance. The first time these good-looking girls drove down the Champs Elysées in an open Landrover wearing their red caps they brought traffic practically to a standstill. One unexpectedly cold November morning Sir Hugh acknowledged the girl's salute as we went into the building and added cheerfully, "Well Corporal, winter draws on."

She blushed as red as her cap and replied, "Not today, Sir."

Sir Hugh disliked paper work and spent even less time in his office than his predecessor. The Press described him once as being "the finest tiddly winks player in the Army". He must have been the only four-star British general never to have been through any Staff College. He had commanded the Royal Welch Fusiliers in Norway in 1940, his brigade captured Madagascar from the Vichy French, then he commanded a brigade in Burma in 1945 and more recently he had endured the frustration and political interference of commanding the ground forces in the Suez operation in 1956.

I only had to point to a map and say, "I bet no general from SHAPE has ever been there," for him to say, "If you can set it up, Roy, I will go."

Naturally the first place to which he wished to return was Pothous in Norway where his regiment and the remnants of the Irish Guards fought a difficult rearguard battle in 1940. Having hidden in a slit trench, and fearing his position was being given away by a mooing cow whose udders were heavy with milk, he enticed her closer and milked her into his steel helmet. But as their retreat continued the cow followed him all the way to Narvik.

The most fascinating part of our tour of inspection was at Kirkenes in Finnmark, where Norway shares 196 miles of frontier with the Soviet Union. It was depressing to see the same Russian watchtowers, wire fences, searchlights and swathes of earth devoid of all vegetation that I had already seen across Central Europe and in Eastern Turkey, an area where for hundreds of years there had been no restrictions whatsoever on travel. In 1920 part of this area was transferred to the newly independent nation of Finland, including the ice-free iron ore port of Petsamo. The Russians, however, annexed the whole region in 1945 and the border between them and Norway then became the deepest channel in the River Pasvikelv which is always shifting and thus gives the Russians a reason to make difficulties.

Like the Italians, the Norwegians have retained a few horses for resupply in the mountains using fjord ponies who will refuse to walk on snow unless they have each hoof strapped in a leather cup attached to a small snow shoe. There is an elite Norwegian unit which spends many weeks on patrol on the border. Each soldier proudly carries a Lapp Knife strapped to his calf boots. It is difficult to live at Latitude 70, where the sun never sets from May to July and where there is perpetual darkness from November to January. Eating every meal in darkness had a strange effect on me and I began to lose all sense of time. There seemed little for the population to do in the winter darkness and I suppose it's no wonder 40% of the population is under the age of fifteen.

The last night of our visit was marked with a dinner given by local civic dignitaries and Norwegian officers, an all-male occasion. Suddenly the door opened and, instead of the usual male steward, a blonde waitress in her forties came in. Having encountered perpetual darkness for the first time and having not seen a woman for days she was a sensation. As she bent forward to place a plate of reindeer meat and sweet potatoes before me she blew softly in my ear which nearly gave me convulsions. When I returned a year later I was saddened but not surprised to learn that she had gone off with an American jazz trumpet player.

On our way back we visited Danish defence installations. The big NATO problem with Denmark was how to secure and mine the exits from the Baltic before Russian air and sea invasion could seize them. We were told we would stay one night on the island of Langland at Traeneker Castle, home of Count Ahlefeld, who had once been looked after by the same nannie as Valerie. Sir Richard Gale had bought an enormous bunch of flowers in Copenhagen for his hostess. He gave them to me to look after when we boarded a Fast Torpedo Boat and I had to stand on deck for the crossing. The wind and rain began to shred the flowers and so I placed them inside a torpedo tube. Sadly when the flowers were presented to our charming hostess they looked very bedraggled. The castle was built of pink stone on top of the only high ground on the narrow island. The walls of some rooms were covered in Venetian leather which expanded and contracted according to the humidity. On the floor of one room lay a simply magnificent carpet. When I asked about it, I was told it had been a gift from the Shah of Iran who stayed for one night after his abdication.

Every night while we were on tour I would write up my notes, draft DSACEUR's thankyou letters and make a list of the requests he had received and the promises he had made. Sometimes there were hitches in the programme which gave me time to catch up with my report. One such occasion occurred when the American helicopter carrying DSACEUR was forced down by very heavy snow near the Czechoslovak border. We prevailed upon the pilot to come down near a tiny village on the German side of the frontier. We struck out through the snow towards the only Gasthaus I could see, whose owner happened to be a lonely widow. Seated in the warmth of her kitchen clutching glasses of Weinbrandt, we began to thaw out. The widow took a great fancy to General Sir Hugh, snuggled up to him on the bench and let him know with a dig from her elbow "*Ich bin eine lustige Witwe*," which drove the poor fellow out into the snow to await our rescue transport.

Although there were some nations in NATO who had fought each other and were now prepared to forgive, there was a marked reluctance to co-operate between two NATO allies, Greece and Turkey. We were taken on a remarkable tour by the Greeks of the frontiers with Albania, Yugoslavia, Bulgaria and Turkey. Bulgaria had sufficient forces either to cut through Greece to reach Kavalla on the Mediterranean, or to capture Turkish Thrace, but not if Greece and Turkey coordinated their battle plans. Sir Hugh asked the Greek general if he had ever spoken to his Turkish counterpart. He said he had not. Sir Hugh then asked a terrified Greek soldier to walk across the frontier bridge near Alexandroupolis with a field telephone and connect it to the Turkish Military exchange. He then suggested that the Greek general should invite the Turkish general to a meeting in, say, a month's time. An initiative which succeeded.

Our wives had been allowed to accompany us to Greece and the party included Joan Stockwell and Franny Wilkinson, wife of the American political advisor to General Norstadt. After following a separate tour, we rejoined our wives in Athens at the end of the tour. In the rush to get the baggage out to the RAF plane, overzealous staff had closed the lids of our suitcases, leaving Valerie still sunbathing in her bikini on the balcony. We smuggled her out of the hotel wrapped in a raincoat and on to the aircraft where she did a rapid change just in time to join the ceremony and farewell reception given by our kind Greek hosts in the VIP lounge.

On my return to Paris we attended a special opera performance hosted by the President, General de Gaulle, in honour of the Shah and Empress of Iran. The settings were memorable, *Les Fleurs* and *Les Incas*, but the music was confusing.

In 1962 I heard that I was soon to be posted, so I went to Vienna to ask an old friend in the British Embassy, Edward Sniders, as to whether it was time to change my career. It was not, but he took me to the Volks Oper where Adele Leigh was the lead in *The Gipsy Princess*, a wonderful evening and we had supper with her afterwards.

My sadness at leaving SHAPE in 1962 was mitigated by being sent on a six-month course at the Joint Services Staff College in Latimer. This was an excellent course for officers of the three services, police, civil servants and several officers from the Commonwealth, to learn about each other and co-operation at all levels. Among the students was an ambitious and articulate twenty-seven-year-old Nigerian major called Emeka Ojukwu. He told me that unless he was made an ambassador or a general at the end of the course he would be very disenchanted with his government. Needless to say he was not promoted and a few months after his return to Nigeria he appointed himself President of Biafra and started a bitter civil war which he lost and fled to Guinea.

Before leaving Latimer I was able to produce a pantomime called "Outward Bound" which made fun of our tri-service traditions and procedures. There was a lot of talent, especially among the Royal Navy officers. We wrote and organized the show in just ten days. It was great fun, at any rate for the cast!

Resigned to returning to command a squadron of armoured cars in Germany, I was then delighted to learn that I was to be promoted to command three hundred horses in the Household Cavalry Regiment at Hyde Park Barracks. Now, at the age of thirty-seven, I really had to learn to ride. I was determined to follow a recruits' equitation course and pass out of riding school just like any other trooper. So, as Commanding Officer, I started a grim twenty-week course, beginning at the crack of dawn, in the riding school. The only concession made was that it was my horse which got ticked off, not me, with remarks such as "I said half sections left *not* right, Black Beauty". The last four weeks were spent getting accustomed to riding in a helmet, cuirasse, gauntlets, buckskin breeches, jack-boots and carrying a drawn sword. Of these it was the helmet which could cause the greatest discomfort.

The first Hyde Park Barracks had been built in 1795 on a narrow site beside the Royal Park. It was pulled down in 1876 and the barracks I inherited had been occupied since 1880. It now fell well below modern standards. Originally there was no mess hall for the men who ate on six-foot tables in their barrack rooms; the meals had to be collected from distant kitchens in hay boxes. The rooms were built to sleep thirty men, including those with wives who initially had been expected to sleep behind a curtain of army blankets at the far end. In about 1946 a kitchen and mess hall were built into the attic on the third floor. This was reached via slippery outside iron stairs. There was no heating except from an ancient cast iron stove and the warmth which rose up from horses in the stables below in the yard. Sanitation was awful until a disused stable in the yard was converted into 'the ablutions'. However, with a lot of help from David Tabor, now Colonel of the Household Cavalry, we persuaded the War Minister, Mr John Profumo, and Miss Jennie Lee from the Opposition to inspect the barracks. Unfortunately it was a fine day and the place was looking quite pleasant. However, with soldiers pouring buckets of water down the iron stairs and spreading the manure and horses' bedding out to dry more liberally than usual, we got both sides of the House to agree to a new barracks. It was pulled down in September 1965 and replaced by the present modern barracks with its controversial tower block designed by Sir Basil Spence.

Soon after Valerie and I had moved into a flat above the old officers' house, we acquired Daffodil, a miniature Pekinese not much bigger than a Drum Horse's hairy hoof. She soon lost an eye to a stable cat but after that she learnt to look after herself. An animal with tremendous courage and intelligence, she would always run ahead of me as I walked around barracks. Troopers would warn their less alert colleagues with the cry, "Eyes down, 'ere comes Daffodil!"

It was from then on that I was known as Colonel Daffodil and even, so I am told, as 'General Daffodil Sahib', many years later, by some Gurkhas.

When the State Visit of the King and Queen of Greece took place the Sovereign's Escort was provided by the Royal Horse Guards under the command of Ben Wilson. There was a certain amount of hostility to them from Greeks in London. I inspected the Escort lined up in barracks and, last of all, took a close look at Ben. There was a huge bulge under his sheepskin which covered a large leather holster precariously carrying his own long-barrelled luger pistol, which might fall out any moment at a trot. I asked how he hoped to dispose of his sword and take off his gauntlet if he ever wished to use the weapon. We had no time to resaddle the horse but were just able to secure the gun with string. Needless to say, firearms were never carried.

Ben created another stir when an attractive nightclub hostess arrived at the barracks in Knightsbridge with a bundle of five pound notes and asked if she could buy Major Wilson's horse, Joe. The guard were suspicious at seeing so much cash, the police were called to check if it had been stolen and they accepted that it had all been well-earned. However, the Army, she was told, could not just sell off their horses to people off the street. She returned four days later, clutching more bank notes, having discovered that the hunter was Ben's private property. The unexpected publicity had revealed Ben's address to his creditors who began to close in. Ben was only too happy to accept her £350!

The stage management of ceremonial occasions in London is preceded by much detailed planning very similar to that of a gigantic stage production. The script or order of events and commands is memorized, the costumes or uniforms for each player have to been clean and correct in every detail, fanfares and music selected, cues and timings understood and tested. The choreography or drill movements, normally related to fixed marks on the stage floor, become traffic islands, manhole covers and lamp posts which must all be checked the night before a parade to ensure that the Borough Council have not moved them. All props such as carriages, microphones, red carpets, colours and standards are prepared; then there have to be understudies, vets and horse ambulances, technicians and police and, of course, the audience must be controlled and programmes sold.

The only aspects different from the theatre is that there is no prompter for the officer on centre stage who might also be riding an unpredictable charger, no lighting script because the show is at the mercy of the weather and there are never any curtain calls or rave reviews in the newspapers, only photographs of the man who fainted or dropped his musket. The British public take the precision and dignity of these great State Ceremonial events for granted and perhaps that is the way it should be.

After two years in command at Knightsbridge I was told I was to command the Royal Horse Guards (The Blues), an armoured car regiment stationed in Germany. It was twenty-one years since I had joined the regiment as a trooper and both I and the Army had changed since then. Did I really want to go back to that depressing North German plain? Perhaps I should consider it was time to change career. Our second son, Robin, had been born in the Military Maternity Hospital at Woolwich. We had already moved home eight times in ten years of married life, and my parents had given up all hope of ever returning to Romania. They had settled with my grandmother, Gui, who still spoke no English, at Rye in Sussex. Perhaps the time had come to stop wandering.

I sat down to think things over with Daffodil on my lap. From the bathroom I heard my son, Alexander, ask, "Mummy, when Daddy dies, do you think I can have his sword and helmet?"

Suddenly the telephone rang, an officer just back from the Regiment in Germany enquired, "Colonel, we were wondering whether you would be prepared to produce a pantomime next Christmas, and if so, we hoped you might persuade the Band to come out?" A pantomime with a band, now that was a challenge I could not refuse!

Soldiering in the British Army of the Rhine BAOR had become a serious and competitive business, which was a pity. There were many senior officers who quite rightly expected very high standards from their brigades and divisions and were only too keen to test their new tactical concepts and theories on how to hold up the overwhelming Warsaw Pact tank forces should they ever cross the border and head for the River Rhine. The Queen's Royal Irish Hussars' and the Royal Horse Guards' mission was to provide a Covering Force from the moment the border was crossed by the Russians. One of the commanding officers was half-Greek and the other half-Romanian!

I was fortunate to have as my second-in-command Dennis Daly, whose abundant commonsense and cheerful encouragement was just what I needed. He and his wife did much to sustain the 'regimental family'.

Every few months SACEUR tested the readiness of his forces by issuing a code word which meant that every unit from every nation had to load up all its vehicles as for war and be out of its peacetime location within two hours of receiving the message. It is a measure of the efficiency of Rhine Army that this was always achieved, well most always.

A few weeks before I took over there had been a NATO alert at 1130 pm. The Duty Officer in the Blues was Captain Simon Crisp, who received the dreaded code word "Quick Train" from Corps Headquarters on the telephone and returned somewhat mystified to his bottle of port, having passed the message on to nobody. The following morning the Commanding Officer, Harry Hopkinson, noticed that the garrison town of Herford was empty of troops. His suspicions were increased when he saw, parked in a sidestreet opposite his barrack gates, the Russian Military Mission (SOXMIS) car with its occupants sound asleep. They had been waiting all night to follow the regiment to its new battle locations. He persuaded the Russians that they were wasting their time and to go away. He then raised his regiment and got them moving in thirty minutes, reporting to Headquarters that he had terrible radio transmission problems.

During the next eighteen months we served under Brigadier Mat Abraham who really knew the art of ground reconnaissance. He had served in the 12th Lancers in North Africa in 1942–43 and been awarded the Military Cross twice. His particular hobbyhorse was keeping binocular eye-pieces dry and how to maintain an unbroken covering force against a diagonal enemy thrust. The exercises he set us were always interesting and covered great distances.

Eventually we returned to Windsor once again and exchanged our comfortable German married quarters with central heating and big rooms for the frugal discomfort of the British equivalent military housing. Naturally, before leaving Germany there was another pantomime which I recall began outside the barrack gates, with the Regimental Corporal Major, Bill Stringer, and myself both half-asleep in wheelchairs, dressed in Russian uniforms, bemoaning the state of a regiment which could not even bother to get out of bed when SACEUR had taken all that trouble to press the alarm button.

After I gave up command of the Blues in 1967 I was appointed to be in charge of a department in the Adjutant General's Branch called PS12 in the Ministry of Defence. I asked how many soldiers I would have under command and was told not one. I was to concern myself with all cere-monial events in Britain and British military participation overseas in events such as trade weeks and tours by units such as the King's Troop and Bands. I was expected to notify families about casualties in places like Aden, argue the case for umbrellas for women soldiers, look after the interests of military bands and process the new titles and uniforms of regiments being amalgamated.

In despair I formed up to Major General Basil Eugster, GOC London District, and complained that I had been a reconnaissance officer all my life and that this was a job which had always been specially suited to a Foot Guard. He let me go on and then said, "Roy, I did that awful job once. You jolly well now do it."

Ten years later, when I heard I was to be Commander British Forces in Hong Kong (an appointment he had once held), I passed him again in the Burlington Arcade and he paused just for a moment to say, "I told you, Roy, that job would not do you any harm!" and he walked on.

After a miserable eleven months an unexpected death resulted in my promotion to Colonel and immediate dispatch to be Chief of Staff to Major General Chandos Blair who commanded the Second Division at Lubbecke in Germany. He was a delightful person to work for and even the most difficult military operations like withdrawing tanks and troops at night over the fast-flowing River Weser became a great adventure and really tested everyone. In winter Chan flooded the tennis courts outside the officers' mess and, with his little band of Scottish drivers, batman and clerk, challenged all-comers to curling matches.

In 1970 I was made responsible for all the tank and armoured car regiments located in Britain which formed part of the Third Division. These included the Scots Greys (Micky Blacklock), the Blues and Royals (Bill Boucher), the Royal Hussars (Clive Robertson) and the 14/20th Hussars (Mike Palmer). My headquarters was in Tidworth, a garrison whose streets and buildings resounded with Indian names. Our home was in Zouch Manor, a house supposedly haunted by a headless drummer boy. It had a wonderful walled garden full of vegetables and fruit, and beneath the chestnut trees the garden was full of yellow aconites, hedgehogs and squirrels. I was once lucky enough to find an ancient hand axe buried in the lawn.

Tidworth has a magnificent small arena in which the last military tattoo had been held about thirty-five years earlier. I was determined to stage another, and having discovered an old plan of the underground lighting circuit, I got Aubrey Jackman who ran the Lansdowne Hotel in Bath to produce a tattoo mainly from our own resources, which was attended by thousands of people and paid for itself. Sadly after two years when I left Tidworth, my successors discontinued the tattoos.

The Tidworth Three Day event, which Major Christopher Ross who worked in my Headquarters ran in his spare time, was another popular and very successful activity, which also ceased when I left. I tried hard to turn Tidworth House into a club and interviewed six married couples in order to find a manager and cook. There was one outstanding pair whom the selection committee preferred and I said we would telephone the successful applicants that evening. This was duly done and after a lady's voice answered, I said, "Mrs Smith, it was such a pleasure meeting you and your husband today at Tidworth House. I have good news for you."

There was a gasp from the other end and a hysterical voice cried, "I have never been in Tidworth House in my life."

Her husband had foolishly given us the wrong number to ring. His plan to disappear from home with his mistress failed and we lost a most promising club manager!

There were several interesting NATO exercises in which Britain had a role both in Denmark and in Northern Norway. I was able to visit the Allied Mobile Force deployed and to judge the effectiveness of the airportable reconnaissance squadron in the snow. The white camouflage nets belonging to units assigned to that role must have been used at countless Christmas parties in gymnasiums ever since.

In 1973 I was selected to attend the National Defence College of Canada, which meant a return to Kingston, Ontario, and indeed to Fort

Frontenac. This was a year-long course attended by senior officers from the Canadian Defence Forces, civil servants and businessmen. The British sent a sailor, a soldier, an airman and a diplomat, as did the Americans. Many senior Canadians had had very little opportunity to travel or study the political and military geography of the rest of the world. There may indeed have been almost too much travel on the course for some of them to absorb, but to me it was a fascinating year and I was able to take Valerie round the High Arctic, to Resolute, Baffin Island and Inuvik, quite apart from visiting every Canadian province, including the North-West Territories and the Yukon. One tour was to study the Colonial legacy left by Portugal in Brazil, Spain in Colombia and Britain in Guyana. Another took us round the world, Alaska, Japan, Malaysia, Singapore, Indonesia, India, Kenya and Cameroon. Before each trip we listened to lectures about the problems of each country and on our return we had to produce papers and make presentations.

During a trip to Israel a few of us met that remarkable lady, Prime Minister Mrs Golda Meir, and then, after calling in on the United Nations Command in Cyprus, we went to Egypt where the Suez Canal was under observation by Swedish troops of the United Nations. I went full of admiration for the achievements of Israel, a tiny country surrounded by hostile neighbours, but much of this sympathy vanished as we learnt more. We were furthermore upset when after a long day on the Golan Heights the rabbis came round the hotel to make sure we had not ordered any hot dishes. When we arrived in Egypt their officers told some whopping untruths. They knew we did not believe a word, but they were so friendly and relaxed that by the time we left our sympathies were all with the Egyptians!

This was followed by a tour of Eastern Europe which included my first return to Romania after leaving the country at the start of the Second World War thirty-five years earlier. As in every other Communist country we visited, the Romanians had a programme of briefings by military and government officials which included visits to industrial installations, dams and collective farms. It was with relief that I was able to excuse myself to the Canadian Directing Staff and, accompanied by a Canadian Admiral, Andy Fulton, hired a big black car which came with two guardians, a driver and a charming female interpreter.

We drove first to Cimpina to see the home of Nicolae Grigorescu, an impressionist painter whose work captures all that I associate with old Romania, shepherds surrounded by tall green grass and wild flowers, beautiful sloe-eyed girls with shawls around their heads, teams of glistening oxen dragging wooden carts and lines of huddled Turkish prisoners. We then drove the short distance to Doftana, where, instead of heading for the old prison and shrine to Communism, I asked whether we could look at my old home. From the top of the dusty road which winds down into the Doftana river valley I had spotted the house amongst tall pine trees on the hill beyond the river. There too was the lush green water meadow where the gypsies had always made camp before the Communist State decreed that they were no longer free to be nomads. We crossed the long narrow bridge over the River Doftana and drove through wooden gates, up the drive past timber huts which now stood where the lawns had once been, and then up to the house, which seemed unchanged.

A friendly custodian greeted me with surprise and explained that Doftana had become a holiday home for the children of railway workers. She offered to show us round and I wondered whether it would be foolish to mention the guns I had greased up and hidden in the eaves of the attic for my father so long ago. The rooms all seemed to be much smaller than I remembered and when she opened the door to the attic, opposite my old bedroom, I could see that there had been an important change.

"Oh, you seem to have put on a new roof," I said, looking at the hideous sheets of corrugated iron. "Do tell me, what happened?"

"Oh, we had such a terrible storm five years ago which, because the house was already weakened by the earthquakes, took off most of the roof," she replied. I wondered if the guns had been discovered.

"There used to be such a wonderful collection of objects in this place," I volunteered hesitantly, and she continued, "Oh yes, the Gendarmes came and took away some very strange packages." There was, she admitted, still some of the original furniture in her bedroom, but the beautifully carved sideboard, chairs and dining table made from railway sleepers had been removed to the Folk Museum in Ploesti.

As we turned to leave the attic I glanced above the door and noticed a small shelf with a candle stub on it and remembered, "Why that's where Florica put her knickers before making my bed." I crossed the landing and went into what had been my bedroom. The window was open so I looked out. Yes, there was the sloping roof. The door to Florica's room in the white cottage was still ajar and there was that friendly walnut tree which I had slid down on that balmy night so long ago.

I left glad that Doftana was still a happy place and being well cared for within limited resources. It was late afternoon as we drove slowly back to Bucharest, past fields of maize and yellow sunflowers and a few oil wells which seemed to have given up trying to extract the last dregs from an exhausted oil field.

When I got back to my hotel room I was surprised to find a knotted brown handkerchief in my wardrobe, which I felt quite sure had not been there that morning. I took it out, untied the knot and was astonished to find inside a wad of crisp Romanian bank notes. Taking money in and out of any Communist country has always been a well-documented process and any suspicion that I might have come by this sum by exchanging dollars or selling a pair of shoes could have placed me in very serious difficulty. I had been quite ready for a knock on the door in the middle of the night and to be confronted by a beautiful naked girl, closely followed by police and sinister men in leather jackets with flash cameras. The theory held by the KGB, and probably MI 5 too, was that, when blackmailed with such photographic evidence, Englishmen, and only the English, would be prepared to betray their country rather than let their wives or members of their Club know the awful truth about a night behind the Iron Curtain. They never for one moment tried to blackmail a Frenchman or an Italian, for example.

My Canadian friends gathered around a bottle of Canadian Rye whisky to decide what I should do with the bank notes. Could it be that my departure from the set programme had prompted the Secret Police to set a trap, working on the assumption that there must be somebody who knew this large sum of money was in my room, then no matter what I did I would be in difficulties? If I bought an expensive carpet, I would be asked to show money exchange receipts. If I flushed the money down the water closet there might be provision in the plumbing for its interception. If I burnt the money the ashes had to be put somewhere, and if I did nothing then the authorities might get bored with waiting and 'discover' the money in my room. We decided to act quickly. We put the money back into the handkerchief and returned it to exactly where I had found it and then jammed the door with a tiny wedge cut from the back of a drawer, so that it remained firmly shut. The hotel management were requested to open the jammed cupboard door so that I could use the space. This was achieved by a carpenter, an interpreter, a security man and the manager.

"Goodness gracious! What on earth is that?" we asked as the cupboard door opened. We asked them to remove the handkerchief and untie the knot. The manager was asked to count the money on the table in front of five witnesses and provide a receipt which I still have. It had been a close call.

There was a gap of five months after my return from Canada while the Military Secretary's office decided what to do with me. This was very demoralizing because, not knowing where we would eventually be living and not having a home of our own, our possessions went into store and we lived in an awful block of army flats in which the bedroom was just twelve feet from the South Circular Road in Putney. I was given various studies to complete and Courts of Enquiry to chair about costly disasters.

A particularly unpleasant man from the security services called to find out more about the incident in Romania and asked us what debts we had, whether we had paid for our car and television set, how much did we drink, did we gamble, listen to Radio Moscow, did I have any friends overseas, did I or Valerie belong to Corin and Vanessa Redgrave's Workers Revolutionary Party?

Valerie was as deeply hurt, as I was, at this crude bullying performance and I was on the verge of resigning. However, soon afterwards I was very happy to be appointed Commandant of the Royal Armoured Corps Centre at Bovington and Lulworth. Dorset was familiar ground because Valerie had been brought up in East Lulworth during the war and I had been at school in Sherborne. Apart from containing all the armoured training schools and the most comprehensive Tank Museum in the world, for the first time I now was responsible for vast stretches of unspoilt countryside including four miles of seashore. It seemed that all senior military visitors to the United Kingdom whom the Ministry of Defence did not know what to do with were sent to the RAC Centre; these included the United States Secretary for Defence, James R. Schlesinger, who was so interested that he stayed an extra four hours.

There were two achievements which gave me great pleasure. The first was providing a swimming pool for the Officers' Mess. A young officer had pointed out that there was an incredible bargain offer only open for three weeks until 1 January 1975 costing only £15,000. Naturally we had no funds but I had discovered that the mess had over £30,000 of good wines in bond. The price of each bottle was already far beyond the resources of most officers and they reflected many years of work by a dedicated Mess Secretary who was in despair when I directed that half the stock should be sold. After engineers and an architect had checked the suitability of the site between two wings of the mess, we ordered the pool and wrote to General Sir George Cooper whose headquarters was in Taunton telling his staff our plans. After six weeks a charming reply came saying what a splendid idea but we must on no account start work until the Department of the Environment had given their approval, which might take many months. Well by then the water was already flowing in, so I thanked them for their helpful letter and said nothing. The pool was completed when the Chief of Defence Staff, Field Marshal Sir Michael Carver, came to unveil a portrait of himself in the Mess. He much admired the pool and I knew that we need not worry about Taunton any more. To this day the pool continues to provide pleasure to Mess members and their families. We gave a farewell dinner on his retirement to the Mess Secretary who had built up the huge wine cellar. Sadly he died that night.

My second lasting achievement was to preside over the creation of footpaths across the ranges which had been closed to the public for over fifty years. I was told to form a working party to decide the best way to complete a missing link in the West Country coastal path which runs for 510 miles. This meant opening up the area between Lulworth Cove and Kimmeridge Bay and giving public access to Tyneham village and Worbarrow Bay. The area was and still is of exceptional interest to ecologists, botanists and naturalists, but there was also the constant problem of dangerous unexploded shells.

I let it be known in the press what I was trying to achieve and was taken aback by the number of different groups, all with conflicting interests, who insisted on having a say in our decisions. I refused to have a public meeting but agreed to meet every single one of them individually and listen to their ideas. It was soon apparent that they nearly all had tunnel vision focused solely on their own aims to the exclusion of anybody else's needs.

For instance one group wanted the path to follow the exact line of the cliff tops, but the bird watchers said this would upset sea birds nesting below. Geologists wanted the fossil forest avoided, archaeologists wanted the path to avoid the iron age hill fort, others wanted there to be access for caravans and tents and so on. But there was always something they said which I felt sure we could incorporate, whilst the other ideas we would consider. I promised to let them all have early copies of our minutes and decisions, and if there was no comment received within 48 hours we would go ahead. This formula worked well and with the necessary help from the Government to pay wardens, with no camping or fires allowed, no stalls allowed to sell anything, no motorcycles or horses on the paths, we opened a route across one of Dorset's most beautiful areas, which had been left totally unspoilt by farmers or modern developers. I was delighted when a magazine whose editor, Rodney Legg, had been a constant critic of the Army, was generous enough to say in his editorial under the heading "In Redgrave Park":

"The virtual conversion of a major army range from a weekday training ground into a weekend public park has been masterminded by Brigadier Redgrave. He has coped successfully with balancing traditional military activities and new mass access plans.

"Redgrave who deserves 'Public Relations Officer of the Year Award' for his achievement leaves Bovington in November." And so it was to be. All good things had to come to an end but I was taken completely by surprise to be told that my next posting was to be that stimulating and exciting city, Berlin.

Chapter Twelve

THE UGLY WALL

She really was a lovely girl but her story had been just a little too glib for my friend, a British intelligence officer in West Berlin. He was suspicious too that she had known exactly where to find him. She had made him an offer which in those days was a dream package. She had a lover, a Russian signals Captain at Army Headquarters, who would provide us with intelligence for one year in return for asylum and a new life in the West for them both.

The British told her to come back in a week while they thought about it. Having already been rejected by the French, she made her way to the Americans who promptly believed every word without checking it out. They then provided her with money, a list of subjects in which they were interested, codes and the address of a 'safe house' in West Berlin. Three months later the French arrested her on firm evidence that she was working for the KGB.

I called on the French Garrison Headquarters during one of my regular trips from Rhine Army Headquarters because I was curious to know what had happened to the lovely spy and asked a charming captain in the Chasseurs Alpins. He opened the door into his outer office where I saw her sitting behind an old Remington typewriter, her long legs sheathed in apricot-coloured nylon stockings from the US Post Exchange shop.

"Zee Americans were not very 'appy. I am now looking after her very carefully, how do you say, day and night," he whispered and closed the door. Sex and intelligence work were then typical of life in divided Berlin.

Twenty-five years later, in November 1975, I became the British Commandant Berlin. When news of my appointment was released, my photograph appeared in the Berlin press, alongside a picture of the naked body of Vanessa Redgrave taken from the film *Blow Up*. I realized things had not changed much. I wondered if the cut and thrust of intelligence, politics and diplomacy was still as active as I imagined. I was not to be disappointed.

If I could summarize my activities over the next two years it was to keep up the morale of the Berliners by ensuring that our tenuous lines of communication with West Germany stayed open and, together with our French and American Allies, to try to defuse as quickly as possible every diplomatic crisis that arose between ourselves and the Soviet Union, which might otherwise have threatened the hard-won concessions our diplomats had taken years to achieve.

There had always been a wall of some sort around Berlin, founded by Albrecht the Bear in the 12th century, until 1866 when the old city walls were demolished leaving only a few of the great gates such as the Brandenburger Tor. Then, quite suddenly, ninety-five years later, on 13 August 1961, the Communist government of East Germany constructed a new wall, immense and ugly, not to protect the city from invasion but to divide it. Until it was pulled down in 1989, the Wall remained a sad, sinister sight cutting a thirty-mile swathe across the centre of Berlin and then encircling the outer limits of the Western Sectors for another seventy miles.

From the top of a small artificial mound built by the Royal Engineers it was possible to see over the Wall what lay beyond. A ten-metre strip of yellow sand, carefully raked every week, in which every footprint made by bird, animal or human, stood out clearly. The next two hundred metres had been cleared of all vegetation and contained at least two wire fences, alarms, trip wires, television cameras and areas in which Alsatian dogs ran loose. Behind all this there was a tarmac track lined with flood-lights, along which armoured cars and motor cycles patrolled between concrete watch towers manned by twelve thousand East German frontier guards. This formidable obstacle could only be approached from outside the city, through an exclusion zone several kilometres wide, whilst within Berlin all windows and streets that looked out on or crossed the new border were blocked, all except Check Point Charlie, manned by French, British and American military Police.

In 1977 the East Germans decided to make the ugly wall more attractive, at least where it ran through the centre of the city. They painted both sides white, thus presenting Western graffiti artists with a platform for their work and East German machine gunners with a background against which escapers were clearly silhouetted. Three metres of land on our side was actually their territory. This had enabled the East Germans to erect the wall and to carry out maintenance works which included placing a concrete pipe along the top of the wall, thus denying escapers any finger-hold. This three-metre strip was the cause of many complaints from the Russians who were powerless to prevent West Berliners who lived in the shadow of the wall from using the land for their rabbit hutches or hen coops.

Although the Berlin Wall had been built by the Deutsche Democratic Republic (DDR), the Allies would only speak to the Russians about matters concerning Berlin. Much of the day-to-day government of the city – education, health and the economy – had been handed over to the Berlin House of Representatives. All matters concerning arms, security and access to Berlin remained our direct responsibility. Legally Berlin was still an occupied city as it had been in 1945 and therefore subject to Military Government under the Four-Power Agreement which had been modified in 1971. This included laws which still prevented Berliners even flying a model aircraft or possessing any weapon, even replica antique swords.

Allied military personnel had the right, provided they wore uniform, to move freely throughout East Berlin. This meant that officers had to wear mess kit to see, for example, a magnificent production of *Spartacus* at the Deutsche Staatsoper in the Linden Allee in the Russian sector. Every day each of the Allies despatched a military 'flag patrol' through Check Point Charlie to drive round East Berlin reminding the people they were still part of a single city and never to give up hope. The Russians seldom came into the West, worried perhaps at the effect the sight of so much prosperity might have on Russian conscript soldiers. In 1977 the Russians came under pressure from the DDR to demand that we should stop our patrols and thus remove a visible sign to the East Berliners that they were still living in a four-power city.

To our amazement this Communist request received a very sympa-thetic reception from a senior official in the Foreign Office, who, possibly taking advantage of the fact that the Foreign Secretary, Dr Owen, was overseas, indicated we should negotiate direct with the DDR. This would have threatened our status and would have been a complete contraven-tion of the well-established procedure that the Allies dealt only with the Russians on matters concerning Berlin. It was only with the support of Percy Cradock, our Ambassador to the DDR in East Berlin, Sir Oliver Wright, Ambassador in Bonn, and General Sir Frank King, C in C Rhine Army, that my impassioned protest against permitting any weakening of the Allied status was upheld. Instead I suggested that the Russians should start visiting the Western sectors of the city. Initially this resulted in

Russian military cars getting hopelessly lost until they were supplied with Deutsche Marks and allowed to buy maps of Berlin from our bookshops.

Percy Cradock's Head of Chancery at the Embassy in East Berlin was Catherine Pestell. She was witty and highly intelligent and I always looked forward to her visits and lucid summing up of the latest developments. As a supplementary means of secure communication between ourselves, I gave her a photocopy of my Eskimo dictionary of which I felt sure nobody else in Berlin could possibly have a copy. This gave us much amusement during the tense days that followed.

Access into Berlin was only allowed along three roads, three railway lines and three air corridors, but the Allied Forces and their dependents could only use the centre routes. The air corridors into Berlin were ten miles wide and aircraft were restricted to a ceiling of ten thousand feet, acceptable perhaps in 1945 for ancient Dakota transports but not for modern jets. Only Pan Am, Air France and British Airways were allowed to fly into West Berlin, no other airline. This infuriated Herbert von Karajan, renowned conductor of the Berlin Philharmonic, who had his own private aircraft. The Russians sometimes threatened to interrupt these regular Allied flights with military air training exercises. The drama would then be played out in the Berlin Air Safety Centre which had been established after the Russians walked out of the Allied Kommandantura in 1948 and was one of the few places where officers of the Four Powers still worked together. It was located in the old Palace of Justice where Hitler's opponents had been tried in 1944 and brutally strangled with piano wire from a crossbeam in the great hall.

A British Military train travelled daily from Berlin to Brunswick in West Germany. The train carried a small British military guard who locked the carriage doors, maintained a radio link with Berlin and Helmsted, and ensured that there was a seven-day reserve supply of rations in case the train was held up. The blue coaches of the British Military Train carried the badge of the Royal Corps of Transport and a Union Jack on their sides and the train was often drawn by a steam engine, of which there were plenty still to be seen in East Germany.

The inland waterways enabled heavy cargoes to be transported from West Germany in barges along the Mittelland Canal right into the heart of Berlin. This canal runs parallel to the centre autobahn and then through the Havel, a long lake beside the Grunewald, into the city.

I decided that our arrival in Berlin should be by road instead of on the customary British Airways flight. Valerie and I were driven by Sergeant Forrow in a large heavy Daimler to Check Point Alpha at Helmstedt on the Hanover–Berlin autobahn. A happy detachment of French, American and British military police carefully checked our documentation because the slightest misprint could, if the Soviets were being difficult that day, result in hours of delay. Two hours later, having lost a Union Jack in the high wind crossing the River Elbe, we reached Check Point Bravo at Staaken through the south-west corner of the Berlin wall. We were met by the Minister John Lambert and Brigadier Lennox Napier. Twenty-four hours later we had unpacked nineteen packing cases, hung the icons and paintings, shaken 286 hands and caused a protocol upset by paying a visit to two local dignitaries in the wrong order.

British Commandants were given the use of a fairy-tale "gingerbread" house called the Villa Lemm beside the Havel. It had been built in about 1904 by Dr Lemm who made a shoe polish based on turpentine. His marketing became highly successful when one tin in every hundred contained a silver Mark. The magnificent gardens ran along 200 metres of waterfront and contained enormous weeping beech trees, a tennis court, a large swimming pool, a boat house and a circular two-storied pavilion beside the lake in which Einstein was said to have once played the organ to a host of small boats anchored offshore.

Contact was maintained with the Russian authorities at many different levels and, although it sometimes took ages to settle a problem, they did abide by the documents that they had signed. The main difference between us was that the Russians claimed to have handed over their sector of Berlin to the East German Government, whereas the Allies maintained that they had no right to do so unilaterally in breach of wartime and postwar agreements on Berlin. However, a great many steps had been taken to ease life and access for Berliners and West Germans when the Quadripartite Agreement was signed in 1971.

My personal contacts with Russian officers were generally limited to social occasions which were cordial and friendly. One morning a Russian Colonel arrived at my Headquarters, which was located in the old 1936 Olympic Stadium. He was in an agitated state and asked to see me. He was shown in and in good English explained that he had a very serious matter to discuss. Now it was quite normal that whenever a military column passed through Check Point Bravo there was always friendly chat between British and Russian soldiers while the documentation was being checked, and small items such as magazines and cap badges were exchanged. Although this trade was unofficial, the Colonel conceded we were both happy to tolerate it.

"But what that regiment from Wales who returned to Berlin yesterday afternoon, did to my men." He paused, priding himself on his knowledge of English idiom. "It was not quite cricket, you understand, General?"

"Please tell me what happened, Colonel." I offered him a cigarette.

"My soldiers do not have wives or girlfriends like yours in Germany. The magazines *Playboy* and *Penthouse* mean a lot to them. Imagine their feelings when they discovered that from the middle of each magazine the double-page picture of a beautiful naked lady was missing!"

This, he pointed out, could easily destroy all the good will we had built up between us and make many new difficulties on the access routes. I told him not to worry, they would have their pictures today. I telephoned the Commanding Officer of the Royal Regiment of Wales suggesting that he should go round the barrack rooms collecting as many pinups as possible, and take them down to the Russians at Check Point Bravo without further delay. Thus yet another international crisis was swiftly averted.

There was, needless to say, a steady stream of visitors to Berlin, many of whom stayed at the Villa Lemm, where it was wonderful to have the staff and rooms available. The house staff were under the somewhat haphazard control of Corporal of Horse Bradley, who had been posted to be my driver in England until I discovered he still needed L Plates. A complaint to his Colonel at Windsor, Bill Boucher, produced the suggestion "Why don't you try him out on making a dry Martini?" which of course marked a turning point in his career. His wife was a cinema usherette in Burnley and refused to come abroad, so he lived alone in a flat in the old coach house. One day he fell asleep leaving a chip pan on the stove which burst into flames. He had already smashed two fire extinguishers which discharged foam all over him before Corporal Riglar showed him how to do it and smothered the flames. The emergence of the dazed, ghostly figure of Bradley covered in foam from the blackened kitchen was a truly remarkable sight.

Riglar was made of sterner stuff. He was at a German party in Gatow village when one of the Villa Lemm gardeners produced a knife and threatened to kill him unless he danced with his wife, Trude, who weighed well over 100 kilos. They danced a few turns round the room until Riglar seized his chance to disarm the gardener and gave the weapon to Trude who seemed a sensible lady. An hour later the gardener, by now very drunk, had seized the weapon and advanced on Riglar who leapt out of the window to fetch the local Police Wachmeister.

I was horrified one winter afternoon to see the Villa Lemm chimney in flames. I raised the alarm and ran up to the attic, then climbed a rickety ladder to the rooftop which was covered in snow. The Berlin newspapers reported that the Commandant had climbed onto the roof and saved his house with armfuls of snow and, as usual, printed the story alongside a picture of a topless young lady. The Berlin Fire Brigade did not commend the method as safe to Berliners. I agreed.

Valerie filled the house with flowers and placed a biscuit tin in every bedroom. One night she awoke and was disappointed to discover that her tin was empty. Half-asleep, she completely forgot that we had guests to stay, crossed the landing naked and entered a guest room to help herself from a box between the twin beds. The guests, whom we scarcely knew, switched on the light as she was leaving. Being British, absolutely nothing was said at breakfast.

Among the visitors to Berlin was a group of very left-wing Members of Parliament who preferred to stay away from the British garrison and their families. They seemed determined to pick holes in the amenities of the beleaguered garrison even though it cost the British taxpayer nothing. They were unwilling to be shown the Wall, Check Point Charlie or to see the practical results of thirty years of 'democratic socialism' in East Berlin.

A special effort was made by the Green Howards to give them lunch with their soldiers. Each MP was seated at a table with men from their own constituencies. It was a dismal failure because the MPs were clearly ill at ease and made no effort to converse. I was worried to see that their helicopter flight over West Berlin was going to take them up the Havel past the Villa Lemm. Realizing that their attitude was unpredictable, Corporal of Horse Bradley, in charge of my house staff, was instructed to lower the Union Jack on the Villa Lemm and replace it with the French tricolour while the helicopter flew the MPs over the city. When I was asked whose was that fine house I replied, "It belongs to the French who always do themselves very well, gentlemen."

They had refused to stay in the British Military transit hotel used by all ranks and their families, but insisted on being booked into a very expensive hotel. That evening they had a simple dinner with the Green Jackets, a meal which was unexpectedly interrupted by an emergency 'Call Out' which originated from SHAPE in Belgium. The MPs were taken to witness the tanks of the 5th Inniskilling Dragoon Guards pouring out of barracks heading for their battle stations through the night. As there was nothing else for them to do, their escorting officer drove them to a company position beside the West Wall on the other side of which Russian soldiers were carrying out some sort of night exercise. The sky was red with flares, there was the sound of machine-gun fire and streams of tracer bullets filled the sky, to the thump of Russian artillery shells exploding. We hoped the MPs may have noted the steady resolution of our forces facing an awesome threat. It was just possible that the reality of why we were in Berlin began to dawn on them.

Their visit was followed by Mr Fred Mulley, Minister of Defence, who had a few days earlier been photographed sound asleep next to Her Majesty The Queen during an RAF flying display. He could not have shown more interest in the garrison and its activities, a point much appreciated by the garrison and noted by the German Press who stressed how wide awake he was.

I wrote to my mother-in-law, Margaret Wellesley:

"The social whirl continues without a stop and so do all the political and other strange events I partake in. This morning I have been visited by the Turkish and Korean Ambassadors, the head of Berlin police, two French reporters and a sad man from the British Council. It is a constant and extraordinary series of surprises each day and great fun. I have already lodged my first protest with the Russians and drunk a few vodkas with them too. Winston Churchill is coming to stay soon and so is Clare Hollingworth and Henry Stanhope. We are having a big press party for them with editors from every newspaper."

Clare Hollingworth had been in Romania in February 1941 and helped the Embassy staff with the evacuation of British Families, including my mother.

Of course all this meant a lot of work for my unpaid wife. She wrote to her mother:

"We have just had the most hellish three days. Eight Ambassadors and three four-star Generals came to Berlin for a conference, and six brought their wives. They had to be entertained, talked to, taken to the opera, concerts and museums, fed and bedded (six stayed in the house), met and seen off. Dinner for thirty on Tuesday, and forty on Wednesday, by last night I had a screaming migraine."

During the Queen's Birthday Parade week she wrote:

"Wonderful dinner party for the Duke of Kent in the pavilion, such fun, Scots Dragoon Guards Piper, candles on the boat house, forty-five guests. After the parade a reception for 1500 in the Olympic Stadium, then a lunch party here. There was a ball for 450 that night in the garden, next day two garden parties and another reception. Robin [our son] worked out on his calculator that 2180 people passed through the house in five days."

Every four months one of the Commandants became chairman and presided at our meetings in the Allied Kommandantura Building. Major General Joe McDonough, the American, did not really enjoy his posting to Berlin, but General Jacques Mangin, grandson of the legendary defender of Verdun in 1916, fitted in perfectly to the international scene. Each of us had a Deputy who was a diplomat in the rank of minister or ambassador, whose staff bore the brunt of the endless discussions with the Russians over the interpretation of the Berlin Agreement. John Lambert, who subsequently became ambassador to Tunisia, was brilliant at settling the most delicate political questions and understanding the Germans. He was succeeded by Francis MacGinnis who had been Councillor in Bonn. There were two exceptional diplomats in the British Military Government who both achieved high rank, David Gladstone and Christian Adams.

Once a month we all six met at one of our homes with the Governing Mayor of Berlin, initially Herr Klaus Schutz, who left Berlin to become ambassador to Israel, and then with Herr Dietrich Stobbe. If these men ever resented having to explain to the Allies what they were doing, they never showed it and they both earned our sincere respect. We were also most fortunate that it was the Berlin Government who paid almost all the costs of our stay in their city.

Soon after my arrival the Rt Hon James Callaghan flew into the RAF base at Gatow. The Royal Regiment of Wales were about to celebrate the Battle of Rorke's Drift and had decorated the Headquarters building with memorabilia. He good-naturedly accepted a Zulu spear and shield from my ADC, Captain Hammon Massey, just before going out to inspect their guard of honour.

I thoroughly enjoyed taking US Vice President Nelson Rockefeller and his wife Honey to look at the Berlin Wall at the Brandenburg Gate. This was in spite of the extraordinary activities of the CIA who turned up armed to the teeth with a light machine gun lying behind a wall of sand-bags in the back of a huge station wagon. A British Royal Military Police corporal, armed with an ancient revolver, could scarcely believe his eyes.

Among the duties which the Allied Commandants shared was that of visiting Rudolf Hess locked up in Spandau Prison which was in the British sector. He was the last of seven Nazi war criminals who were spared execution at the Nuremberg War Crimes trial and had been a prisoner for thirty-five years since he flew to Scotland in 1941. It is doubtful whether history has ever recorded a case in which the prolonged custody of a single man, who posed so little a threat to society, could prove such a costly undertaking. The maintenance cost of a prison built in 1881, which had contained six hundred prisoners in 1945 and now had one, was enormous. Each nation provided a military guard of thirty-four soldiers every four months who manned six watchtowers and the main gate. Within the prison there was a team of six warders from France, America, Russian and Britain, a total of twenty-four. The original British warders had all served in the Shanghai Police in the 1920s and were about as old as Hess.

The administrative staff of the prison and warders' mess all had to be non-Germans, cooks, clerks, carpenter, electrician, waitress, about ten in all. Finally each nation appointed a Prison Governor. There were also doctors, medical orderlies, and the French padre, as well as officials in my headquarters who dealt with the Spandau Prison budget, supplies and maintenance. Thus at times seventy people were assigned to looking after Spandau Prison and Rudolf Hess.

On my first visit I was accompanied by the Russian prison governor, a Colonel, who was determined to ensure I did not grasp Hess's hand or call him anything other than Prisoner Number 7. His interpreter, a lieu-tenant, understood English and translated every word I spoke. Hess had tidied up his cell and was standing to attention at the foot of his iron bed wearing a white shirt buttoned up to the neck with no tie and black pinstripe trousers. On the ceiling of his cell was a large map of the stars in a night sky which he had probably not been able to see for a great many years. His black bushy eyebrows were unmistakable from the photographs I had seen of him as Deputy Führer.

I introduced myself and said I was the new British Commandant and suggested that he must have seen a good many.

"Fourteen," he replied, "but you are the first to speak to me in my own language." By then I had begun to talk to him in German.

The Russian Colonel was clearly put out, because, as Hess also spoke French and English, he was always going to find it difficult to monitor my entire conversation. There was a library in an adjoining cell and I usually looked to see what Hess was reading before starting the conver-sation. After each visit I tried to improve the conditions in which he lived by asking for items such as a bedside table and a lamp, a coffee machine, a floor mat. Each request had to be approved by the four prison Governors and it was invariably refused by the Russian who had to refer to Moscow for final approval. This could take weeks.

Hess was allowed one newspaper by each of the four powers, so he received *Die Welt, Tagesspiegel* and *Frankfurter Allgemeine* from the West, and from the East *Neues Deutschland*. All these were censored before he could read them by Armenian clerks who cut out any mention of Hitler, National Socialism or himself. After Hess had read them they were carefully put through a shredding machine so that no one would ever know what had been censored!

It was no use complaining about the rules because they had been agreed by the Allies in 1946 and, although the Western nations were now anxious to see them modified, the Russians steadfastly refused to alter any rules. Indeed their censorship of his outgoing letters was petty and irritating to the Western Governors. Hess would be invited to rewrite the offending pages of his letter or it would not be posted. An example of a passage to be deleted and reluctantly agreed by the other Governors in order not to delay transmission of his letters any longer showed how sensitive to criticism the Russians had become. Hess had written:

"You'll be saying my letters are not exactly easy to read either and unfortunately you will be right. I am afraid it is to do with my age and need to write small, being limited to four pages, and I can't do anything about that either."

Hess was only allowed to receive 1200 words a week. His wife missed a week and so wrote an extra-long letter the following week. The Russians, sticking firmly to the rules, cut the letter in half and only gave him the second part after three days of remonstrations by the Allies.

The British Military Hospital had a complete floor sealed off and retained solely to accommodate Hess and his warders and guards if he fell ill. He particularly appreciated the care and attention he received from the Queen Alexandra's Royal Army Nursing Corps and, possibly in an attempt to return to hospital, he made a clumsy attempt to cut his wrist with a butter knife in 1977. This infuriated the Russians who indicated they would punish the old man severely and remove all the concessions to his spartan regime which had taken successive Commandants years to negotiate. This was firmly resisted by the Allies, whereupon the Russians said they would deny him any reading material and lock up the cell which contained his library. This punitive gesture was foiled by General Mangin who put the key in his pocket and walked off.

Hess had once seen television in the British Military Hospital and let it be known that he would dearly like to watch television as no doubt did many of his warders. The Russians naturally said they could not agree and added that there was far too much iron inside the prison to make reception possible. I was advised by the French prison governor and the American Minister to stop rocking the boat by always asking for improvements after each visit. So on my next official visit I began by asking what was it that the warders needed in order to make their own mess more attractive and comfortable, and these items I promised to supply. As I was about to leave, Hess asked if I would consider providing him with a television set. The Russian Colonel shook his head and mentioned the technical problems. I concurred, but then suggested, "Look Colonel, he is such an old man that he will never understand or believe our reasons. Why not let us demonstrate to him that with so much metal around there will never be good reception?"

The proposal was accepted and when I was back at my Headquarters in the Olympic Stadium I called the Chief Signals Officer, Freddie Lockwood, and asked him whether it was surely not beyond the wit of man to make a TV set work inside Spandau Prison. A few days later we gathered outside Hess's cell for a demonstration before the four prison governors. Freddie, who liked amateur dramatics and was a bit of an actor, switched on the television set. The picture was incredibly distorted, there was no sound and the sceptics and Russians were smiling as Freddie appeared to be getting more and more frantic. Then, with a bit of deft fingerwork, he gradually achieved perfect reception and so it was agreed that a television set could be placed in an empty adjoining cell where censored programmes relieved the monotony for warders as well as for prisoner Number Seven.

Work to raze Spandau prison to the ground began in 1988 a few hours after Hess, aged 92, was found hanging in peculiar circumstances in a shed in the prison garden. I wish I had had a chance to look round the prison once more before it disappeared because beneath the cells there was a basement which contained five punishment cells each with a smaller cage inside. There was no light but a torch revealed that the walls were covered with scratched messages from condemned men. Upstairs there was a white-tiled execution chamber where there had been a guillotine and an iron bar from which prisoners were hanged. On the floor there was a trap door through which bodies were dropped into a truck waiting to remove the corpses. Records show that there were 1200 political prisoners executed in this way just before the Second World War began. The room had been used as an operating theatre during the last few weeks of the Battle for Berlin in April 1945 and subsequently for operations on some of the seven original war criminals sent to Spandau after the Nuremberg War Crime Trials.

The Russians could never bring themselves to forgive Hess for his "responsibility" for the deaths of millions of their people. Even though he was already a prisoner of war in Britain long before Germany invaded the Soviet Union, his mission had been to persuade Britain to stop hostilities and to unite with their fellow Saxons against the real enemy, the Soviet Union and Communism. In June 1940 Hess visited a military operations room on the coast of Belgium and as he gazed at a map showing Operation "Sea Lion", the German invasion plans for the southeast coast of England, he was heard to muse aloud, "We should not and have no wish to fight Englishmen who are so akin to us. We should both be able to live together in freedom."

It has been suggested that Prisoner No 7 was not really Rudolf Hess, born in 1894 in Alexandria. This sensational revelation was based on a glimpse of Hess by a young doctor while he was putting on his shirt in the X-ray department of the BMH Berlin. It seems that the scars of the wounds received in 1916 when he was a pilot and mentioned in his records could not be clearly seen and it was therefore presumed that the real Hess must have been murdered and replaced just before his flight to Scotland.

It is just possible that a switch of identity papers took place in the chaos after 1918, when Hess became a small-time gangster. But it is incredible that Hess, whose appearances between 1939 and May 1941 were numerous and well-recorded by his friends and personal staff right up to the day he left, could have been replaced by an identical lookalike at the last moment. Indeed for this new man to have also been trained to fly a newly designed twin-engine fighter, an ME 110E, and navigate alone with few aids over the North Sea, to make a precision landfall in Scotland, is impossible.

Finally to find a man willing to remain locked up for more than forty years without saying a word about not being the real Deputy Führer seems incredible. To me Hess looked exactly as I expected. Those sent to identify him by Winston Churchill had no doubts. It was the circumstances leading up to his dramatic decision to leave Germany which will continue to be debated. The Reverend Paul Oestreicher from Amnesty International came to see me in order to get permission to visit Hess. I told him that this could only be at the expense of one of his regular monthly family visits, which he was reluctant to do. He said that the purpose of his visit was to reassure Hess that he had not been forgotten by the outside world. I pointed out that censorship regulations were precisely directed at preventing Hess from knowing that anyone was interested in his case. I vouched that his conditions were the best we could devise within the parameters of 1945 prison legislation and that Hess might not take kindly to a visit, however well-intentioned. I explained that Hess was a very strange man, a proud man who often resented efforts to better his lot.

The Russians never ceased trying to approach allied servicemen for low-level information and at one time they targeted married American soldiers who were in debt. An agent would appear at a soldier's married quarters while he was at work and offer his wife precisely the sum owed, in return for some tiny item such as an internal telephone directory or a copy of a forces basic training manual. We discovered that they were, not surprisingly, listening to all private calls made from Berlin to the West and were quick to follow up remarks such as "If only Hank can raise $400 all our troubles with that Hire Purchase company will be over".

The trouble was that, having once handed over a basic training manual or telephone directory and cleared the family debt, the soldier was easily blackmailed.

In a subsequent operation we picked up two KGB colonels in plain clothes who had gone to meet an off-duty American soldier in a gasthaus. An hour later we arrested two more KGB officers who had gone to look for them. There was of course nothing we could do to them that would not have prejudiced the security of our men visiting East Berlin. I met one of the Russian Colonels at a Queen's Birthday party given by the British Mission in Potsdam. He was wearing a uniform with green KGB facings and I expressed surprise that he was still around after the nonsense he had made a week earlier. He assured me I would see him around for a long time yet but he would be more careful in future. He then asked me who that officer was with green facings to his mess kit. Seeing that he was a Colonel in the Royal Army Dental Corps, I replied that they were both in the same line of business and I gathered from the dentist that a most confusing conversation then took place between them.

Berlin had always been a hive of intelligence service activities. In the early days the British had dug a tunnel deep into the Russian sector whence they could tap the telephone cables to the Russian Headquarters at Zossen Wunsdorf. This worked well for about a year until we received a warning that the East Germans were carrying out road works and would discover the tunnel within a few hours. When the workmen's drill broke through the ceiling they discovered American signal wires, US Army boot imprints, packets of Camel and Lucky Strike and chewing gum wrappers.

The Americans, who at that time had many rival intelligence agencies, did not know who was responsible and received a blast from the Russians.

In the 1970s a secret Russian twin-engine fighter was in difficulties over the British sector and asked permission to make an emergency landing at RAF Gatow or at USAF Templehof. This was refused by their control who insisted they got back to the East at all costs. They failed to make it and crashed into the Havel between the Villa Lemm and Spandau. The Russian military guard at their War Memorial in the British Sector climbed into a bus and raced off to where they thought the plane had crashed. They were spotted on a small knoll scanning the lake by a Military Police patrol who swiftly encircled the bus with a broad white ribbon and forbade the Russians to step outside it. A hessian screen was erected to hinder observation while the Royal Engineer sub-aqua club were called in to locate the wreck. During the night all sorts of experts arrived to investigate and next day we handed back a body. The Russians accused us of capturing the second pilot, which we strongly denied. Eventually, when the wreckage was lifted out of the water and handed back to the Russians the second body was found compressed into the nose cone.

There was a small-time German informer in the Berlin Brigade Headquarters who emptied the waste paper bins every evening. Items which looked interesting he removed to a private cache beneath an old pram behind the building, which in turn were examined nightly by a sharp-eyed Lance Corporal in the Intelligence Corps and replaced. One night I was telephoned and asked to return to the office because the man had recovered a document marked Secret which had not been properly destroyed. To remove the document, which the spy must surely have noticed, would have given away our surveillance and blown any chance of following him to his controller. So we took a risk, the document was put back and a week later we brought the operation to a successful conclusion.

I never ceased to admire the thoroughness of German planning before the start of any venture. This often began in the home. The Sunday stroll through Berlin's beautiful woodland was a ritual for young families and couples who had to decide what hat to wear, which feather to stick in it, which walking stick to carry and in what cafe to enjoy a slice of Apfelstrudel or chocolate cake afterwards. I once spotted in the distant undergrowth a superb example of attention to detail. Two walking sticks stuck in the ground on which perched two hats, an amorous couple lay on a green cloak and from a branch two jackets rocked gently in the breeze on coathangers which had been taken just in case of need.

Escapes over the wall into West Berlin became very rare as the East German authorities increased their hold on the population. Even the sewers which flowed under the wall had been blocked with wire and traps. Brigadier Charles Grey, who commanded the Berlin Brigade, wanted to test the feasability of military operations in the sewers. It proved to be a dangerous undertaking because of pockets of poisonous gas. At one moment when we were very disoriented I was astonished to hear the theme music from the 1949 film *The Third Man*. It turned out to be my ADC Hammon Massey who had brought a tape recorder with him.

A young man trying to escape to the West remained under water several hours breathing through a tube. He dragged himself out near the Reichstag and with great difficulty made his way to a small building which happened to house the British Military Police detachment behind the Russian War Memorial. He was exhausted and his vision was blurred. There were two door bells; one would have summoned the Russians who would have returned him to East Germany on their bus, the other brought a Lance Corporal Military Policewoman who helped him inside.

There were other refugees and I referred to them in a Christmas Message in 1976:

"During the past year nearly four thousand refugees from Eastern Europe arrived in West Berlin and for the first time were free to do and to say just what they wished without any fear. A number of these people chose to risk their lives by climbing over the Wall, an obstacle which this year you have watched being strengthened and through which an escape has become increasingly perilous.

"That precious individual freedoms which they sought still exist in West Berlin is largely due to the presence of the British servicemen and civilians, who, together with our French and American allies, continue to protect this great city and thus encourage its prosperity."

After high winds one November night six top sections of wall fell on to our side, but all landed within the three-metre strip except one concrete pipe which rolled further and was picked up by our soldiers. In due course the East Germans climbed over and replaced the five sections. A request was then received through the Russians, "Give us back our piece of wall."

The Chief of Staff, Tony Pielow, who had recently been Defence Attaché in Belgrade replied, "Certainly, just come to the Military Police Lost Property office and sign for it like anybody else." They never came.

Two bodies were spotted in thick bushes against our side of the wall. They were clearly dead and may have been shot escaping. We suggested

205

to the Russians that they might like to retrieve the bodies, which they did at night with great difficulty by digging a tunnel beneath the wall. Later we learnt that they had been West Berlin homosexuals who had made a death pact. The Russians sent us a bill for the autopsy which we disputed.

I used to say to the Russians, "We arrived in Berlin long before you did. Come and look at the four thousand graves of British and Commonwealth airmen buried in the British Sector." No doubt bearing this in mind, the Russians notified us that workmen clearing a building site in East Berlin had found the wreckage of an RAF Lancaster bomber and the bones of its crew, which had been shot down during 1940–1945. An impressive ceremony then took place on the Glienike Bridge leading into Potsdam and famous for being where the Soviet Union returned Gary Powers, the American U2 spy plane pilot who had failed to take a cyanide pill after he was shot down. Four black metal boxes, carried by eight very tall and smart Russian soldiers, were handed to an RAF funeral party in the middle of the bridge. They were followed by a lorry filled with wreckage whose part numbers might have helped to identify the aircraft. Group Captain Ray Tavanyar RAF gave the Russian commander a plaque to commemorate the event. The dead were never identified, but, because of their dark blue uniform, were presumed to be from Canada or Australia.

A few months later the Green Howards returned the body of a Russian soldier found by a contractor buried beneath 1½ metres of earth in a zinc bath. He had no identity discs, but the leather bottom and linen uppers of his boots were as worn by the Russian Army in 1945.

West Berliners were exempt from military service and so the city attracted a lot of young people who had become 'permanent' university students until their mid-thirties. Among these were several intelligent, affluent and disturbed potential terrorists who joined the Red Army Faction or the Bader Meinhof Gang. These movements were devoid of any political or moral aims except to destroy the existing establishment. They had kidnapped a Berlin politician, Peter Lorez, President of the House of Representatives, and held him for weeks until the police rescued him. He never fully recovered from his ordeal.

In order to illustrate how dedicated these people were I would show visitors a seven-inch black leather mini-skirt worn by a murderess which had not one but two pistol holsters stitched inside. The young lady in question escaped from the women's prison in Berlin with the help of a crooked lawyer, a dentist and a wax impression of her teeth which also contained an impression of the key to her cell.

An arms cache in a wood in the French sector was watched for nearly three weeks by Berlin police in a skilful and most professional manner. When the terrorists flew into the city on the eve of the annual Allied Military Forces Parade the police, in their understandable wish to conclude the stake out, let it be known, much too soon, that they had made arrests, and so were unable to capture the remaining three terrorists. A search next morning through the woods along the parade route revealed another cache almost opposite the saluting stand where I and my fellow Commandants were to stand. It was a strange feeling standing there during the march past knowing that we had not yet arrested all the gunmen.

There was a certain rivalry between the Allies as to who could be the smartest on parade. The French made a sensational opening by dropping free-fall parachutists all along the parade route. The Americans tended to integrate their women soldiers in the ranks where they sometimes looked incongruous in steel helmets and tight skirts trying to match the strides of much taller men. I recall a small lady dwarfed by her enormous tuba marching in the rear rank of the 956th US Army Band. The British played safe and put their nurses and women soldiers into open vehicles. But it was the French who stole the show. They picked their prettiest long-legged Air Force women and placed them all together marching eight abreast at the head of their troops, to the great delight of the Berliners.

British cavalry regiments have always given their armoured vehicles a name, often reflecting their interests, such as the names of hunts or racehorses, although I do remember Chaos, Calamity and Catastrophe. The French tanks had evocative battle names such as Sambre, Verdun and Austerlitz, while for many years the Americans just carried numbers on the turrets. On this particular parade they appeared with large boards bearing names such as Bastogne, Guadalcanal and Lundy's Lane, an engagement fought near Niagara Falls in the war of 1812 against the British. As we three Allied Generals saluted, I made an aside to my American colleague,

"Surely, you have got that wrong, Joe. We won that battle."

"No, you did not" he whispered. "It was a draw!"

In the Grunewald was the only hill in Berlin, built entirely with the rubble from bombed buildings. It was high enough to give a line of sight, if it were possible, all the way to the Ural Mountains. The British Forces Broadcasting Service had its transmitter on top and we discovered that many Germans in the East listened to BFBS. I thought that if we could increase the strength of our signal we would be heard in Poland. I was told by the ever-cautious Foreign Office that this was contrary to an International Protocol which limited our signal strength. I asked myself when did the Russians ever allow such small matters to influence them. We announced that we were going to repair the aged radio masts and everyone remarked how much clearer BFBS had become afterwards.

Berlin was a wonderful place in which to live, not only because of its museums, theatre, opera and the Berlin Philharmonic Orchestra under Herbert von Karajan, but also for its woods and lakes and, of course, wonderful crisp dry air. There was so much going on and such good will towards the Allied forces in the city. At Christmas a multi-national carol service was held in the ruins of the Blue Church with Holy Night sung in three languages to the same tune. The Governing Mayor used to give an annual lunch party to Allied soldiers in the Schoneberg Town Hall, which was always a success. There were a small number of British who had always lived in Berlin, some since the First World War. They were mainly widows or nannies. They had lived through the Second World War, endured all the bombing and insults from their neighbours, and many lived in East Berlin. They were all collected and brought to the Villa Lemm for tea by the Foreign Office staff. It was much appreciated and very touching to meet these old people.

After about eighteen months Valerie was beginning to feel the strain and wrote to her mother:

"I am beginning to get a bit oppressed by this place and can now understand why people say it gets so claustrophobic: wherever you turn you meet the Wall. It is also very difficult to get to know people whom you only meet at official parties and receptions. None of the military wants to be thought to be sucking up to the General's wife!"

Then there was always the problem of security:

"Things are getting a bit of a strain with the Russians who are getting tougher and there are more terrorists in town. People follow Roy to see who is following him! They are putting extra dogs and guards on the gates and patrols in the garden at night. Extra security locks in the house, four different telephones in the bedroom and a radio telephone in Roy's dressing room. He says he can't get me a gun. So what with the constant sound of Russian gunfire from the other side of the Wall 800 yards away and the deliberate sabre rattling, I find it is all a little frightening.

"I watched the November Revolution Day Parade at the Russian War Memorial last Saturday. I saw them goose-stepping and shouting, 'Three Cheers for Mother Russia', then a reception full of Russian Generals in bright blue uniforms, gold shoulder boards and rows and rows of medals. I had a nightmare afterwards of being interrogated in a floodlit cell."

Valerie's father, Arthur Wellesley, was an eccentric who would much rather have made the stage his career than the Army. He had joined the Royal Tank Regiment in 1929 and commanded a troop of Vickers Light Tanks on the North-West Frontier in what is now Pakistan in 1935. This was the first operational use of tanks since 1918. He retired in 1957. Some years later he had been invited to spend a weekend in a splendid country house and discovered on arrival that he had forgotten to pack a spare pair of underpants. Ever resourceful, Margaret, his wife, lent him a pair of her silk pants which proved to be much too large until they were secured by a tuck and a safety pin. Driving back to the Royal Hospital in Chelsea he realized that his first appointment was to be with a tailor in Savile Row. In the event the tailor did not bat an eyelid when he saw Arthur's voluminous silk bloomers.

When Margaret died suddenly in 1982 a dear neighbour thought quite seriously of setting up house with Arthur. On the spur of the moment she asked him whether he would give her a memento of Margaret. He was delighted to help and rushed upstairs to return with an object hastily wrapped in drawer-lining paper. It was her false teeth! Sadly, they never did get together!

Over seventy nations had diplomatic representation in West Berlin; many were Germans who relished the status of being an honorary consul representing a distant Central American country, because it put them on the protocol list. The position of the Warsaw Pact countries, who all ran hostile intelligence networks in Berlin, was different. They had to be considered as still being our wartime allies, because that is what they were when the war ended in 1945, and time stood still in Berlin. I discovered that the most effective hold I had on them was to threaten to withdraw their NAAFI shop cards and cut off their supply of whisky. This worked wonders, especially with the Czech, who had been stocking up his cellar in the Tatra Mountains for months.

Every two years the British Brigade, then under the command of Brigadier Charles Grey, staged the Berlin Military Tattoo in the Deutschlandhalle. His theme for 1977 was to celebrate the Silver Jubilee Year of Her Majesty Queen Elizabeth II's Reign. I was delighted to be associated with such a wonderful show produced by an outstanding and imaginative man, Major Michael Parker. The music under the inspired direction of Trevor Sharpe, Director of Music Coldstream Guards, was provided by twenty-three different bands and augmented by the Choir of the Welsh Guards and the Morriston Orpheus Choir from Wales. Their renderings of Vivat Regina and Crown Imperial were magnificent, but my favourites were The Slaves' Chorus from *Nabucco* and the Ode to Joy. Thousands of Berliners completely filled the hall for ten performances, and I watched them all. I was delighted when the President of the Federal Republic, Herr Walter Scheel, made a surprise visit. One could not fail to be deeply moved at the conclusion as six hundred musicians marched off to deafening applause and the strains of that old Berlin favourite by Linke, *"Die Berliner Luft"*.

A steady stream of world leaders visited West Berlin, every one made extremely welcome by the Governing Mayor and people of the city. I remember in particular Vice President Walter Mondale accompanied by yet another discourteous, arrogant pack of CIA agents who managed to upset both the Berlin and British Military Police. The receptions which accompanied these visits were ruled by the protocol list. On one occasion in my home my wife found a senior British diplomat altering her seating plan.

"You must have Monsieur X on your right because he is the doyen of the diplomatic corps," he insisted.

"He has been seated next to me at the last three dinners I have attended and is such a boring person," she retorted, "and this is my home but I will suggest to him that he might like a change."

Of course it worked perfectly.

It was not long before I noted that we had had our 301st official guest to stay at the Villa Lemm. My entertainment allowance was not anything like enough to cover all the entertainment I was expected to provide. As we did not have any other source of income than my pay, I considered it a little unfair to find myself so out of pocket.

Valerie wrote, "We will be entertaining the British Ambassadors to Paris, The Hague, Bonn, Brussels, NATO and the DDR next week. Someone in the Foreign Office told me the Ambassador in Bonn gets £18,000 entertainment allowance and we are supposed to keep up the same sort of standard with many more people staying, on one 18th of that!" However, we did achieve an increase and my ADC Hammon Massey, who was handing over to Patrick Bailey, was shown how to calculate these expenses in a manner acceptable to the finance office.

Russian parties were always a little sticky once the obvious subjects for conversation had all been tried. I once asked a Russian Admiral, "On what sort of ships did you serve, Admiral?"

His platinum teeth fillings flashed in a weak smile, "Iron ships."

For Valerie common topics of conversation with Russian wives were limited to children, their home in Russia and food, which all had to be translated by a Russian Lieutenant. On one memorable occasion she lifted up the podgy hand of a general's wife and glanced at her palm. The lady hesitantly asked whether she would read it for her. Valerie had no idea how to set about this apart from having watched her mother in action. She began cautiously, and every word was translated by the interpreter and eagerly listened to by the other wives. She then noticed a well-developed love line in the lady's hand and suggested that there might be a good-looking, dark-haired man in her life. The Russian lady began to blush and so she developed the theme with the poor woman getting more and more flushed. After this they all wanted their palms read, but she wisely refused. When I got back to my office I asked the staff whether we had anything on the wife of General Y and was told, "Yes, it's the Third Secretary at the Hungarian Embassy." I then asked, somewhat in vain, whether in future I could be supplied with more background information in order to brief my wife beforehand.

It had become known by some Germans that I was a philatelist and so I developed an interesting link with the Spandau stamp club. The military postmark for Berlin was BFPO 15 and I asked the Ministry of Defence what was so secret after thirty years about our presence in Berlin that it required a coded postmark. On the occasion of the Queen's Birthday parade 1976, for the first time in the history of the Forces Postal Services, the location was used on the postmark instead of a code number. Five thousand first day covers were issued, ten of which were signed by Herr Klaus Schutz, Governing Mayor of Berlin, Sir Lindsay Ring, Lord Mayor of London and myself.

A year later there was a magnificent Queen's Silver Jubilee Parade in West Germany at Sennelager and another occasion for a first-day cover. My wife wrote: "We saw masses of people we knew, it was all a bit of a rush because of getting to the Royal Lunch and to the President of the Federal Republic's reception in the evening at Paderborn. Strangely it was the President, who on the spur of the moment, presented us to the Queen."

Every now and then we would allow one of the regiments stationed in Berlin to use the beautiful grounds of the Villa Lemm for a party. At the conclusion of one such occasion on a hot summer night many young people jumped into the swimming pool in their evening clothes and long dresses. The following morning I strolled round the garden before breakfast and noticed that one of the swimming pool filters was blocked. I lifted the lid and discovered that the trouble was caused by a tiny pair of pale blue knickers, which carried a large red letter L on the front. I squeezed them dry and took them to the regular Monday morning staff conference when the Minister and I would be briefed on events of the past three days by the diplomatic staff, the Chief of Staff, Tony Pielow, intelligence and operations officers and public safety officers. At the end of the meeting I produced the pants and, rather like a pantomime Prince Charming trying to find out whose slipper he held, I asked for a report on who the knickers fitted. There was an embarrassed silence from the table until the policeman suggested that at least she must have passed her trade test. I was not to find out who she was until I dined with her and her husband in Hong Kong two years later, by which time the garment had long since been lost.

Six months earlier than expected I was told that I must now move to Hong Kong. This was a terrible disappointment because I knew that I would never again serve in such a stimulating and exciting appointment. I made a farewell speech at the Rathaus Schoneberg, said goodbye to so many friendly Berliners, packed up house for the twenty-third time since we had married and set off once again into a totally different world. At a quick farewell to the military staff in the Olympic Headquarters building I was told that this was a rare occasion when a private soldier could give a rocket to a general. Someone had remembered that soon after I arrived I had spotted a German World War II panzerfaust in the ruins of a building. I had remarked that I had been blown up by one in 1945. Now, having packed my boxes, here was a young private in the Royal Army Ordinance Corps with this large rocket. It can still be seen in the Household Cavalry Museum at Combermere Barracks in Windsor.

I had developed a special affection for the Berliners and especially for their dry sense of humour. This is best reflected in the work of the famous Berlin cartoonist Heinrich Zille 1858–1929. My favourite cartoon is a watercolour which showed the backs of six scruffy Berlin children walking hand in hand, past the gates of a gaunt grey prison, the tallest child, aged about ten, is saying, "Won't father be pleased, when he finishes his stretch, to see how many of us there are now."

Chapter Thirteen

CROWDED ISLANDS

The Trans-Siberian railway seemed a logical way to get to Hong Kong from Berlin, and so I suggested to the Ministry of Defence that I might be allowed to travel on the daily train to Moscow and then change trains for Beijing and Canton. Would they please make the necessary arrangements? This simple request caused consternation and resulted in two dour gentlemen being sent from London to advise me very strongly against such an idea.

The charming French Minister, Pierre Landy, who had been Ambassador in South Korea, sympathized with my obvious disappointment and said, "Roy, you must arrive in Hong Kong in a man-of-war. It is the only way you will ever gain a true first impression of what that place really means."

So I approached the Admiralty in London and made discreet enquiries, only to be told that my dates did not fit their sailings and that there was only a Fleet Tanker calling. I was informed that this could hardly be considered a fitting vessel in which the new Commander British Forces put in his first appearance. I was just beginning to learn the importance of 'face'.

The only route left to me was a twenty-six-hour flight with Royal Air Force Transport Command which flew to Hong Kong once a week. I asked that wherever the aircraft refuelled I should be allowed to get off and spend a week, because I was not even being allowed any leave between the two appointments. The authorities were horrified and said, "What about your luggage? We will never be able to get that out of the hold." I explained that I always travelled light and really did not need any baggage.

So I left the plane in Sri Lanka, where, through the good offices of the Mission to Seamen, I was able to hire a car and driver in Colombo and thus explore that fabulous island. We followed the coast road south to the old seaport of Galle which had been fortified by the Dutch in 1687. I then wanted to visit the nature reserve near Yala in the south-east of the island. Although this can not be compared to the great game reserves of Africa, it nevertheless contains a wonderful variety of snakes, alligators, monkeys and birds. I must have been the only person staying in the camp that day and went to bed early. During the night I was conscious that somebody had entered my room, yet I was certain that I had locked the door and secured the shutters. I turned on the light and there, towering over me, was an enormous fat man in a loin cloth who resembled the muscular half-naked giant who hits the gong at the beginning of Rank films.

"Who the hell are you?" I asked,

"You rang the bell, Sir," he replied. "I am the manager."

The only bell button was on the other side of the room and I could see the pass key in his hand with which he had let himself in. He then proceeded to sit down on the end of my bed, which made me pop up like a jack-in-the-box and on to my feet in a flash. I then realized I was at a serious disadvantage because I did not even have a loin cloth. It was only after a lengthy conversation and with considerable difficulty that I persuaded this lonely fellow to leave. The next day I reluctantly felt obliged to cut my stay short and drove inland to the old colonial hill station at Nuwara Eliya, with its run-down hotels, tea plantations and old racecourse.

In 1841 Hong Kong was an unlikely place in which to start a colony because it was so mountainous, very short of fertile land and because there was practically no water. Lord Palmerston, the Foreign Secretary, was most dissatisfied with the spot chosen and described it as "a barren island with hardly a house upon it".

At the Treaty of Nanking in 1842 Sir Henry Pottinger secured not only a favourable commercial agreement, but, contrary to the instructions he had received from the new Foreign Secretary, Lord Aberdeen, he managed to secure the whole island as well.

The *Illustrated London News* of 8 November 1845 published a long account which described Hong Kong as a dreadful place. There was a dry burning heat when the sun was up and a foul gaseous smell which came out of the ground when it rained which produced fever and a speedy death. Every solder or sailor was expected to catch fever, dysentery or diarrhoea at least four times a year. The Chinese, it seemed, were all smugglers or vagabonds and Europeans had to sleep with pistols under their pillows. Nevertheless the colony survived those first traumatic years and trade with the mainland began to flourish.

British troops fighting in the Anglo-Chinese wars of 1856–58 and 1859–60 found that Kowloon, on the mainland, was a much more healthy place to build a military cantonment. So the British Consul in Canton, Sir Harry Parks, managed to secure the perpetual lease of Kowloon as far as Boundary Street and of Stonecutters Island. In 1898 at the Convention of Peking, in a move intended to make the defence of Hong Kong more efficient against a possible threat from Russia, the New Territories and 235 islands were leased to the British for 99 years until 1997.

Hong Kong has two outstanding assets. Firstly its magnificent harbour, which was the main reason for the British presence in the first place, a harbour which is used by ships from every nation trading with China. Its second great asset are the Chinese people who have moved in over the years. Their adaptability, industry and enthusiasm are renowned. They have flourished because they were allowed to operate with a minimum of controls, unlike the rest of mainland China.

The two appointments of Commander British Forces (CBF) and Major General Brigade of Gurkhas (MGBG) had previously been held by two officers, a Lieutenant General and Major General, but in yet another series of sweeping defence cuts the Headquarters was now to be moved into the naval base at HMS *Tamar* and only one general, in the lower rank, was to carry out all functions. I was to advise the Governor on matters affecting the security of Hong Kong but remain responsible to the Chief of Defence Staff in London. The Armed Forces were primarily to maintain stability and sustain confidence in the United Kingdom's intention to maintain the British position in Hong Kong. The garrison consisted of five Royal Navy patrol craft, three Gurkha and one British infantry battalions, engineers, signals and transport units, a Royal Air Force helicopter squadron and an Army Scout helicopter squadron.

There was to be no reduction whatsoever in my responsibilities and indeed within a year the number of ships, soldiers and aircraft in the Command had to be increased to handle an unexpected massive influx of illegal immigrants. I have never had to work so hard but then I would certainly never have been given the job of CBF if it had meant promotion!

All my attempts to meet my predecessor, Lieutenant General Sir John Archer, were unsuccessful. I had never taken over a job from someone who just did not want to communicate and I desperately needed a few tips. Fortunately Brigadier Derek Crabtree, the Chief of Staff, Captain Bob Mowland, Royal Navy, and Group Captain Dan Honley, Royal Air Force, were a tremendous help to me.

Twice a week CBF had to attend the Governor's Executive and Security Committee meetings. My apparent 'loss of face' among the Chinese at my lower rank was compounded because I now had to sit on the Governor's left instead of his right! None of this bothered me in the least because I had experienced nothing different.

The Governor, Sir Murray MacLehose, was a distinguished and much respected figure who literally towered above the Chinese who surrounded him on his tours around the colony. He handled the meetings firmly and gave everybody a fair hearing. He was also my Commander in Chief and sometimes expected the Armed Forces to carry out tasks which were beyond the capability of the resources which the Ministry of Defence in London, to whom I was also responsible, had allotted to Hong Kong. Consequently there were moments when I found myself sandwiched between conflicting interests.

Our first home was in Flagstaff House, the oldest building in Hong Kong, completed in 1846 for Major General C. D'Aguilar and which had been occupied by successive commanders ever since, except for the period 1941 to 1945 when four Japanese Admirals used the building, one of whom was the only occupant of Flagstaff House known to have been executed for war crimes! I was to be the last to live there because, as part of a new Defence Costs Agreement, the house and Victoria Barracks, in which it was located, were to be given up in four months' time to the Hong Kong Government.

I wrote at the time: "We are installed in a house bigger than the Villa Lemm, albeit for only three months. It is very humid, about 96%. Last night it was 100%! There are masses of smiling Chinese house staff who may not understand a word I say but nevertheless are incredibly willing. There are huge fans in the ceilings of every room and tiny electric heaters in every clothes cupboard to cope with humidity. I have been gluing corks to the back of every painting and icon to keep them off the wet walls. I am glad I did not bring my stamp collection!

"Neither drink nor cigarettes are Duty Free which is a blow! The cost of living is very high but the allowances are better than in Berlin. The roads are full of expensive cars including over three hundred Rolls Royce which belong to wealthy Chinese. The ancient Daimler saloon with which I have been provided broke down in Kowloon yesterday. We got out and pushed it, flag still flying, into a nearby fire station and telephoned for help!"

Today Flagstaff House, which was called Headquarter House until 1932, is surrounded by highrise buildings and the view it must have once enjoyed of the harbour right below has gone for ever because of an enormous programme of reclaiming land from the sea by filling it with rocks from the mountains. In the garden there was a unique flock of sulphur-crested cockatoos who loved the flowers on the cotton trees and are said to have been released from captivity in 1941 just prior to the Japanese occupation. The garden contained Royal Palm trees, a white Jade Orchid tree and a rare red Frangipani. Beneath them there were two tombstones, to "Wong" Siamese Cat 1923–1933 and "Wise" born Bloemfontein 1904 died Hong Kong 1907.

A new house was built for CBF in 1978 high up on Barker Road just below the Peak, with a magnificent view and graceful verandas. I went to have a look and wrote: "There are over one hundred people working at the house each day! Just think of the problem of getting a plumber or carpenter in London. There are lots of little old ladies in wide-brimmed flat hats carrying baskets of tiles, bricks indeed everything. The metal work for the balustrades are fashioned on the spot by men beating hot rods with hammers. The windows are smoky laminated glass from Australia, the green roof tiles come from Japan, the floor tiles from Germany, there is air conditioning throughout, from America. It is going to be easier to run than Flagstaff House."

The staff, which numbered seventeen at Flagstaff House, had to be reduced to eight. I wrote to my predecessor who had known them all for two years for his advice, but he declined to help. So I left it to the Chinese to decide among themselves who should move up the mountain to live in the new house. They explained to me that in order to secure 'good will' it was important to consult the Gods and ask them to decide what would be an auspicious day on which to move. The occasion would be marked by taking the two magnificent stone lions, which guarded the entrance to Flagstaff House, up the mountain to sit outside the new Headquarter House. So it was that at breakfast one morning I noticed that a little table had been laid in the porch between the lions. It was covered with dimsums, rice cakes, fruit and a colourful display of ribbons, flickering candles and smouldering paper money. The result of this consultation was that if I wished to live in a happy new house and if the Chinese staff were all to enjoy good 'fung shui', then the move had to take place two weeks earlier than I had expected.

My resourceful ADC, Rupert Litherland, told me at the conclusion of a splendid farewell dinner party in Headquarter House that he had been asked by a Hong Kong film company whether they could borrow the now vacant residence for a film they were making. The house belonged to the British Forces for another two weeks and the prospect of raising money for our welfare funds seemed most attractive. It was only after my son Alexander, on holiday from the University of Washington in Seattle, became a film extra that he told me the scantily clad daughter of the Chief Secretary, Sir Denys Roberts, would be stepping out of a pink cake onto the same dining room table. When I learnt the film was to be called *Emmanuel II*, a sequel to a successful erotic film, I did not want to know any more! However, I felt sure that when the film was shown nobody could possibly remember that the British Forces had owned the house at the time the film was made.

The money which the film company paid enabled us to place an order with a local shipyard for two large junks for recreational use by servicemen and their families. This proved to be a godsend to those cooped up in tower blocks or living in the new Joint Headquarters building, HMS *Tamar*. The junks were delivered on time and named *Tinker Tailor* and *Soldier Sailor*.

Before finally leaving the house I asked the Queen's Gurkha Engineers to search for buried treasure. At midnight on 26 December 1941, just before the surrender to the Japanese, General Maltby, GOC China Command, and his ADC Ian MacGregor had wrapped up the colours of the 1st Middlesex and 2/14 Punjab Regiments in oil paper and put them into a wooden box. They dug for about an hour and a quarter into very hard soil to a depth of about 3 feet and placed the box inside, covering it up with earth and rows of plants in pots.

When the prisoners were released from the horrors of Japanese captivity in 1945 they found it impossible, from the rough plan they had made, to locate the spot because so much had changed. All subsequent searches have failed and it could be that the box and its contents disintegrated. The metal parts of the Royal Hong Kong Defence Volunteer Corps colours were, however, found twenty-five years after their hasty burial.

A similar search took place a few months later in the basements of Government House where it was believed the silver and some paintings by Chinnery had been hidden in a secret room. Once again, in spite of using modern devices, the hidden chamber could not be located.

On 5 July 1977 Valerie and I walked out of Flagstaff House and down the drive. The Gurkha Guard Commander hauled down the Union flag, folded it up and gave it to me, together with a huge brass door key to Flagstaff House.

Shortly after my arrival I was invited as guest of honour to the first of many Hong Kong charity dinners attended by several hundred people in a Kowloon hotel. To my horror a raffle-ticket seller approached me at the top table and, after an embarrassing search, I found a crumpled ten dollar bill in my pocket. There was more embarrassment when, surrounded by people spending a lot of money, I could only buy one ticket. My Chinese hostess then spoke earnestly to the Boy Scout ticket seller in Cantonese and the dinner proceeded. After speeches the raffle draw began and my hostess clutched my arm and urged me, "Look at your ticket, General. You really must look at your ticket."

I protested that I never won prizes, but, as I by then half expected, the very first ticket, slickly drawn out of the depths of a silver urn, for the top prize was mine. Then, as she dragged me to the fore to receive a most handsome prize, I remembered her conversation with the ticket seller. I thanked the organizers for inviting me, wished their endeavours every success and requested whether, as a great favour, would they now auction the object. The consequences of indebting myself to any organization would only have brought requests for a landing craft or a bulldozer or a helicopter to perform some mammoth and politically sensitive task. Nevertheless I was acutely conscious of the need to maintain the good will of the people. The Garrison was greatly helped by twelve hundred locally recruited Chinese soldiers who manned the landing craft, various boats, drove staff cars and trucks, worked as store-keepers, cooks even as fingerprint experts with the Royal Military Police.

We were to be assisted from time to time by the Royal Hong Kong Regiment (The Volunteers) and by the Royal Hong Kong Auxiliary Air Force. There were about 260 seagoing Chinese civilians in the Royal Navy patrol craft and a further 700 Chinese sailors in ten ships of the Royal Fleet Auxiliary Service. I was just getting used to the polyglot nature of my command when I discovered that there was even a well established company of Sikhs who guarded the ammunition stores on Stonecutters Island.

The Royal Navy worked closely with the Marine District of the Royal Hong Kong Police whose patrol craft merit a page and a half of *Jane's Fighting Ships*. They were responsible for search and rescue operations in the South China Sea. Its team of clearance divers worked in conjunction with Police and Customs in the recovery of drugs and stolen property and in salvage operations.

The Royal Air Force carried out search and rescue and medical evacuation from remote islands. They also had a role, as did the Army, fighting brush fires, using the Sims Rainmaker underslung water bucket which was filled by dipping into the sea. Their prompt arrival often extinguished fires which started after Chinese had attended to the graves of their ancestors on remote hillsides, where, after cleaning the bones, they lit candles and joss sticks. They then hurried back to the nearest road to catch a bus home, invariably forgetting to blow out the flames. After a spate of fires I gave orders that the slightest trace of smoke must be doused. This was highly successful, but not before a few family groups got soaked.

The first opportunity to get a change of scene from Hong Kong was to visit an exercise in Fiji accompanied by my new MA, Squadron Leader Peter Gooding RAF. Our first duty was a Kava Ceremony designed to impress visitors with their warlike qualities and then to calm them down if they still had hostile intentions. This was held in a huge hangar where a hundred Fijian soldiers were seated cross-legged in an open V formation. They chanted in wonderful deep sonorous voices, led by an enormous man seated at the base of the V. I was placed on a small chair facing him and watched fascinated as he crushed a large twisted yellow kava root into a wooden bowl between his knees. What would he do to me? Two men trotted up with a hollow tree trunk from which they poured water into the bowl. Baskets of strange fruits and vegetables were placed at my feet and then a large pig on a spit. After a lot more chanting, a virile little man filled a coconut shell with the white liquid from the giant's bowl and began shuffling towards me. I had no idea what to expect. Was it going to be hot, or bitter, or alcoholic? I had been warned to drink it all without hesitation and then shout "Bulla". With my lips and tongue already numb, I praised their military achievements in the Lebanon and begged them to keep and enjoy the pig and fruits. Afterwards a Fijian officer told me that an American Admiral, Commander of the Seventh Fleet, had failed to do this and had ended up with the pig and fruits being dumped onto his pillow in his hotel bedroom.

After Fiji I was delighted to visit New Zealand where I was driven by a large Maori female soldier called Sergeant Connie Watiti. A full and interesting programme had been prepared for me by the Chief of General Staff, Major General Brian Poananga. Sergeant Watiti was determined that I should not miss a moment so we travelled great distances at high speed, never stopping to spend a penny. On the third night we arrived in Rotorua. She turned to me and, with a charming smile, commanded, "And now General you are going to take me out."

I hesitated. "Of course Connie, but this place looks dead."

"Just you wait until I put on my glad rags," she replied.

It turned out to be a most amusing and unusual evening. Before we parted she gave me a wooden carving of a rainbow trout "From Connie your Grand Prix driver."

A few months later a New Zealand mortar platoon came to Hong Kong by private arrangement in exchange for a Gurkha platoon. All went well until a Chinese girl claimed that she had been molested by a New Zealander, many of whom were Maoris. Publicity would have put an end to a popular venture so Brigadier Michael Carleton-Smith insisted that there should be an identity parade. Faced with the entire New Zealand detachment who all looked much the same we were greatly relieved when she decided to withdraw her allegation.

The increasingly onerous task which we faced in Hong Kong was the interception of Illegal Immigrants (IIs), who were beginning to pour over the land border from China into the New Territories. Hong Kong was already one of the most densely populated places in the world with an average density in 1976 of 4487 per square kilometre, but in the metropolitan areas, such as Kowloon, there were 25,400 people per square kilometre. Any II who evaded capture and reached the overcrowded cities had to be regarded as having reached a safe haven from which it was almost impossible to winkle them out, and certainly this might prompt their relatives to start a riot.

During my first year we intercepted a staggering total of 96,000 IIs and returned them to China. It was estimated that perhaps a further 110,000 evaded capture. Each II caught meant a soldier having to get up from his hide and catch them physically because they never opened fire. To me, coming from Berlin where just one successful escaper over the Berlin Wall would be greeted as a hero, this was a complete contradiction. However, there was neither the housing, water, food nor work in the Colony to support so many unhappy desperate people. We were directed to return them all to China within 24 hours.

News of such massive repatriations resulted in my receiving a death threat from the 'Overseas Chinese World Federation' posted in Long Beach, California.

"You are wrong, You insult us Chinese people in such a way that we decide to kill all the British whites in Hong Kong unless you do the following:–

1. Stop arresting Chinese escapees. They are more miserable than Vietnamese refugees, They have nothing with them. They have no food or clothing. Vietnamese refugees have gold bars with them and are richer than four million Chinese people in Hong Kong. If you continue arresting Chinese escapees we shall kill you.

2. Abolish the immigration office at Lo Wu. Those who are granted permission by the People's Republic of China to enter Hong Kong can enter without permits. (This of the prestige of the People's Republic of China and it brooks no insult.)

3. Do not force people in the New Territories to vacate their homes. Hong Kong cannot again sell an inch of land there.

If the above mentioned cannot be done, then we twelve million overseas Chinese shall unite with the five million Chinese in Hong Kong to kill all British whites in Hong Kong."

British regiments posted to Hong Kong imagined that they were all set for a pleasant two years, but in reality they endured greater separation from their families or from the comfort of barracks than they ever experienced doing four-month tours of duty in Northern Ireland. The 1st Bn the Royal Green Jackets, the 2nd King Edward VII's Own Gurkha Rifles, 7th Duke of Edinburgh's Own Gurkha Rifles and 10th Princess Mary's Own Gurkha Rifles all spent over six months a year on border duties or overseas training.

It could take foot patrols up to four hours exhausting climb carrying radios, batteries, weapons, food and water up the mountains which faced the northern border with China. Every time an II was spotted they had to be intercepted and subdued if necessary, then walked up to a collecting point. I proposed that RAF helicopters should lift patrols into the more difficult positions, but the Political Advisor, ever cautious, said it might break an agreement made twenty years earlier during the Korean War not to fly aircraft near the border. I pointed out that the Chinese Communist forces, who were also trying to intercept IIs, could not possibly object. Eventually the Governor allowed the RAF to fly in the border region.

Between 300 and 600 IIs were being caught every night, on some busy nights nearly 1000. We were fast running out of plastic handcuffs which could only be locked once and then had to be cut off. For nearly two years the work load on the soldiers required operations rooms and observation posts to be manned and quick reaction forces to be ready round the clock.

Many soldiers only averaged five hours' sleep in twenty-four. Ambush positions were by necessity without protection from burning heat, humidity, torrential rains and typhoons, and in winter from freezing winds, rain and frost. IIs were pursued through heavy undergrowth, down into steep rocky gorges and through swamps. Although the majority surrendered quietly once caught, others put up a fight. Every company had an arsenal of captured weapons; fortunately casualties were mainly limited to knife wounds. Not once did any British serviceman shoot an illegal immigrant.

The Royal Navy normally kept one of its five craft on patrol. Even when augmented by four vessels they had to spend fifty percent of their time at sea. The naval base and seagoing personnel worked at full stretch. The ships were uncomfortable, the patrols were often tedious but always had to be ready to arrest IIs, sometimes in dangerous conditions and then to show compassion in handling them. Every junk, sampan or speedboat encountered presented a different problem for ship's boats, boarding parties, reception and first aid teams. The mixed British and Chinese crews were under constant pressure, especially when the number of illegals herded on the upper deck often outnumbered the crew by three to one.

The Royal Air Force in Hong Kong had only been established to work a five-day week, but now, in spite of reinforcements, the flying effort had to be doubled. The eight Wessex helicopters of 28 Squadron RAF and Scouts of the Army Air Corps needed a very high order of maintenance from ground crews. Circumstances demanded exceptional skill from the aircrews flying over such inhospitable terrain delivering men and supplies, evacuating casualties and arrested persons.

In order to try to get the outside world to know what was happening and to press the point home to the Ministry of Defence in London, Brigadier Mike Carleton-Smith, Gurkha Field Force Commander, took the international press corps up to the border and showed them the bus loads of dejected captured illegal crossers being taken over the bridge at Lo Wu back into China. One hour before sunset the reporters were driven to Lin Ma Hang and shown the ineffective wire fence which ran along the border, with pathetic strips of torn clothing flapping from the barbed wire. Then they were urged to look north into China at the steep slopes of China Mountain. These they could clearly see were covered with hundreds of would-be crossers, looking down on us, choosing the best route and waiting until dark to cross the wire. It was like a shot from the film *Zulu*, thousands of warriors waiting on the hills before swooping down to attack the South Wales Borderers at Rorke's Drift.

The more determined IIs now began to swim through the Mai Po Marshes or across Mirs Bay from China, risking shark attacks or at least severe jelly fish stings. This meant that we now had to deploy troops on the flanks of the New Territories and every single battalion was soon committed. Every day a dawn patrol was flown by the Army Air Corps along 250 miles of coast line. This revealed where boats had arrived during the night. Patrols were then dropped by RAF helicopters further inland to intercept these unfortunate people.

Initially all arrivals from mainland China could easily be distinguished by their simple blue or grey Chinese clothing. Then their friends in Hong Kong began to post them jeans and T shirts as worn in Hong Kong, which were put into plastic bags to keep dry whilst they swam across. The beaches soon became dotted with piles of old Chinese clothing, but the refugees usually made landfall on most inaccessible shores which no Hong Kong resident could possibly have reached on foot without getting their clothes filthy. Consequently the new arrivals in clean white T shirts and blue jeans were once again easily spotted. The Royal Navy, anchored in Mirs Bay, could pick up many IIs on their radar screens. It was fortunate that neither the British nor Gurkha servicemen could understand a word of Chinese, because the heart-rending stories of hardship and danger endured by those unfortunate men and women would have made our task very much more difficult to carry out.

At the same time as trying to stem this flood of immigrants from mainland China we were faced with another threat from the South China Sea. Thousands of Vietnamese boat people were on the move. We intercepted an incredible 76,000 Vietnamese refugees, some of whom had already escaped into Southern China, did not like what they found and had now decided to move on to Hong Kong. Very few ships' captains, including naval vessels, were prepared to stop and offer help to these desperate people because it then became practically impossible to find a country prepared to accept them. Consequently, when they were intercepted by the Hong Kong Marine Police they were in terrible shape. Here too they had to be caught at sea and interned before they made a landfall and disappeared into the cities.

The Hong Kong Government let it be known that the captains of ships which smuggled Vietnamese into the colony would be prosecuted and fined. A ship crowded with Vietnamese which was boarded by the Royal Navy just outside Lantau Island appeared to have been seized by the passengers. The Captain, who must have been a bit of an actor, was on the bridge surrounded by a villainous bunch holding a knife to his throat.

"They forced me to steer for Hong Kong," he pleaded. "I had no alternative." When the Vietnamese who had all paid the Captain with their life's savings realized that the 'resettlement arrangements' he had promised them were fiction, they told the truth and eventually were given back their gold which had been hidden in the ship's propeller shaft casing.

A dramatic landfall by a Vietnamese steamer was made on Lamma Island. The ship's captain had selected the most intelligent Vietnamese, put him in a wheel house and given him a course to steer at very slow speed towards a sandy beach. The crew then launched a speed boat and, taking the passengers' money with them, raced off to Portuguese Macau fourteen miles away. The inexperienced helmsman missed the sandy beach and hit the island beneath a cliff. There were hundreds of passengers already ashore and scrambling up a slope when the RAF deposited the duty platoon of Gurkhas on the top to intercept them. We then began sending the Auxiliary Air Force twin-engine Britten-Norman Islander out every evening up to 200 miles to see what else was coming our way. This was flown by off-duty Cathay Pacific Airline pilots and helped us to position police launches to intercept them.

How to reduce the number of Vietnamese refugees held in camps in Hong Kong became a constant problem to the Government, because no nation wanted them. United Nations law stated that the first country of refuge was obliged to keep the refugees. Therefore it was decided to repatriate to China all those who had not come direct from Vietnam. Fortunately this miserable task was given to the Hong Kong Police who collected the refugees in the middle of the night and took them to the border where the Chinese, embarrassed that they had not liked China, put them on to a train for the interior, probably never to escape again.

After visiting my son Alexander at the University of Washington in Seattle, I flew to see friends in Kingston, Ontario. Flora Macdonald, who had been at the National Defence College, lived in Kingston and was now the first woman to become Minister for Foreign Affairs in Canada. I explained to her what was happening to tiny Hong Kong and she agreed that Canada would take at least 2000 Vietnamese. When I returned to tell the Hong Kong Government about this unexpected offer, the FCO were upset and disapproved strongly of this amateur approach, which had not been made through their proper channels.

During my passage through immigration controls in Seattle I was much delayed by officials who even cut into the lining of my suitcase. Being aware that those fellows take things very seriously and have little sense of humour I kept my mouth shut. Eventually as no end seemed to be in sight I said, "You might like to know that we British do not treat American Generals and Admirals like this when they come to Hong Kong. The last war between our countries was in 1812." Complete silence. The immigration official continued to stare at his computer screen.

"Are you sure that the Redgrave on your screen," I asked gently, "does not have the first name of Vanessa? Such a wonderful actress, but one whose Left-wing views I have never shared".

There was the faintest blush to his cheeks as he handed me my passport and walked away. On my return I was met by my MA, Major Mike Taffinder, Royal Marines, who once inside the Daimler produced with a great flourish a telegram. "This is wonderful news, Sir. You have been awarded the KBE." I was quite amazed and only wished my parents had been alive to share my pleasure. There was a down side, however, in that I had to pay for champagne at the monthly Tripehounds lunch for Chinese and British businessmen and officials in the Hong Kong Club!

I flew back to London where I addressed a meeting called by the Chief of Defence Staff to explain what was happening in Hong Kong and to stress that we were getting very tired indeed. It was accepted that the Armed Forces in Hong Kong could not possibly maintain the high level of activity much longer, because, apart from exhaustion, their basic military skills had been completely neglected for the past six months. The First Sea Lord, Admiral Sir Terence Lewin, listened to me sympathetically, invited me to lunch and I was treated to a spectacular and most enjoyable journey from Westminster to Greenwich in his barge.

Within days the 1st Bn the Parachute Regiment was flying out to Hong Kong. The Royal Navy sent two SRN Hovercraft and *Scimitar*, a fast Motor Torpedo Boat, a flight of Sea King helicopters and the 42nd Commando Royal Marines with rigid raider boats, whilst the RAF increased their helicopter strength. I was very relieved that there was now a chance to rest some of the Gurkha Field Force. Their operations had been amazingly successful. I doubted whether many of the businessmen in Hong Kong had any idea of how much we were doing to prevent them from being swamped with refugees.

My Chief of Staff, Brigadier Tony Boam, who had served in the Scots Guards and later was to become CBF himself, prepared a paper for me to send to the Ministry of Defence on behalf of all three Services. It concluded:–

"That the operations conducted by the Armed Forces in Hong Kong against illegal immigration were in excess of normal peacetime military service and entailed exceptional hardship together with physical dangers.

"That such operations were sufficient to justify recognition by the award of a medal.

"That the medal should be a theatre medal and award open to all military personnel serving in the colony for a minimum of 30 days from 1 June 1979."

This excellent case was turned down, I strongly suspect, on advice from the Foreign and Commonwealth Office, who predictably felt it might damage relations with the Chinese People's Republic, whose population had been constantly trying to escape into Hong Kong. I do not believe that the FCO can have had any idea from their sheltered offices what discomforts and strains the Armed Forces had been enduring for many months or the slightest idea what a boost to morale the issue of such a medal would have been, especially to the Brigade of Gurkhas, Royal Navy and Royal Air Force.

One of the joys of Hong Kong was being able to sail to some of the distant islands, my favourites being Ping Chau on the Chinese side of Mirs Bay, Crooked Island and Tap Mun where we ate a bowl of rice and fish next to two obvious illegal immigrants. Lieutenant General Sir Richard Ward, CBF in 1970, had built a small two-bedroom bungalow on a remote shore of the Sai Kung peninsula which could only be reached by ship or helicopter. This was known as Wardhaven and could be used by officers and their families for short holidays. I have an enduring memory of watching Valerie and our younger son Robin sailing in the bay when they were surrounded by a school of dolphins. These played around the dingy for twenty minutes allowing their noses and tummies to be touched before suddenly disappearing. It was always a paradise, except once when we got caught there in a typhoon and I got stung by hornets.

There were several holiday chalets on Hei Ling Chau Island which also contained a Detention Centre. All Servicemen and their families were entitled to stay there and the Armed Forces made a grant to the TOC H who ran the holiday complex. Sadly, fewer and fewer people wanted to go there and the place was losing money. An RAF officer who had decided to spend Christmas with his family there explained that he had taken a bottle of claret to drink on Christmas Day but had been forbidden to do so by the TOC H staff. We heard from other holidaymakers that the only way to get a glass of beer was to visit the prison officers' mess, which of course was making a fine profit. A dour deputation from TOC H in Northern Ireland came to see me. They were pathetically obstinate and quite unwilling to take a more pragmatic approach. They grimly reminded me that "Happiness does not come out of a bottle, General."

"Some of mine," I regretted, "does come out of a bottle. You must realize that you are no longer dealing with gin-sodden soldiers of long ago. If you are unwilling to recognize the legitimate needs of my men and their families, we must close the leave camp."

Which, sadly, is exactly what happened. Luckily the two new junks were in use by then. I was just beginning to understand how bigoted some people could be.

Hong Kong was a rest and recreation centre for the United States Pacific Fleet. I was invited to lunch on USN ship *Midway*, an enormous aircraft carrier. It never ceases to amaze me how over two thousand men can be kept busy and happy in a confined space. At lunch there was a refreshing glass of Pimm's on the table which turned out to be cold tea. I offered the Admiral a chance to hold his reception ashore at HMS *Tamar* where they could drink what they wanted. This offer was much appreciated.

The Hong Kong Police and the Royal Military Police viewed each visit with some apprehension. Whereas in one year there was not a single drug-related offence among the British Armed Forces, the prevalence among US servicemen initially was high but this improved greatly before I left. The fact that US warships are completely dry meant that the first thing their sailors did when coming ashore was to drink a few pints of beer in the Royal Navy South China Fleet Club. The next stop was usually the Wanchai red light district where the "Washington", the "Popeye", the "Suzie Wong" and "Red Lips" were magnets to emotionally starved seamen. Indeed the only foreign sailors who kept clear of the delights of Wanchai were those on a French frigate. I congratulated the French Capitaine de Fregatte on the good behaviour of his sailors.

"You must understand, mon General," he replied "we are based on that enchanting island, Tahiti. We have come to Hong Kong for a rest!"

A lady whom one might kindly say had been pensioned off from the Wanchai nightclubs applied to Headquarters British Forces for a War Widows' pension. She claimed she had married a Scottish soldier in 1940, presumably in the Royal Scots, and that he had been killed a year later. She needed money now to buy her one room home. As evidence she produced a photograph of her wedding, a diminutive Chinese girl in white, clutching the arm of an enormous Sergeant in the Black Watch. A glance at his medal ribbons showed that the date was well after 1940 and even after the Korean War, so we sent the picture to his Regimental Headquarters in Scotland. They knew exactly who he was, a happily married sergeant in a Scottish police force. We never told her the truth but were able to pass on a substantial cheque which I believe came from his regimental funds.

The disappearance of Alice Chan, a well known old stager from the Kowloon bar scene, was marked by a lament in the Royal Military Police report for the benefit of the Queen's Own Highlanders who had just arrived in Hong Kong. The last verse went:

> "But weep for poor Alice, and the way she went,
> She fell doon a hole and into wet cement;
> And instead of her proppin' up mony a bar
> She's proppin' up part of the auld MTR!"

The MTR was the Mass Transit Railway, Hong Kong's new unmanned underground railway system in the process of being built at the time. Typical extracts from such reports were:-

"Red Lips' known as 'Granny's Ghetto', continued to be an irresistible magnet to tourists and servicemen alike. All girls are over forty and the oldest sixty-five. They cater for all tastes. Business has never been better."

". . . Several cases of VD were traced to fifteen Thai girls operating from a noodle stand in Hong Lok Rd . . .'

". . . 'Disco Den' in the China Fleet Club . . . popular haunt for Filipino Amahs during visit of US Navy . . . offering all services . . . memories of Subic Bay . . . possibly sent by employers to offset sharp rent increases"

Then there was the "luckless member of 1 Royal Green Jackets who attended a pyjama party given by Wrens of HMS *Tamar* . . . was discovered in a toilet sleeping off effect of the party neatly wrapped in a sheet. Personal effects incl money was stacked beside him but his suit and pants vanished . . . still missing . . . maybe he was overdressed for the occasion."

Once when I visited the British Military Hospital I met an Australian Chief Petty Officer with dressings on his arm and face,

"What happened, Chief?" I asked.

"It was Anzac Day," he replied.

"What happened to the other fellow?" I hesitated to ask.

"He's upstairs in the operating theatre."

I was looking forward to my first visit to Australia and to meeting Australian soldiers. My father had told me how in 1941, in Vichy French Syria, a fight had broken out between the occupying force of Australians and French troops waiting for repatriation to France. A Foreign Legionnaire was being hard-pressed by two Australians in a bar and in desperation he cried out, "*A Moi la Légion*". This is a call for help to which anyone who has ever served in the Legion is honour bound to respond. Passing outside was French General Catroux, who, on hearing the cry, entered the bar and went straight up to the two drunken Australians, the three stars shining on his Kepi.

"Do you know who I am?" he asked the first soldier.

"Oy Bill, here is another geezer who does not know who the hell he is!" he replied and swung a punch at the General. The situation was saved by the timely arrival of the Military Police.

There was also the delightful story of several hundred Australians waiting in a camp in the Canal Zone in Egypt for a ship to take them home. They had nothing to do except to parade every morning for a few minutes in front of a dapper major from Movement Control. This immaculate officer always wore a monocle much to the astonishment of the soldiers on parade. On the third day every single man had a substitute monocle in his eye. The major said nothing and carried on with his inspection. At the conclusion he turned to face them before dismissing the parade, paused to take the monocle from his eye, threw it high in the air and caught it neatly in his eye socket. "Now try and do that, Damn you! Dismiss." They loved him for it.

One of the great pleasures of being MGBG was that I could visit the Brigade of Gurkhas wherever they were stationed. The 6th Queen Elizabeth's Gurkha Rifles were in Brunei, which provided some exceptional jungle training, indeed we ran a jungle survival course run for pilots of all three services should they ever crash into a rain forest. Sadly lumber logging had begun to make terrible inroads into the jungle and caused soil erosion and the silting-up of rivers.

A most unusual case happened in Brunei when a Gurkha rifleman disappeared in the jungle. When his body was found it seems that he had fallen into a shallow ravine and had made no attempt to climb out, although he was uninjured. It appeared that he had just willed himself to die. He was broken-hearted, it seems, having been jilted by his girlfriend in Nepal. A poem found among his possessions described her heart as being as cold as the icicles which hung from the glacier high above her village in the Himalayas.

Once a year I had to make my report to His Royal Highness the King of Nepal in Kathmandu. These were ideal occasions on which to visit on foot some of the villages in either East or West Nepal from where our recruits came. It was strange to see soldiers going home on leave, marshalled at the end of the runway in Kathmandu and being told to report back in three months, before setting off to walk for two or three weeks back to their homes in the mountains.

A tragic accident occurred in the Gurkha family lines in the New Territories when a soldier returning after a long period away picked up his son and raised him to the ceiling, forgetting that in British-designed quarters there were rotating fan blades, which seriously injured the child.

In West Nepal at Pokhora and in East Nepal at Dharan there were small British bases which ran recruiting, demobilization and pension payments. There was also at Dharan a small hospital where military doctors treated Gurkhas and their families for illnesses which they would probably never see in England. Because there were so few beds available, doctors had to decide what were the chances of a patient surviving before accepting them, especially those who had suffered snake or rabies bites several days earlier.

A girl in her early twenties was sitting on a low wall beside the vehicle workshops, while an artificer Warrant Officer was using a welding torch to reduce the size of a large 1914-pattern artificial leg. These had been found in the corner of the Army Depot in Didcot and sent to BMH Dharan. She had fallen off a buffalo down a mountainside and lost her lower leg. Two weeks later I passed her on a mountain trail returning to her village with her brother. She was on crutches, carrying her new leg on her back pack, to be worn only on special occasions.

Every six months a British Gurkha officer would carry out a trek paying out pensions to old soldiers on the way and listing the works that needed doing such as water supplies, suspension bridges, or recording the need for new medical centres and schools. These were all in due course processed and discussed with the Government of Nepal before the money was provided from the Brigade of Gurkhas Welfare Funds which are well supported in Canada and America as well as Britain. It must be one of the most efficient and cost-effective charities in the world.

It was a little unexpected after Berlin to discover that even in Hong Kong, where everybody was busy making a commercial success of their lives, there was still a terrorist threat. The fact was that in 1976 there had been more than 110 terrorist incidents in Asia. The threat came from groups elsewhere in the world who had an axe to grind and might find it easier to explode a bomb and escape in Hong Kong than anywhere else.

There was the Moro Liberation Front who threatened Philippine Government offices and Philippine Air Lines. There were assassination groups from South Korea, Malaysian Muslims and the Palestinians. The most difficult killers to detect were educated, well-off intellectual fanatics who were mentally allied to the Red Brigades, Bader Meinhof or the IRA. These people might choose to swoop into Hong Kong which typified capitalism and a small governing colonial minority.

The Royal Hong Kong Police were well trained and prepared for such contingencies. A small team from Britain had given them special training in tactics, using the underground headquarters deep beneath Victoria Barracks from which the courageous defence of Hong Kong had been conducted in 1941.

At a social gathering in a bar afterwards one of the British instructors hit a Chinese police officer with a knuckleduster and quite rightly was arrested and charged with assaulting a police officer. I was informed that if he was found guilty there were only two sentences, six months in prison or six strokes with a cane. I warned the Governor that this man would probably go for the flogging and that if the British newspapers got the story there might be an outcry. The Governor, however, refused to believe it would come to that. A member of the Army Legal Services handled the defence and at one stage there was a fair chance that there might even be an acquittal, since the accused claimed it was only by sheer chance he had found a knuckleduster in his pocket. The prosecution countered by bringing a table into court, taken from a bar they had visited the previous night, which bore the unmistakable imprint of the defendant's knuckle-duster.

As expected, he asked to be flogged rather than go to prison. I warned the Governor and General Sir John Stanier, in London, that the sentence would be carried out in twenty minutes by a Sikh prison officer and that it was not an unusual event in Hong Kong and unlikely to attract any local attention. The man, whose injuries were severe, was taken to the Military Hospital and flown back to Britain in due course, without his knuckleduster.

Early one morning, I think at 4.30am, I received a call to get down to the Operations Room as soon as possible because one of Her Majesty's ships was in danger of being captured by the Chinese People's Liberation Army. One of the SRN hovercraft had been about to start a morning patrol and had come close inshore to where Deep Bay joins the Mai Po Marshes, when its engine failed to start. As it was close to the Shum Chun River which marks the border, soldiers of the PLA who had been lurking in the reeds, swooped out in two small boats and boarded the stranded hovercraft. The crew of four, including an eccentric bearded Lieutenant Commander, had been quick to lock themselves inside the hovercraft.

I immediately remembered the USN *Pueblo* incident when the North Koreans seized an American ship, which made no attempt to defend itself and to whose assistance no ship came, before it and the crew were ignominiously taken into captivity. This simply was not going to happen now. I ordered a company of Gurkhas and the RAF squadron of Wessex helicopters to stand by, the Royal Marine Commando and their rigid raiders to close in and the Army Air Corps to maintain observation. Captain Bob Mowland RN, the senior naval officer in Hong Kong, despatched a patrol boat up to Deep Bay to put the vessel under tow.

The next step was to warn the Governor and the Political Advisor, David Wilson, who became Governor ten years later. I also informed the Chief of Defence Staff in London. I realized that diplomacy takes time and with the Chinese it could take ages. The situation became a little more tense when the Chinese brought up a launch with a heavy machine gun on a mounting and pointed it at the hovercraft, whose captain now chose to reveal that he was shipping water slowly and that in due course his battery terminals would be under water and communication with us would cease.

The Royal Navy immediately sent Commander Robin Sheriff and an interpreter from the Royal Hong Kong Police to parley with the Chinese, who made them sit on the deck with a machine gun pointing at their chests. The Commander took a firm line and stressed that the Chinese troops had mistakenly entered Hong Kong waters, that they would get into terrible trouble with the Headquarters of the People's Liberation Army and maybe even greater difficulty with their Government in Beijing once we let them know through diplomatic channels what had happened. He also stressed that as both the PLA and ourselves were trying to intercept illegal immigrants, what on earth were they trying to achieve?

To me there was a similarity to the incident thirty years earlier on the interzonal border in Germany when the Russians had captured a young officer in my squadron and a show of force had worked. However, just as I was about to start making a show of strength the Commander's reasoning proved successful and the Chinese withdrew. By six o'clock that evening the hovercraft had rejoined the Fleet. It was not quite such an emotional reunion as that when HMS *Amethyst* escaped down the Yangtze River to rejoin the Fleet and was cheered to the echo by other ships. Nevertheless there was quiet satisfaction at the manner in which the Armed Services, diplomats and Royal Hong Kong Police had co-operated.

The British still maintained a token presence in the United Nations forces in South Korea by sending a platoon from Hong Kong to form part of the Honour Guard. It was extraordinary to visit a country which was still at war twenty years after it finished, but such was the tension between North and South Korea that young Koreans spent the entire period of their military career service in a slit trench watching the North. There was some justification, I supposed, when the American General explained to me how the North Koreans were still digging tunnels beneath their position and, although it was possible to hear the digging, it was almost impossible to intercept. He estimated there were now several tunnels through which men could move four abreast which stopped just short of breaking through the demarcation line. He showed me the building astride the 38th parallel in which acrimonious meetings of the United Nations took place with the North Koreans, all watched by reporters through the windows. I told him that if they could only hold meetings in private without the Press watching, as we did in Berlin with the Russians, it would result in a lot more being accomplished and less display of histrionics.

One of the joys of my first visit to Korea was the wild life. Standing in the long grass in the neutral zone between the two sides in Korea I spotted a group of magnificent tall Manchurian cranes. In Hong Kong in a restricted area just south of the frontier village of Sha Tau Kok, there was a large colony of cattle and little egrets, Chinese pond herons and night herons. About 1000 birds nested in a 'fung shui' wood, including a few of the world's rarest birds, Swinhoe's egret. There were a few Chinese porcupines with black and white quills in Hong Kong and a creature I never saw, the Chinese pangolin (scaly anteater). Once, when visiting a Gurkha position at Nim Wan on the east coast, a Gurkha Major asked whether I would like to see a huge python which had confronted a rifleman in a slit trench. He showed me a skin about ten foot long,

"What happened to the flesh?" I asked.

"Oh the villagers came up and begged for it. They are cooking it now."

There were several venomous snakes in Hong Kong such as kraits, cobras and green bamboo snakes, but there were few reports of people being bitten. The more poisonous a snake the greater is the delicacy to Chinese gourmets.

The Armed Forces and Royal Hong Kong Police requested some improvements to the border fence which was raised to fourteen feet. This did little to contain the influx of immigrants who still managed to scale the fence in twenty seconds.

Meanwhile yet another threat now developed from the direction of Macau. Gangsters would charge huge sums guaranteeing to land passengers into Hong Kong or to smuggle in contraband, using high-speed motor boats which they were prepared to write off and still make a profit. There seemed nothing we could do to catch them because the Royal Navy patrol boats were not fast enough. The motor torpedo boat had trouble with its gas turbines, the hovercraft were never in the right place at the time and the Royal Hong Kong Police vessels lacked that extra speed needed to overhaul these speedboats.

I tried to get political approval to our stationing an RN patrol ship in the mouth of the Pearl River off Macau, just to give us enough warning to place ships in a position to intercept. Although we had sounded out a Chinese Admiral privately who had no objections, there was once again much FCO diplomatic sucking of teeth and hesitation for weeks before agreeing. Meanwhile we achieved our first success when a speedboat was spotted approaching Hong Kong waters by the Royal Navy tug *Claire* which nearly burst a blood vessel trying to cut across its bows. An Army helicopter then shadowed it, while the Gurkha quick reaction platoon were lifted by the RAF Wessex and and the Royal Hong Hong Marine Police blocked the entrance to Hong Kong harbour. The smugglers veered off towards Telegraph Bay near Aberdeen and ran their boat at full speed twenty yards up the beach. The RAF Wessex landed the Gurkhas about two hundred yards inland and a great game of cops and robbers then took place until they were all caught. Several very angry British residents telephoned the Governor and my Headquarters to complain at such unseemly behaviour by the military on their private beach, but then it was probably the first indication they had that we actually had an immigration problem.

The obvious solution to these speedboats would have been to hover a Wessex helicopter overhead and let the downdraught overturn them, but this was considered a foul by the Governor and FCO, and not allowed. I then heard that in New Zealand deer were caught in nets dropped by helicopter, but the RAF had good technical reasons for saying this was impossible. In the end it was co-operation between all the security forces and the goodwill of the Chinese inhabitants of Hong Kong, once they realized that their own quality of life was at stake, that reduced the influx of illegal immigrants.

In 1980 I knew that I would have to retire at the age of fifty-five and thus began a series of farewell journeys to Brunei, Fiji, New Zealand and Australia, which coincided with military exercises in those countries and of course one last visit to Nepal.

Hong Kong had been an incredibly interesting appointment, I was so lucky to be sent there but it had not been much fun. There had been so little to laugh about, people were terribly serious and naturally pre-occupied about the future and making money. There could never have been the feeling that the Forces were part of Hong Kong and shared any ideals in common with the people, as had been the case in Berlin. We were most grateful to have enjoyed wonderful hospitality from Leo Lee, Sidney Chung, Horace Kadoorie, Run-Run Shaw and many others who must have been terribly worried about the future of Hong Kong, but never let it show.

Just before leaving we tried to make an incognito visit to Macau which I had not been allowed to do. My cover must have been blown because on arrival I was told that an entire hotel had been reserved for us. This was alarming until I discovered that there only were four bedrooms. Julian Mellor, the ADC, had even arranged a visit to the theatre, which sounded great. When we went there it soon was evident that Valerie was the only woman in the audience which was made up of the Chinese equiv-alent of men in dirty mackintoshes. The awfulness of the programme was overshadowed by a young lady, possibly East German, called Kiki Railroad. Her arrival in Macau probably marked the end of the line for her when she rode her red motorcycle into a glass water tank and then performed a languid striptease which had the Chinese all chattering with excitement.

The farewell Valerie and I were given was one of the most moving occa-sions of my life. It was not just goodbye to Hong Kong but also to a lifetime in uniform. It all began with a farewell to the Chinese Military Service Corps drivers and to the house staff outside Headquarter House. This was followed by a guard of British and Chinese sailors at the entrance to HMS *Tamar* and finally another guard of honour provided by the 2nd Queen's Own Gurkha Rifles outside the Headquarters on the waterfront. Then a moment to say farewell to the Joint Headquarters

Staff and to members of the Hong Kong Government. Finally we boarded HMS *Wasperton* with our son Robin, who was on holiday from Gordonstoun School, to sail over to Kowloon. As she cast off, there was a crash and clouds of gunsmoke as the Royal Navy saluting battery began to fire their guns, the Royal Marine Commando rigid raiders weaved patterns around us, the Hong Kong Fire Boats turned their jets of water high into the air, every ship's hooter seemed to sound, Royal Navy Sea King and Royal Air Force Wessex helicopters flew past and Army Air Corps helicopters brought up the rear with spectacular plumes of coloured smoke. It was hard to keep back the tears. What a wonderful send-off!

Chapter Fourteen

ONLY FADE AWAY

We arrived in England after five years abroad and with no longer any guarantee of further employment or a home of our own. Fortunately we were able to move in with Valerie's parents at the Royal Hospital where Arthur Wellesley was a Captain of Invalids. She reminded me that she had not married me to provide lunch every day and she soon became a freelance negotiator with an Estate Agent in Chelsea.

I was given one last task to conduct a group of senior officers from many different countries, who were attending a course at the Royal College of Defence Studies, around Canada, the United States and Mexico – a most enjoyable and interesting experience. Just before leaving London I was reassured that at least somebody was worrying about my future. It was a telephone call from a Resettlement Officer at the Ministry of Defence whom I had never met.

"Have you found a job yet, General?"

"No." I snapped ungratefully.

"Am I right in assuming that you speak French?"

"Yes," I replied cautiously.

"Well, I have an interesting offer. A bilingual General is being sought to take command of the Armed Forces of the Republic of Chad in Central Africa. You would be Commander-in-Chief and the job will be very well paid. They reckon it will only take six months for you to get them organized and tell them what needs doing. By the way you would be supported by a New Zealand Air Commodore who is a helicopter specialist."

"Have they got helicopters?" I asked.

"Well," he hesitated, "Not yet, but soon. You will be given enough money to buy all the equipment you need."

"Surely, is there not a Civil War going on in Chad?" I asked in horror "Which side do I get? Who gets the Armoured Car and Camel Squadrons?"

He did not know. I told him it was a crazy mission which no British officer would ever take on.

I then discovered that it was linked to powerful business interests who had their eyes on mineral deposits in the Tibesti Mountains. Three weeks later the Ministry rang again. "Would I, for £20,000, fly to Faya-Largeau for ten days and tell them how to win the war?" I wonder if they ever found anyone to advise them.

We bought a terraced house at the World's End in Chelsea which we could just afford with the gratuity the Army paid me and our combined savings. In keeping with our neighbours there was an outside closet in the back yard and the house next door still retained gas lamp wall fittings. We unpacked our packing cases, many items unseen since our wedding, hung up the icons and pictures in the first house we had ever owned and went to Dorset for Easter. When we returned the house had been robbed, our icons and silver stolen. We were in despair.

I took the first job I was offered and became the Director General of the Winston Churchill Memorial Trust. This was fascinating work which encompassed a huge variety of subjects and the selection of exceptional men and women for Travelling Fellowships which the Trust granted each year.

A further four-year link with the army was established when I was appointed Honorary Colonel of the 31st Signal Regiment Volunteers. Based in London, they had an active role in support of SHAPE in Belgium. One third of the regiment were well motivated women who wanted a change from working in banks or large London stores. Once, when visiting a squadron encamped in a forest in the Belgian Ardennes, I was stopped by a sentry from the Queen's Gurkha Signals attached to the regiment. He was supported by a steel-helmeted lady whose blue mascara mixed uneasily with the black camouflage cream on her face.

"What is it like doing guard duty with a good-looking girl?" I asked the smiling Gurkha soldier.

"Oh General Sahib, they will never believe me when I get back to my unit in Hong Kong!"

After three years I became one of the few non-political Chairmen of a District Health Authority, that of Hammersmith and Fulham. This was often a bed of nails because of constant cuts to our budget by a vacillating and niggling Ministry of Health. Unbelievably, all Health Authority meetings had to be held in public. This slowed up all proceedings and decisions because a handful of strident ladies and bearded, red-eyed, emotional left-wing men all felt they should be seen to object to every motion, whatever it happened to be. Nevertheless I was always able to get general agreement without resorting to a vote except when we decided to amalgamate with Victoria and Westminster and to form Riverside Health Authority, which I welcomed because it did away with my job!

Various unpaid Health appointments followed, of which being Chairman of the Charing Cross Hospital Special Trustees was by far the most worthwhile, thanks in no small measure to the support given by the Secretary, Graham Buckley, and the Treasurer, Jim Reader.

Our sons Alexander and Robin married girls from Denmark and Australia respectively and live nearby. They each have a son and daughter, Sofia and Caspar, Thomas and Catherine, and now there is Anna. My sister, Ioana, whom I had hardly seen since I left Romania, now lives next door.

However, it is travel which has occupied me since I retired and has yet to be written about. In 1983 I travelled alone in China at the invitation of a Chinese General whom I met in Berlin. A most extraordinary and exciting experience. The next year, accompanied by a Danish hydro engineer, Konrad von Rauschenberger, and an Inuit girl interpreter, we went to North-West Greenland visiting remote Inuit settlements.

The following year I travelled with Lieutenant Commander Angus Erskine to Svaarlbad, then to North East Land and a close encounter with a polar bear.

In 1986 I travelled with three companions and a Tibetan girl interpreter two thousand kilometres overland from Kathmandu in Nepal to Lhasa in Tibet and back to Nepal, some of it on foot. Donald Saunders, whom I had known as a boy in Romania, had organized the trip.

A year later I went to the Hudson Bay to photograph hungry polar bears as they gather waiting for the sea to freeze hard enough to bear their weight and be able to resume seal hunting.

For the past few years I have had lots of pleasure as a guest lecturer on many tours organized by Andy Cochrane of Noble Caledonia to Turkish North Cyprus. I also gave talks in Mexico and Guatemala, Albania, Fiji and New Zealand and on the *Caledonian Star* visiting Egypt, Libya and Tunisia.

By far the most exciting journeys were into the Arctic Ocean, to Bear Island, to Spitzbergen and, thanks to the services of a Russian nuclear icebreaker, twice through the pack ice to inaccessible Franz Josef Land.

As I reflect on my life with yet another one-eyed "Daffodil" at my feet and the only icon to escape the burglary on the wall, I realize how incredibly lucky I have been to have held appointments which offered so much independence, variety and excitement. I am deeply conscious too of the patience and understanding my wife has shown all these years.

With deafness rapidly increasing I was prevailed upon to go before a War Pensions Medical Board in South London. I arrived five minutes early and had dressed slightly shabbily in order to enlist their sympathy. I rang the door bell and was greeted by two cheerful ladies who led me upstairs,

"We have never had a General before, have we Mabel? We had better measure him and weigh him," said the largest of the two who led me to an antiquated set of scales with weights. Having done that, Mabel went to a table on which were the remains of their coffee break. She picked up an empty bottle and waved it at me.

"We are going to need a specimen from you," she chortled.

"But I have only come to get my ears checked out," I stammered.

"You won't get no War Pension without a specimen," ordered the fat one. So I did what I was told and left them to play with a bundle of coloured litmus papers, whilst I was summoned to meet two elderly doctors who could not have been kinder. One clutched a millboard covered by a faded piece of green paper from which he questioned me.

"What exactly were you doing when damage occurred to your ears?"

"Do you really want to know? I was peeing against my armoured car rear wheel," I replied, "when all hell broke loose." This and all my other answers were noted down with the equivalent of a quill pen. They then said they would test my ears, but I showed them the printout of sophisticated ear tests made at British Military Hospitals in Hanover, Tidworth, Woolwich, Berlin, and the Charing Cross Hospital. No they said, they had their own method.

"Put your finger in your good year and repeat after me, Forty-two!" I could not believe he was serious so I stayed silent.

He came closer and shouted, "FORTY-TWO".

I misheard, sat bolt upright and replied, "Forty-three."

"You are very deaf. We will see what we can do." He shook my hand. I said that as Chairman of a London Health Authority I would sing his praises. Nine months later I began to receive a small pension. Today, when I am almost stone deaf without hearing aids, I am most grateful to those two patient retired doctors.

In the autumn of 1999 my sister Ioana and I decided to go back to Doftana for one last look at our Romanian home. From afar we could see the house on a hill above the River Doftana but an ugly scar below showed there had been a huge landslip. The rusty iron gates, with corrugated sheeting wired on to prevent anyone seeing inside, took a while to unlock. Dingy barrack blocks had been built in between the trees, not only had the house been damaged by successive earthquakes but arson had destroyed the first floor and the roof had collapsed intact. The house was now a gloomy mess hall to 350 children for only five months a year because there was no central heating. There was virtually no sanitation. The gardens had been neglected for fifty years, not a shrub or rose, fish pond or lawn remained. There was nowhere for those children on holiday to play except on the cracked concrete 'Tennis Court'. The Director of the Holiday Home was a most useless and disinterested person, only too happy to draw one year's salary for a few months' work. It was depressing, grotesque and we should never have gone. We scuttled away without looking back.

In Bucharest my birthplace, the Athene Palace Hotel, was now the Hilton Hotel, but it still retained the old name over an entrance. Capsa's, the old coffee house was being rebuilt. At Cotroceni Palace, in Queen Marie's salon which had been beautifully preserved, we saw her diary written in English and the white grand piano which our mother, Micheline Capsa, had played in 1918.

On the highway leaving the city there is an impressive memorial to Aviation Heroes of 1916–1918. We stopped the car and crossed to the centre island where to our surprise and great pleasure found enscribed *Nicu Capsa, Major Pilot Killed 1918*.

Finally, before leaving Romania we drove high up into the Carpathian Mountains and stopped to look down at the gentle green slopes and at the little churches with onion-shaped roofs and wooden tiles. There were groups of peasants with scythes cutting grass and making small conical hay ricks, as I had always remembered. Then we heard sheep bells tinkling as a huge flock came up from the valley below, surged over the crest, accompanied by two dogs and three shepherds wearing crude pointed leather boots, their white shirts hanging outside their trousers and with black conical felt hats and leather shoulder bags. Somewhere I heard laughter and then a flute, it was magic. Just for a moment I knew I was back to my childhood.

INDEX

Note. Abbreviation: Major General Sir Roy Redgrave (author) = RR. All British regiments appear under British Army